Bit Rot

Douglas Coupland (pronounced KOHP-lend) (born 30 December 1961) is a Canadian writer, designer and visual artist. His first novel was the 1991 international bestseller *Generation X: Tales for an Accelerated Culture*. Since then, Coupland has written twelve more novels, which have been published in most languages. He has written and performed for the Royal Shakespeare Company and is a columnist for the *Financial Times*. He is a frequent contributor to the *New York Times*, *e-flux*, *Dis* and *Vice*. In 2000, after a decade of generating web graphics, Coupland amplified his visual art production and has recently had two separate museum retrospectives: *Everywhere Is Anywhere Is Anything Is Everything* at the Vancouver Art Gallery, the Royal Ontario Museum and the Museum of Contemporary Canadian Art; and *Bit Rot* at the Witte de With Center for Contemporary Art in Rotterdam and Villa Stuck in Munich. In 2015 and 2016, Coupland was an artist-in-residence in the Paris Google Cultural Institute.

Also by **Douglas Coupland**

Fiction

Generation X
Shampoo Planet
Life After God
Microserfs
Girlfriend in a Coma
Miss Wyoming
All Families Are Psychotic
Hey Nostradamus!
Eleanor Rigby
JPod
The Gum Thief
Generation A
Highly Inappropriate Tales for Young People (with Graham Roumieu)
Player One
Worst. Person. Ever

Non-fiction

Polaroids from the Dead
City of Glass
Souvenir of Canada
Souvenir of Canada 2
Terry
Extraordinary Canadians: Marshall McLuhan

Bit Rot

short stories + essays

Douglas **Coupland**

WINDMILL BOOKS

1 3 5 7 9 10 8 6 4 2

Windmill Books
20 Vauxhall Bridge Road
London SW1V 2SA

Windmill Books is part of the Penguin Random House
group of companies whose addresses can be found at
global.penguinrandomhouse.com.

Penguin
Random House
UK

First published in Great Britain by William Heinemann in 2016
First published in Canada by Random House Canada in 2016

First published in paperback by Windmill Books in 2017

www.penguin.co.uk

A CIP catalogue record for this book is available from the British Library.

ISBN 9780099510895

Text design by Andrew Roberts

Printed and bound in Great Britain by Clays Ltd, St Ives plc

MIX
Paper from
responsible sources
FSC® C018179

Penguin Random House is committed to a
sustainable future for our business, our readers
and our planet. This book is made from Forest
Stewardship Council® certified paper.

Contents

Before We Begin . . .

When the pioneers crossed North America from east to west, the first thing to be thrown off the family Conestoga wagon was the piano, somewhere around Ohio. Then, somewhere near the Mississippi River, went the bookcase, and by Nebraska off went the books . . . and by Wyoming, everything else. The pioneers arrived in the Promised Land owning only the wagon and the clothing on their backs. They may have missed their pianos, but in the hard work of homesteading, they didn't have the time or energy to be nostalgic.

There are many different sections of short works in this book, all written since 2005. Each section came about in a way that, at the time, felt random and one-off-ish—but now I look at them together and see they essentially vindicate all the furniture I've tossed from the back of my wagon, year by year, over the past decade. If you were to go on Google Maps and look down from the stratosphere at these pieces of shed weight, you could connect their dots and trace my odd voyage from the twentieth-century brain to the twenty-first. I may miss some of those pianos I threw off my wagon's rear end, but if I hadn't, then I'd be stranded somewhere *back there*, and that would be intolerable.

I've titled this collection *Bit Rot*—a term used in digital archiving that describes the way digital files of any sort spontaneously (and quickly) decompose. It also describes the way my brain has been feeling since 2000, as I shed older and weaker neurons and connections and create and enhance new and unexpected ones.

Some of the stories in this compendium come from the novel *Generation A* (2007), and I really scared myself when I was writing them. They flowed directly from spending two years deeply immersed in the writings of Marshall McLuhan, and they explore how language, literacy and numeracy feed the technologies we make, and then how those technologies feed back into language. In the novel these stories were integrated into the larger narrative and made a certain sense, but I think the stories work far better extracted from it. These stories capture the sense of being in a foreign country and losing your passport, credit cards and money—and the only thing you're left with is limited Internet access at a small café that's only rarely open and has a low-speed connection. The local people are indifferent to you and they speak as though from *Finnegans Wake*, and you know that, should you ever get home, home will be a very different place than when you left it.

The pieces in this book also, to me, evince a shedding of all my twentieth-century notions of what the future is and could be. By 2007 I realized that the future that was once this far-off thing on the horizon was coming closer quite quickly, and then somewhere around 2011 or 2012, the future and the present merged and became the same thing—*and it's now always going to be this way, and we are now always going to be living in the future.*

These days I express ideas through visual means to a great extent. My books have always contained unrealized ideas for art installations and works, particularly the novels dealing with tech, such as *Microserfs* (1995) and *JPod* (2006). A much shorter version of this book was created as a "catalogue" to coincide with a show in Rotterdam at the Witte de With Center for Contemporary Art.

(This show moved on to Munich's Villa Stuck Museum in fall 2016.)

My thanks go out to Defne Ayas of the Witte de With for her ideas and energy and hard work in taking any number of seemingly disparate ideas and weaving them together so that they reveal an overall pattern and logic—the true meaning of curation. Also my thanks go to the Witte de With's Samuel Saelemakers for his time and energy and hard work helping to realize the exhibition. And thanks to my editor, Anne Collins, for always being in the helicopter in the sky above me, connecting all of my dots that I'm too close to the ground to see.

Douglas Coupland
Paris, 2016

Vietnam

I am Private Donald R. Garland from Bakersfield, California, as nice a place to grow up in as you can imagine—good folk, and California was booming. My mother used to put sour cherry pies out on the lower edge of the Dutch door, just the way they cool down pies in cartoons, and it was pleasant that way. Please call me Don. On August 5, 1968, I was on an unarmed film reconnaissance mission of rivers in the Bong Son region, and I was killed when my Huey Cobra's pilot got shot by a sniper from I don't know where. The rear blade snagged the remains of a napalmed tree, and the tail boom severed. It took maybe seven seconds in all. The last thing I saw was an orange explosion approaching my face like lava flying down a Hawaiian slope.

I'm thinking about what I just said and how *Nam* it sounded. That was the thing about Nam. Everything about it was so alien that all you had to do was say a few place names with a few military flourishes and *boom!* It was like I was describing life on Mars, not something real that was actually happening to me, and closer to my parent's house than, say, Vienna or Sweden. For people back in Bakersfield, reading about Nam was ... I don't know ... like forcing them at gunpoint to read a Chinese menu closely, and no matter what you asked for, all they'd bring you was machine guns and dog soup.

My death in Bong Son was expensive. Aside from the costs of raising an American child born in 1949, there were the added costs of my attending San Diego Military Academy—it probably set my old man back thirty grand—plus all the US government money it cost to start a war overseas and then pay to fly me over, peel my potatoes, wash my laundry, buy me weapons, and put me in helicopters with pilots like my pal Len Bailor, taking off in a Huey filled with canisters of film that were to have been processed and shown on CBS TV. Len always got off on that—maybe our footage would be shown right before Red Skelton or *Bewitched*. It cost the Vietnamese way less money to send one of their nineteen-year-olds to war. The math's not hard: grow up on a rice paddy, get a Soviet-made AK-47 (for free) and bingo, it's wartime. That's what Len called asymmetrical warfare.

I often wonder if someone in Washington looked at the cost of sending over people like me and said, "You know what, this is *not* sound Keynesian economics. We put too much money into raising this guy in—where? Bakersfield, California?—sounds too expensive already. His mama probably put out pies to cool on a window ledge—just so he can end up dying in a fucking Huey Cobra crash? And how much does one of those things cost? How did someone that *expensive* end up in the shit? This is nuts. Don't we have cheaper people we can send off to that godforsaken shit-hole? Isn't that the reason we allowed Mississippi to be part of the country? . . . Where's Lyndon?"

"In his office, watching TV."

"He is not watching TV. He is watching *TVs*. All three TV networks at once. He's paranoid. He's gaga."

The moment I landed in Nam I knew there was no way we'd win the war over there. Sure, we had all these Hueys and fighter jets and shit, and Ann-Margret came and performed for the USO in Danang in '66 and '68, but we had expensive people like me playing with big, expensive toys that would never stand a chance against inexpensive—basically cost-free—gook soldiers playing with lots of essentially free Commie toys. It's some sort of historical law.

David and Goliath? Plus we were always getting crabs and syph, DEET burns, blister beetle scabs, and foot rot and ringworm . . . It was unholy.

God, I was homesick in Nam. Nothing was familiar and everything stank, and man, those latrines with ventilation provided by Satan! I was grateful for the orders and discipline—otherwise I'd have cried all day. I always wanted to be on potato-peeling duty, except I went to a military academy, so they'd never have me doing that kind of chore. I'd have liked to be peeling potatoes because at least a potato's a potato and you know what it is and that it comes from the northern hemisphere. Potatoes don't have shuddering diesel engines that stink in your face, making sleep impossible, and potatoes aren't yokels with teeth that look like handfuls of dice randomly stuck into gums inside heads with the intelligence quotient of Popeye cartoons . . . but I'm just being mean.

We were all just babies over there. We shouldn't have been there. It was stupid. We all knew it. April 1968: 48,000 men drafted and 537,000 troops in Nam. Those pansies burning their draft cards in New York City were totally right to do so, even if they did suck dick. I don't think I met even one person in Nam who thought we were going to win someday. We all knew we were fucked. Maybe Ann-Margret thought we'd win. We just didn't want to get killed . . . but then, obviously, I got killed, so . . . just more proof us boys were right.

I'd like to talk to Mr. Washington General Guy someday . . . but time no longer exists for me, so what's a day? I'd ask, "Sir, why did you think it was a good idea?"

"Who said any of this was a good idea? How old are you, boy? Let me see—Private Garland?"

"Call me Don. I was a month shy of nineteen when I was killed."

"Boo hoo, Don."

"Sir?"

"Nam was obviously a total fucking disaster. There, are you satisfied?"

"But wait—how long did you know it was a total fucking disaster, sir?"

"Christ. Right out of the gate. If you want, I can go through my Day-timer and find the magic moment when it dawned on me that it was all a colossal goatfuck."

"Actually, yes, sir. Could you, please?"

"Here it is: a telex from March 7, 1966. *Mr. Bob Hope demands that he and Miss Margret be provided with Sealy Posturepedic mattresses with custom-molded foam pillows for her impending visit.*"

"And?"

"That's all. I read that specific telex, Don, and something inside me died. I don't think Ann-Margret even knew the Nam reality. The reality was that Bob Hope had been in Nam before and he knew what a cosmic shithole that place really was, and he buckled at the thought of Ann-Margret witnessing the whole truth, because if she knew, then that would show in her performances. And then the troops would get spooked, and it would have just put the doom on fast-forward."

"But me . . . and all the other guys like me who got killed."

"You were cannon fodder. What else do you want me to say?"

"Excuse me?"

"Don't play dumb. You and all the other guys—and women too, for that matter, goddamn dykes mostly—just cannon fodder. This somehow surprises you, Mr. Military Academy Graduate?"

"Tell me more."

"This is getting tiring. The thing about males from about seventeen to twenty-two is that nature rigs your brains—don't ask me how—so that you're susceptible to even the stupidest fucking ideas, whatever they may be. And you're out there carrying a rifle or a scimitar or—fuck, I don't know . . . If it's not the war, maybe it's just a bitter, fucked-up English teacher who wants to poison you by making you hate all the writers he or she hates—I used to study English, and I remember those teachers. They didn't care about what was good or bad—they just wanted to poison young brains. And that was just English classes. It wasn't even something as visceral as putting dumbfuck rich boys from Bakersfield, California, out in some godforsaken toe-rot shithole like Bong Son to die useless, overfunded deaths."

"I see."

"Don, when was the last time you saw a guy in his thirties ditch his family and run off to certain death in some goatfuck war? Never. It's a brain thing. Males from seventeen to twenty-two are genetically fucked. They'll do anything for anybody and they'll think it's the right thing. They have no sense of risk assessment."

"That's kind of cynical."

"Brother, young dumbos like you have been going off to war to fight for crazy batshit stuff since the dawn of man. Makes me embarrassed to be human sometimes."

"Thank you for your candour, sir."

"You're welcome, *Don*."

You maybe think I must be angry for having been sent off so cynically to die in a pointless war with no clear good guys or bad guys, where young men were turned into zombies and ghouls and where everything good in the world was covered with a mixture of gasoline and Styrofoam pellets and then set alight.

But what you don't know is that I went to a museum once, in Toronto, Canada, in—1965?—and it was summer and my parents were arguing and my brothers were being a real pain, and I simply walked away from them, walked up echoey travertine stairs to another floor, into the rooms where they kept the displays of taxidermied life on Earth, and it changed the way I thought. Walking through those chambers didn't feel like a boring school field trip:

it was the most wondrous trip ever. I looked inside the glass display cases and they had an Alaska king crab with red prickly legs longer than my daddy's arms, and there was a skeleton of a triceratops, and there was an extinct passenger pigeon, and a fungus that secreted a red blob shaped like a soccer ball. And there were foxes and butterflies and deep-sea creatures with little dangling light things in front of their mouths, and there was a clamshell the size of my car's trunk and . . . I just looked at all of this *life*. So much life. Life in every shape and form and size, and I just stood there and thought, *Here it is. I'm alive, just as everything here in these cases was once alive. So what is it, then, this thing called life? This thing called life that I share with all these creatures here.*

My parents were furious when they found me. I'd been gone an hour and we still had to visit some kind of castle thing a few miles away. But I didn't care if they were mad, because I had been shown a small window in time. And I knew I'd been given something precious in my just sixteen years on this planet, a chance to share the Earth with those other creatures. It kept me going when I was in the shit.

I thought, *I could be a Butterfly fish off the Australian coast.*

I thought, *I could be a leopard in a Kenyan tree, waiting to pounce on prey below.*

I thought, *I could be one of those stray dogs who loiter outside the mess tent.*

I—you—we—anyone could be a coral reef, a cuttlefish, a gust of pollen or a bright yellow mantis longer than my foot. I was alive!

My name was Don—Donald Garland—and now I'm gone, and I miss you, Earth. I really miss you dearly.

Black Goo

The first time I ever visited a McDonald's restaurant was on a rainy Saturday afternoon, November 6, 1971. It was Bruce Lemke's tenth birthday party and the McDonald's was at the corner of Pemberton Avenue and Marine Drive in North Vancouver, BC. The reason I can pinpoint this date is that it was also the date and time of the Cannikin nuclear test on Amchitka Island—a Spartan missile warhead of between four and five megatons was detonated at the bottom of a 1.5-mile vertical shaft drilled into the Alaskan island. The press had made an enormous to-do over the blast, as it was roughly four times more powerful than any previous underground detonation. According to the fears of the day, the blast was to occur on seismic faults connected to Vancouver, catalyzing chain reactions that in turn would trigger the great granddaddy of all earthquakes. The Park Royal shopping centre would break into two and breathe fire; the Cleveland Dam up the Capilano River would shatter, drowning whoever survived in the mall three miles below. The cantilevered L-shaped modern houses with their "Kitchens of Tomorrow" perched on the slopes overlooking the city would crumble like so much litter—all to be washed away by a tsunami six hours later.

⌧

I wrote the above paragraph in 1992, twenty years after that trip to McDonald's, and no, the world didn't end. It never does.

Looking back on the nuclear paranoia and fear that defined the emotional texture of the Cold War—not just for me, but for much of the world's population—I see now that the nuclear threat was a bogeyman constructed largely to terrify citizens into okaying massive defence budgets without debate. Fear sells.

There's nothing like the fears you acquire between the ages of, say, ten to fourteen. They seem to go in the deepest and colour your world the most strongly. A common question I ask people whenever film discussions come up is, "What is the movie that scared the shit out of you when you were eleven or twelve—the film that you were probably too young to watch, but you watched it anyway, and it totally screwed you up for the rest of your life?" Everyone's got one. Mine was *Lord of the Flies*, but other common answers are *The Exorcist* and *Event Horizon*. The point is that we all know that magic window in time when one is most susceptible to fear.

$\boxtimes$

In the early hours of Tuesday, September 25, 1973, two freighters, the *Sun Diamond* and *Erawan*, collided at the entrance to Vancouver's main harbour area, Burrard Inlet, dumping over fifty thousand gallons of bunker oil into the water. Bunker oil is the nastiest, stickiest, creepiest oil there is. In the oil distillation process, bunker oil is what sticks to the bottom of the tank. It's like molten tar, brutally foul, jet black and, on a warm day, the consistency of magnetic black diarrhea. It sticks to everything and it doesn't come off. An oil-soaked bird is a dead bird. They don't live. They die. There's no happy ending for any wildlife touched by the stuff. Don't ever believe the photos experts show you.

On the afternoon of September 25, 1973, someone thought it would be a great idea for local school kids to come "help," so a bunch of us went down to help "clean things up."

It was a dreadful idea.

We were dropped off in the same parking lot you normally parked in to get to the beach in summer, except there were dark boot-prints everywhere, and you could see streaks on the lawn where people tried wiping bunker fuel oil from their shoes before getting back into their vehicles; litter and newspapers were used for the same purpose. I remember the bus driver saying they could get someone else to pick us up; he wasn't getting any of that in his bus, and then he drove away.

It was confusion. Nobody really had any idea what to do. Well-intentioned people were using bamboo rakes to try to capture bunker fuel globules. You could see the blobs inside the waves as they lobbed in. Undead black zombie jellyfish. Nothing had prepared any of us eleven-year-olds for the foulness of bunker oil, the way it obliterates anything it touches, and its neutron-star black gloss as it smothers a low tide–scape of barnacles and starfish. It felt like a crime scene. It was a crime scene.

Someone gave us brand new rakes that had price stickers on them from the Woolco store in North Van. The government bought rakes from Woolco? They didn't have actual proper cleanup tools on hand?

The government was seemingly no help at all, having no visible plan in place to deal with a spill like that, and its efforts were directly compared to *Monty Python's Flying Circus* by *The Vancouver Sun*.

Someone shouted, "Go down to where the gravel meets the water and start raking. Try to catch the blobs before they break up," and so that's what we did. It was dismal, like trying to capture wheelbarrow-sized chunks of Jell-O with chopsticks. We saw, farther down the beach, that peat moss had been strewn onto gravel and sand to soak up the oil. Logs along the beach, we were told, acted as excellent bunker fuel sponges, and people would be gathering these logs to burn later in the day.

I remember a hippie with something black in his hands coming up to me and two friends: a cormorant completely covered in oil but still alive, and in heartbreaking death throes. "Look what you did."

"Huh?"

"You people from the suburbs. You made this happen. You killed it with your consuming and pollution."

That asshole destroyed any sympathy I might have one day had for hippies, but he made me love all birds and animals in a way I may never have otherwise. So thanks, asshole. And by the way, where did you grow up—in a manger?

In general, local environmentalists showed no pity for the citizens of North and West Vancouver, whose beaches, rocky coves and bays were blackened for miles once the tides began pushing the oil along. (Forty-two years later one can still clearly see oil stain marks on rocks ten miles up the coast.) The environmentalists argued that residents deserved retribution for all the crap the suburbanites were already putting in the harbour—an attitude as arrogant and useless as that of the government. People talk about the 1970s, but they never talk about how much hate there was back then. Hate and pollution. Everyone was looking for cheap, easy targets. Social ideas were evolving, but technologies to make new ideas fully manifest—as well as laws supporting the changes—were evolving much more slowly. Inside the lag time between the two realms lurked hate; everyone hating everything. Nobody looked clean. People still littered. Cars belched blue smoke that smelled like burning plastics. Don't get too nostalgic; it wasn't all plaid bell-bottoms and feathered hair.

✄

After an hour it was obvious we were wasting our time. Two friends and I took a regular bus back to school, where we got a punitive lecture about bailing on community participation. It was 1973 and the fact that three kids had spent the day unsupervised as easy prey to molesters had never troubled anyone. Had we hitchhiked back to school, we probably would have gotten points for being resourceful.

That night I didn't sleep, and I didn't sleep well for a month, and I still sometimes can't sleep when I think about the cormorant.

And don't forget nuclear war was always one ICBM away.

And then somewhere in there I saw *Lord of the Flies*.

¤

The punchline is that not even a month later, in the early morning of October 24, 1973, a German freighter, the *Westfalia*, dumped almost nine hundred gallons of bunker oil in Vancouver's main harbour, and by noon it had washed up on the shore of Vancouver's crown jewel, Stanley Park. The *Westfalia*'s spill was a fraction of what had been dumped the previous month, but you have to add the 1970s everything's-gone-to-shit factor: this smaller spill just reinforced the spirit of the age. Everything was disintegrating back then.

¤

On April 8, 2015, 15,142 days after the *Westfalia* spill, a grain ship, the *Marathassa*, registered in Cyprus, leaked 528 gallons of bunker oil into Vancouver's outer harbour area, English Bay. It was one-eighty-sixth the volume of what had been dumped on September 25, 1973. One would think oil spill cleanup in 2015 would be quick, forceful and inexpensive. Wrong. Federal and provincial politicians were about as functional and helpful as Peter, Chris, Stewie and Brian Griffin drinking ipecac together on *Family Guy*. Finger pointing on all sides. Blame. Retaliation. Lying. Downplaying. Catastrophizing. The one lesson that emerges from what was actually a comparatively small spill is that there still is no effective system in place to handle oil gone wrong, and this is in the centre of a city of 2.4 million people. I shudder to imagine a spill, even a small spill up or down the coast, away from both cleanup protocols and scrutiny.

In Vancouver right now, a company named Kinder Morgan wants to triple the amount of oil carried by the Trans Mountain pipeline and increase the number of oil tankers in Burrard Inlet from five to thirty-four per month. In preparation for (inevitable) future spills, the company "is committed to a polluter-pay, world-class, land-based and marine-spill response regime." Who wouldn't feel better already? I'm stoked!

Also, the BC government is trying to get liquefied natural gas (LNG) out of BC and down to Malaysia and, to do so, is hoping to get in bed with the Malaysian energy giant Petronas. The BC government has seemingly bet the family farm entirely on LNG going to Malaysia, complete with a fantasy number of 100,000 jobs to be created (in actuality, 4,500 during construction and up to 1,500 permanent jobs afterwards, spread around the province). One plant in particular is slated for the end of Howe Sound, North America's southernmost fjord and a place of spectacular beauty that has only recently healed from the toxic and visual blight of both copper mining (closed 1971) and a pulp mill (closed 2006). The selling point in the nearby town of Squamish (which lost all those pulp and copper jobs) is, of course, jobs, jobs, jobs—even though the proposed job numbers are pie in the sky, and the facility is setting the region up for truly devastating disaster scenarios. As a bonus, an LNG plant will blight one of the most beautiful and beloved scenic tourism corridors in Canada. It will be a visual nightmare experienced by every single human being who drives from Vancouver up to Squamish, Whistler and beyond.

Everyone is trying to move energy everywhere—and probably close to where you live. If it's not tankers and pipelines, then it's oil by rail. Remember: when something goes horribly wrong (and it will; even they acknowledge that), it will be written off as a one-time-only human error kind of thing, but it will keep happening over and over. Yes, the world will continue to chug along, but it will be a stained and damaged world.

A wonderful expression comes to mind here, one about trees: "The best time to plant a tree is twenty years ago. The second best time is right now." This could equally apply to planning safe energy. Twenty years pass very quickly. Start digging now.

The Short, Brutal Life
of the Channel Three
News Team

Sandra was sitting at her kitchen table looking out at a sunny day when her front doorbell rang. It was the police, come to tell her that her mother had been arrested for murdering the local Channel Three News Team—two anchorpeople and the weather guy and four studio technicians. Her mother, acting alone, had arrived at the TV studio carrying an oversized rattan handbag and pretended to be a sweet old thing interested in meeting the hostess from a cooking show. The moment she was close to the newsroom set, she asked to visit the washroom, slipped away, removed several guns from her handbag and came back firing. She was knocked to the ground by a surviving cameraman. Her pelvis was fractured and she was in hospital in stable condition. A clip of the event was going viral. The police asked Sandra if she would go to the hospital with them and she said of course, and off they drove, cherries flashing.

The main entryway was cordoned off, but the cruiser was allowed to slip past the security guards and news-crazed media. They elevatored up to the top floor, where a quartet of rifle-toting officers guarded her mother's room. Sandra had always expected that one day she would visit her mother with a broken hip or something similar in the hospital, just not under the current set of circumstances.

"Mom?"

"Hello, dear."

"What the hell were you thinking?"

"I'm more than happy to tell you."

"Wait—where's Dad?"

"He's not available right now."

"Oh Jesus, he's not going to go out and shoot somebody too, is he?"

"Aren't you quick to jump to conclusions!"

"Mom, you killed seven people."

"Good."

Sandra tried to compose herself while her mother serenely smiled. "So, why'd you do it?" she finally managed to ask.

"Our New Vision church group had an enlightenment fasting up in the mountains last weekend. It was glorious. And during group prayer, I was lifted up above Earth, and when I looked down on this planet, it was black like a charcoal briquette. At that moment I realized that Earth is over, and that New Vision will take me to a new planet."

"You're kidding me."

"No, I'm not kidding you, Sandra. Your father and I want you to join us."

"Mom. This is awful. Wake up—*wake up!*"

Sandra's mother looked at her with the same bland face she used when she thanked polite men for holding a door open for her. "You should be thrilled for me, dear. I believe it was you growing up who was fanatical about that escapist comic strip—what was it?—*The Battleship Yamato*? You of all people must understand what it feels like to want to leave a destroyed planet and roam the universe trying to fight an overwhelming darkness."

"It was just a comic, Mom."

"For 'just a comic' it certainly took hold of your imagination. I think you're jealous of me, dear."

"What?"

"You're jealous because right now I'm actually inside your comic book—on the other side of the mirror—and you aren't. But you can be. Join us."

"Mom, just stop it. Why did you kill those people?"

"I killed them because they were famous."

"What?"

"The only thing our diseased culture believes in is fame. No other form of eternity exists. Kill the famous and you snuff out the core of the diseased culture."

"So you killed the Channel Three News Team? They're barely famous even here in town."

"If you watch the news right about now, you'll see that New Visioneers around the world have shot and killed many people at all levels of fame. To decide who is more famous than anyone else is to buy into the fame creed. So we have been indiscriminate."

Sandra's sense of dread grew stronger. "So who is Dad going to kill?"

"What time is it?"

Sandra looked at her cellphone. "Almost five o'clock."

"In that case, right about . . ." Sandra's mother looked at the ceiling for a second, whereupon Sandra heard small cracking sounds coming from the hospital entranceway. "Right about now he's just shot the news reporters covering my shootings."

"Oh God, oh God, oh God . . ." Sandra ran to the window: pandemonium. She turned to her mother: "Holy fuck! What is wrong with you?"

"Is your father dead?"

"What?" Sandra looked out the window again and saw her father's body sprawled on a berm covered in Kentucky bluegrass. "Yes. Mother of God, he is!"

"Good. He'll be on the other side to greet me with the rest of us who have fulfilled our mission today."

Sandra staggered out into the hallway, gasping, but police and hospital staff paid her little attention as they braced for the next wave of wounded, dying and dead. She shouted at them, as if they could understand, "I am so sorry for all of this!" but she was ignored.

On a nursing station's TV screen, newscasts were coming in showing the faces of murdered celebrities from around the world.

Sandra ran back into the room to find her mother glowing. "Mom, you're crazy. Your cult is crazy."

"I want all of your generation to come join me and band together to smash all the shop windows of every boutique in the country, to set fire to every catwalk, to shoot rockets into Beverly Hills. It will be beautiful—like modern art—and people will finally stop believing in the false future promised by celebrity."

Sandra wanted to vomit. Gurneys loaded with bodies shunted quickly past the room's door and her mother went on talking: "In the last days of World War II, the Japanese emperor told the Japanese to sacrifice themselves, to die like smashed jewels. And so I say to you, Sandra, die like a smashed jewel. Destroy so that we can rebuild. We can become a furnace within a furnace."

Outside it had grown dark—not regular darkness—a chemical darkness that felt linked to profound evil. The moon was full. Sandra and her mother caught each other staring at it at the same time. Her mother said, "I wish the Apollo astronauts had died on the moon."

"What?"

"Then it would be one great big tombstone for planet Earth." Her mother popped something into her mouth.

"Mom—what was that?"

"Cyanide, dear. I'm off on your Battleship Yamato. Why don't you come too?"

Sandra ran for help, but the staff were too busy with the wounded, and so she watched her mother die, writhing on her bed, then falling still.

Stunned, Sandra walked back out into the hallway. There was blood on the floor and blood on the walls. It was smeared, and the whole place smelled of hot, moist coins. She heard gunshots coming from the elevator bank, and screaming staff ran down the hallway past her. She saw an orderly in turquoise surgical scrubs coming toward her holding a sawed-off shotgun, and the look in his eye told Sandra that this was a New Vision follower.

He was whistling, and as he came nearer, he said, relaxed as can be, "Looks like you're one pretty darn famous little lady now, aren't you. Being daughter of a mass murderer and all."

Sandra ran into her mother's room and kissed her mother's mouth violently, sucking in the remains of the cyanide. She tasted the chemical as it entered her bloodstream and knew death would be quick.

The whistling stopped as the orderly loomed in the doorway. Sandra said, "Know what? I leave this planet on my own terms, you freak." She was dead before the buckshot pounded her chest.

Nine Readers

Last summer in Reykjavik, I learned that one in ten Icelanders will write a novel in their lifetime. This is impressive, but the downside of this is that each novel gets only nine readers. In a weird way, our world is turning into a world of Icelandic novelists, except substitute *blog, vlog* or *website* for *novel*—and there we are: in Reykjavik.

A defining sentiment of our new era is that never before has being an individual been so easily broadcast, yet never before has individuality felt so ever-increasingly far away. Before the twenty-first century, we lived with the notion of oneself as a noble citizen of the world, a lone soul whose life was a story written across a span of seven decades or so. We now live instead with the ever-gnawing sensation that one's self is really just one more meat unit among seven billion other meat units.

This twenty-first century crisis of individuality expresses itself in many ways. In Japan there is the phenomenon of the *hikiko-mori*. Your child grows up, leaves home and then, after a few years, returns home and never leaves his or her bedroom again. Ever. The rare *hikikomori* will venture out in the middle of the night to visit a local mini-mart, but that's it. In 2010 the Japanese government estimated there were 700,000 *hikikomori* in Japan, with the average age being thirty-one. Yes, you read that correctly: almost three-quarters of a million modern-day elective hermits back with Mom and Dad, and they are psychologically incapable of ever leaving.

Ever.

I suspect these young people are experiencing "atomophobia": the fear of feeling like an individual. After the late-1980s bubble burst, Japan went from being a monolithically homogenized culture, with guaranteed lifetime employment, to its exact opposite: a land of hyper-individuality trapped inside a consumer hyperspace that guarantees nothing, let alone employment. The crazy costumes once worn only on Sundays in Harajuku are now regular, uncommented upon Japanese daywear. One might think that a culture in which its everyday citizens dress in borderline Halloween costumes is a culture of fierce individuality; instead it is a society deeply conflicted about the dark side of enforced uniqueness. "The more like ourselves we become, the odder we become," wrote Australian critic Louise Adler. "This is most obvious in people whom society no longer keeps in line; the eccentricity of the very rich or of castaways."

In North America and England we have the trend of normcore (the *normal* version of hardcore)—a trend so stupid that it's more famous for being a stupid trend than it is for being a trend itself. But normcore actually is something real, a unisex trend that very much exists. England's *Heat* magazine tells us, "Normcore celebrates the ordinary with its reliance on brazenly bland staples such as stonewashed denim, label-less shirts, and pool sandals that bear a distressing resemblance to Crocs. It's the ultimate knee-jerk reaction to not only the meticulously dour Hipster look, but the demands of fashion in general."* Normcore is about dressing to be invisible, the fashion equivalent of renting a mid-size American-made sedan in a large American city: total anonymity

---

* Heatworld, "WTF Is Normcore and Which Celebs Are Keeping up with It?" *Heat* (September 18, 2014). http://www.heatworld.com/Star-Style/2014/07/WTF-is-Normcore-and-which-celebs-are-keeping-up-with-it/

that offers abdication from the responsibility of having to be an individual living in real time in the real world. Normcore says, "Screw it. Go ahead: monitor me on CCTVs. Scan the Internet with facial recognition algorithms. Have the NSA read my emails like tea leaves. I'm going to be deliberately un-unique. *I am going to punish the world with my blandness, and if you scan my metadata, you'll fall asleep before you find anything good.*"

⊕

In the fall of 2014, driving in a taxi on Clerkenwell Road in London, I saw a huge Gap billboard that read: "BE NORMAL."

Huh?

⊕

I wonder if the need for individualism may, in fact, be a form of brain mutation spread lightly throughout a population. I wonder if most human beings are cut out to cope with the psychic vacuum freedom can create. I get the impression from the daily news that there are a lot of people out there, possibly a majority, who don't actually want progress—or the freedom progress brings. Most people seem happy to belong to a group—any kind of group—and they mistrust someone who doesn't feel similarly. And I also get the impression there are a lot of people out there who perceive freedom as an invitation to chaos—which is somehow embarrassing. And I sometimes wonder if feeling unique is an indication of actually being unique—even though it is the feeling of uniqueness that convinces us we have souls and are individuals.

⊕

You have a blog. She posts on Facebook three times a day. They have a website. Sigrid wrote a saga.

The novel made us individuals. The Internet makes us units. Write as fast as you can. Blog like crazy. Vlog your brains out. Be unique. Be the best *you* you can be. One thousand years ago, you assumed that your grandchildren's life would be identical to your own. In 2016 we know that 2020, not even a decade from now, is going to be very different and possibly quite scary compared to what we have now. How shall we dress for the occasion?

Nine Point Zero

The king was up in his hot-air balloon, looking down over his mighty kingdom, proud that he had been born to rule over it and silently happy with his lot in life. It was the middle of a sunny weekday and life in the kingdom was happening as usual: the roads were full, the children were at school, and the last of the lunchtime diners were heading back to their workplaces. That was when the earthquake struck.

It was a nine point zero; within fifteen seconds it had demolished the older, less seismically prepared buildings in the land. After that, the newer buildings began to drop. Throughout the kingdom, survivors did a clumsy dance out onto the wobbling streets to avoid falling debris—shards of glass and masonry.

The noise of the quake was deafening. Such a roar! It was the planet itself shifting and readjusting. The people on the street couldn't even hear each other yell.

The king, up in his hot-air balloon, was the only person who experienced none of the quake's violence, which continued to roar and roar and destroy—a quake that wouldn't stop. By the quake's fifth minute, most of his kingdom's houses were gone and all the dams had broken. Reservoirs had drowned whole suburbs. Office towers had fallen on their sides, and the quake's continuing lunging motions shook them until only twisted steel beams remained.

The king's heart was broken and still the quake continued! Survivors were becoming seasick from the ground's lurching—they lay vomiting on the crumbling parking lots and sidewalks. Trees fell. Birds were unable to land on the moving surfaces and were relieved to sit on the rim of the king's hot-air balloon basket.

Fires broke out and the rubble burned. The king watched, helpless to stop it, tears in his eyes, flocks of confused birds circling his basket.

After ten minutes, survivors truly wondered if they were lost inside a dream; the pounding earth was almost boring, like a carnival ride that had gone on far too long.

After fifteen minutes, there was nothing left to destroy. All the buildings were gone. All statues, all communication towers, all laboratories, all movie theatres, all gyms, all gone.

And then the earthquake stopped.

The king, his nerves in ribbons, sobbed as he landed his balloon atop what was once a mighty supermarket. The quake had shaken it so badly that the remains had settled into a grey powder, beneath which the larger chunks slept, neatly graded by size. As he stepped out onto the dust, he remembered a photo he'd seen of the first footstep on the moon.

The roads and parking lots had cracked open and the pavement fragments above had broken like soda crackers, then shattered, then turned to dust. Front yards had liquefied, swallowing whole houses and trees, which now lay deep within the planet.

The king tried to find survivors, and soon he did: stragglers, caked in dirt and vomit, still seasick and crazed by the fifteen-minute quake, feeling they were hallucinating upon seeing their perfectly intact, well-groomed king.

They began searching for food and water and medicine and liquor, but little could be found in the rubble and dust.

The king helped a middle-aged woman who was picking away at the spot where there had once been a convenience store. She held up a clear bottle of liquid and asked the king what it contained.

"Fruit Solutions with Omega-3 . . . but why are you asking me that? It says so right on the label," he replied.

The woman ripped off the cap and poured half the bottle's contents onto her face to rinse out her eyes; she then drank the remaining liquid and groped through the dust for bottles that were identical.

A former four-lane commercial strip was so destroyed it couldn't even be called a path. There the king found a couple of hipsters in cargo pants and vintage early-1990s Soundgarden T-shirts. They held up some cans and asked the king what was in them. "Who's Your Daddy Energy Drink with Caffeine, Taurine and B Vitamins . . . but why are you asking me that? It says so right on the label." They quickly opened the cans and guzzled the contents, ignoring the king.

The king walked farther and met his old high school teacher, who was alive only because he'd called in sick that day and had been stuck in traffic while taking his Jack Russell terrier to the vet when the quake struck, riding out the fifteen minutes in the padded comfort of his 2010 Nissan Sentra. The teacher said, "Oh, King, hello. Such good luck to find you. Please, please tell me, what does this bottle contain?"

The king looked at it. "Bleach. But why are you asking me that? It says so right on the label."

"It's a funny thing," the teacher said, "but I can no longer read."

"What do you mean?"

"Exactly what I said—I look at the shapes on this label and they look like upside-down Hebrew mixed with right-side-up Korean. No idea at all what any of it says. By the way, I see a tsunami coming. Let's hope we're far enough away from the coast here."

The king had little time to reflect on the fact that the quake had stripped its survivors of the ability to read. A massive tsunami sloshed inward from the coast, turning the recently powdered city into a rich dark brown cake batter that stopped just inches away from the king's royal shoes. A small aftershock jiggled air bubbles from the batter. His world fell silent.

Behind him, a chimney collapsed, the last remaining vertical line to be seen for miles around. The hipsters and the middle-aged lady and the old high school teacher stood beside the king. The woman said, "I'm glad at least one person is still able to read. Otherwise we'd never be able to rebuild from scratch everything that we had before, back to shiny and brand new, as if none of this had ever happened!"

Another tsunami washed in atop the first one, bright red for some reason. Industrial colouring agents? A trainload of cough syrup? Did it matter? The king stumbled over to the teacher's destroyed Sentra, half buried with the remains of the road; he leaned against it and retched. With his index finger, he wrote the words "THE KING IS DEAD" on its dusty window, and when he was asked what he'd just written, he told his subjects, "A map."

Smells

At my gym there's a sign saying, "This is a fragrance-free zone." I thought about it and, yes, perfume in a gym might be kind of weird, like smelling cooking bacon when trying to fall asleep at night. And then last week a younger male gym-goer showed up and as he walked across the floor, everyone's eyes started burning and their nostrils flared. This wasn't because he was, in some way, hot. It was because he was wearing a male body spray. The odour was half industrial, half ultra-cheap soap, and had he been wearing any more, he would have resembled Pigpen from Charlie Brown, going through life with his own visible weather system. Fortunately, the staff at my gym are fearless and they landed on this guy like hawks. He won't be wearing Satan's Tears there again anytime soon.

The incident reminded me of something a teacher friend told me, that the single worst thing to happen to education since the 1960s has been the introduction and wide adoption of body sprays among male teens. "They think it makes them God's gift to women and they have no idea how bad it is. They don't shower after gym anymore—fear of pervs—so they arrive in the classroom and it's like pepper spray in your face. On top of everything, it's highly flammable and you can turn the cans into blowtorches with a Bic lighter. It's a marketing perfect storm."

⊗

One August somewhere in the late 1980s, I returned to my apartment building after two weeks away, and the lobby's smell was unlike anything I'd experienced. The closest approximation was the time a rat got stuck and died in a roach motel in my bathroom in Honolulu. Mix vomit and shit together and . . . ugh, it was staggering. Of course, you've probably already figured out what it was: a tenant died on August 1 after paying the rent. I returned on August 27. My apartment was in a different wing, so I didn't have the smell around me full blast, but I could hear the contractors cutting and crow-barring away every single surface in the offending apartment (and the apartment below it—leakage) to take it all away to be burned. The smell even got into the Formica countertops. And then, the next morning, the building's lobby smelled like . . . cinnamon candy? Huh? Yes, cinnamon candy. It turns out that smell is a vector, and for every smell there exists an anti-smell, and the anti-smell of human death is artificial cinnamon. You learn something new every day, and this is what you learned today.

⊗

I was in California years ago when they were aerially spraying malathion to stop the spread of pests called Mediterranean fruit flies, or the medfly. From the political noise surrounding the event, you'd have thought they were dropping plutonium on the city, but the spraying went ahead regardless. One afternoon I was almost directly below a spray in progress, and I thought to myself, *Well this is interesting—today I get to learn what malathion smells like*. And I did. It smells identical to the playground I spent eight years in, from kindergarten to the seventh grade.

I think everyone has a few unusual smells that bring back happy times and places. On my first trip to Japan, my hotel used an industrial cleaning agent that smelled like artificial peaches.

About once a year I'll smell it in an unlikely place, like a European airport or a mall in the United States, and I'm right back in pre-bubble-collapse Tokyo. I wish they made a cologne that smelled like it. I'd wear it every day. I try to wear Eau Sauvage, but it keeps getting confiscated by airport security screeners because I always forget to not put it in my carry-on.

There are more odours I wish I could bottle: freshly sharpened pencils; a bag of Halloween candy; car exhaust in the 1960s, back when they put lead in it; a freshly peeled tangerine. A smell I don't miss? High-end magazines from the 1990s that were laced with scratch-and-sniff perfume cards. Gag.

A friend of mine worked as a consultant for American Flavors and Fragrances, and he told me that the reason supermarkets have in-store bakeries is because the smell of bread is the one smell, more than any other, that makes people buy more food than they set out to buy. The bakeries themselves lose money. In a similar way, someone told me that the only reason couture designers do couture is to keep the brand healthy in order to sell its fragrance, which is the financial bedrock of most fashion houses.

It's actually pretty rare to find people who wear a lot of perfume or cologne these days. I guess it's like smoking: it's on the way out, no matter how you look at it. But I think it's actually kind of gutsy to wear too much scent: *Hi, I'm going to colonize the space around me with my Jean Patou/Halston/whatever, and if you object, it means you're merely trying to recolonize the space I've just colonized from you—which is pretty much the formula for war. Bring it on.*

And what is the best smell of all? According to surveys, it's the vanilla-y, plasticky smell of Play-Doh, a smell for which most people have potent, 100 percent happy memories. Wouldn't it be nice if you found a Play-Doh scratch-and-sniff in this book right here?

Coffee & Cigarettes

I don't remember how I started drinking coffee. Yes, I do. I worked at a Chevron gas station in high school, and in the back area, we had this hideous powdered coffee called High Point, which I'd never seen before except in a few TV commercials in which Lauren Bacall (who surely must have been cash starved) was its spokesperson. It burnt out my coffee taste buds forever and desensitized me to all coffee nuances for the rest of my life.

I started smoking around the same time—peer pressure. But don't get me wrong, I loved it. I may have stopped smoking on Halloween 1988, but I still consider myself a smoker and sometimes—for some reason, cold, clear, non-windy days are best—I'll be out of doors and inside someone's second-hand-smoke slipstream and I fully experience all those same happy chemicals from age seventeen all over again.

I miss smoking while driving. I miss smoking and talking on the phone, but then I don't talk on the phone anymore—nobody does—so it's kind of moot. I wonder what it must be like smoking while using the Internet. It must feel holy.

◐

The slowness and cluelessness of some Starbucks staff drive me insane. I want a brewed coffee, here's two dollars, so come on, just pour the damn thing. Starbucks needs an express lane. Do they ever count how many customers leave because they don't want to wait for ten minutes behind useless people ordering complicated, useless beverages? I think they must have monetized some sort of algorithm that equates useless, complicated beverages and their ridiculous preparation times versus people who just want coffee. And I know which side wins.

❖

In the summer some guests stayed over at the house, so I tried to be a perfect host and asked if I could get them some cigarettes. I went to a local grocery and, after being shamed over the loud-speaker system, a staffer came to a special zone beside the fire-wood pile and opened a black door and gave me a box with a photo of a diseased lung on it. "That'll be fifty dollars" (or some other insane price). At some point you have to see that the writing's on the wall for smokers.

I'm not sure if those warning labels make smoking even one tiny notch less desirable. Sex and death are the deepest emotional pairing we have as a species. Maybe those pictures of diseased lungs are, in some filthy, perverse, highly human way . . . cool. You're not supposed to say it, but smoking really is cool. It's a fact, and how you choose to not believe it is possibly the last thing that stands between where you are in life now and becoming a full adult.

❖

I once worked with a girl named Anne-Marie, who was allergic to any chemical that ended in *aine*, which meant benzocaine, novo-caine and cocaine. That always seemed like the sexiest allergy possible, like being allergic to glitter balls and to orgies where all the women have crimped hair and the guys have zodiac medallions.

●

Smoking in France is a real eye-opener. All the decisions seem to get made by smokers during their cigarette breaks. I think that in France, smoking is a social filter, and if you don't smoke you'll only ever make it to two rungs from the top, never the top. A very strong memory of France for me is of being in people's apartments and hearing Carla Bruni's music, and playing with bowls of Ai Weiwei's ceramic sunflower seeds stolen from the Tate's Turbine Hall, within a miasma of indoor smoking. Smoking indoors—it feels like listening to smuggled Beatles records in Kiev in 1965. It feels stolen.

●

When did Nespresso conquer the planet—three years ago? I woke up one morning and every hotel I went to on Earth magically had Nespresso machines. The capsules are so seductive and druggie looking—how can you resist? For the same amount of electricity it takes to make the aluminum in one capsule you could probably fuel a suburban household for a week. In a thousand years we'll look back on right now as the Era of Squandered Metals, but our descendants will never know the joy of a custom single hit of coffee that you also didn't have to stand in some ridiculous Starbucks lineup to get.

●

In China everyone smokes, which is just sad. They should have a motto: "China: the Land Where the Air Does Your Smoking for You."

●

My grade seven gym teacher told us that if you quit smoking, it took your body seven years to fully quit, so in my mind I wasn't over the hump until Halloween 1995. Since then the only anniversary that really registers in my brain is Halloween every seven years: 2002, 2009, and this year's a biggie for me. I framed the last cigarette I ever smoked. I knew it was the last as I smoked it. If the house is ever on fire, it's the first thing I'm saving.

Public Speaking

The first time I ever spoke publicly was in March 1991, at a chain bookstore beside Copley Square in Boston. I hadn't given the event much thought beforehand, and then suddenly I was in the backroom, surrounded by cartons and paperwork and being told, "You're on in thirty seconds."

Oh, I thought. I peeked through the door, saw a healthy-sized crowd and had one of those rare epiphanies: *Well, Doug, those people out there just assume you're going to do a good job, so just do a good job*. It was that simple, but it is all I—or anyone else—need to know about public speaking, and it has been saving my bacon for twenty-five years. People generally want everyone to do well on a stage—they really do. And, at the very, very worst, remember what Steven Spielberg once said, which is that people will sit through twenty minutes of anything. Another good piece of advice is that two hundred people sitting in a room together isn't really two hundred people sitting in a room together—it's one audience, and it will have its own temperature and texture, and it is also your audience. Being onstage talking is one of the few moments in your life where you control absolutely everything, and it can be its own high. I remember seeing something online about Pete Townshend of The Who yelling at someone from the front row who had climbed on stage: "F*** off! F*** off my f***ing stage." Words of truth.

Something will always go wrong during a public speaking event. Mine used to almost exclusively take place in bookstores, where, at any moment, one can encounter cappuccino machines, PA systems, crying babies, outside traffic, dead microphones—the list goes on. It was good training because it made me think on the fly. Speaking of flies, I once did a reading event in Ontario, Canada, in a professional theatre with flawless acoustics, and I thought to myself, "Yessiree, nothing could possibly go wrong in a magical stage environment such as this." The first minute on stage, a fly landed on my face. And then another. I swatted them away and the audience giggled, not knowing why I was doing this, and basically I had to speak for fifty minutes with flies crawling all over me. It was probably the worst speaking gig ever.

But wait, there *was* another one that was worse. It was in Quebec, and I'd done a huge amount of work preparing a properly synchronized presentation on I no longer even remember what. But I remember plugging my laptop into the venue's AV system shortly before the event began and watching my desktop scramble, randomize and then fry. *Vzzzzzzzt!* Both the track pad and the mouse stopped working. The venue filled up, and having to speak that day felt like I'd had a stroke in public. It was a terrible, ghastly event, and I'm glad it was about a year before smartphones came out or else video evidence of my shame would live for eternity in the cloud.

◻

One form of public speaking not usually recognized as such is teaching. I've had a few experiences in educational situations and they've been worse than flies crawling over my face. I don't know if it's me or what, but having to speak to college students is like having to address a crowd of work-shirking entitlement robots whose only passion, aside from making excuses as to why they didn't do their assignments, is lying in wait, ready to pounce upon the tiniest of

PC infractions. You can't pay teachers enough to do what they do. Having been in their shoes, even briefly, has converted me into an education advocate. Double all teaching salaries now.

☒

In recent years there's been TED, which everyone seems to have a theory about. It usually has to do with the way TED creates pressure for speakers to make their message nothing less than transformative, while insisting that the passing forward of this wisdom fits into TED's twenty-minute meme delivery system. TED speakers are almost always terrific, but one wonders what they might do with more breathing room, more time for reflection, and without a need to include an orgasm at the talk's end.

☒

Sometimes, if you're feeling lazy, instead of a speech or lecture, you can do an on-stage discussion—which is a little bit like getting away with something. But it's a workaround that also has the potential for disaster. I have learned the hard way that not everybody is comfy with winging it on a stage, and what was supposed to have been a fifty-minute cake walk can sometimes turn into fifty minutes of torture as you try to minimize someone else's paralyzing unease, for you, them and the audience. The only thing worse than this? Q & A. Why do we still do this? Ugh. I was hoping the Internet would somehow kill Q & A, but apparently not. The first question is a softball, the second question is "the hostage taker," which holds the audience captive while articulating often irksome points of view, and question three is the "therapy question," when a needy person forces two hundred people to witness the deficiencies of their id. Basically, talks should be forty-five to fifty minutes with no Q & A, and if too many people start coughing around minutes thirty-five to forty, it's nature's signal to you to wrap things up quickly. It's your audience, but not for much longer.

Shiny

A friend of mine sells hotels in California. If he's having a slow time moving a property, he has a three-point program to speed up a sale. First, he surrounds the property with a planted mixture of annual flowers—petunias work best—in a one-to-one colour proportion of white-to-colour. They make a property look both lived in and loved. Second, he has a tow truck drop off one or two Rolls-Royces. These are dead Rolls-Royces, sold for a few thousand bucks by Los Angeles car-hire companies. Basically, they're husks, but if you park one out front, they become real estate and the property's price instantly rises. Third, he invents affairs between movie stars that took place on the property. A room is a room is a room, but not if Grace Kelly and William Holden spent a lost week there in 1955. It's a strange trait we human beings have, but we seem to love imagining celebrity ghosts having sex.

$\oplus$

I remember being in an airport lounge this past February 21, watching CNN footage of Dubai's seventy-four-storey Torch skyscraper in flames. Bits of burning debris from the fiftieth floor drifted down and set other floors on fire. Like most fires, the burning Torch made for gripping TV, and I remember the guy at the table behind me saying, "It's going to take more than just a pressure washer to get that thing looking brand new again."

⊕

A favourite video of mine from 1983 was for a song called "Shiny Shiny" by the now long-defunct group Haysi Fantayzee. One of its vocalists, Kate Garner, sang and danced in a high-tech Barbarella-style outfit. The video is on YouTube; give it a look. In 1995 I was living in Palo Alto and a photographer showed up to do some shots, and the photographer was Kate Garner (!), which was a fan moment for me but not for her. She'd moved into photography and was now a serious person and really didn't want to discuss her former life as a new wave pop star. She had glasses on and was dressed down, and I guess I can see her point, but I did keep waiting for that moment when she would take off her glasses, unbundle her hair and shake it loose—at which point everyone would say, "By God, Kate Garner . . . you're beautiful!"

⊕

A friend of mine does window displays for Cartier in North America, and he told me this interesting fact: if you place two or more objects in a display case, people will always read the object on the left as being the most valuable, even if it isn't. I would have thought the centre object would be perceived as the most valuable, but apparently not. If anybody knows the laws and rules of luxury and desire, it's Cartier.

⊕

What all these snippets have in common is that in some form, they help us decode the notions of value and beauty that seem to be hardwired into our DNA. Shiny is youth. Shiny is fertility. Shiny is uncorrupted. Shiny smells like the interior of a new car. Shiny is sixty-five golf courses in Palm Springs in the middle of the worst drought in a century. I love shiny because the moment you see something shiny, you know there's going to be something rotten or scary nearby—like the Japanese notion of *honne* and *tatemae*: the public face and the private face. I don't like it when people show me something rotten without first giving me something shiny to compare it to. It's like people who deconstruct music without learning how to play it in the first place.

$\oplus$

In the mid-1980s I attended a Japanese institute on the Hawaiian island of Oahu, where the temperature was seventy-five degrees and slightly breezy pretty much every day of the year. But I was in my mild goth phase and with a few similarly minded locals, we were the only people in Hawaii wearing black sweaters while we cursed the sun. Evil, evil sun.

$\oplus$

In 2000 I was in a Daiei department store in Tokyo and I had an epiphany in the cleaning-products aisle. Fifty brands of bleach and toilet-bowl cleaners and window sprays were all duking it out for my attention, but of course they all cancelled each other out, creating an optical-field effect. The sensation of standing in the aisle and soaking in these bright Japanese pinks and turquoises and baby blues and reds, with all of their noisy katakana labels, was sort of like an experience you might have in front of an Olafur Eliasson piece. It transcended culture and became a biology project. Similarly, aisle seventeen in my local Michaels craft store is a ribbon aisle, with shelves on both sides filled with shiny, blingy ribbon spools. The floor is white. To stand there in the middle of the aisle is not unlike staring at white and coloured petunias planted together in a one-to-one ratio. It makes me feel like I'm engaged in some sort of universal constant, like pi or Avogadro's number.

In any event, I bought around one hundred of the Japanese cleaning-product bottles and took them back to the hotel room and flushed their contents down the toilet, an act that horrifies most people but, if you think about it, it was all going there anyway. And what's the difference if there's a bit of hand dirt or spaghetti sauce residue mixed in with it? That gets you off the ecological hook, morally? These emptied bottles all came back home and went into a dedicated shelving unit, and it became an installation I titled *Tokyo Harbour*. To look at *Tokyo Harbour* is to be seduced by its candy-coloured cheerfulness, except suddenly you start thinking about what was inside the bottles, and cheerfulness becomes toxicity.

In 2011 Japan had the Tohoku earthquake and tsunami. Millions of tons of debris were swept off the eastern coast of Honshu and into the Pacific, where, years later, the refuse began washing up on a remote beach off northern British Columbia's coast: the north tip of the northernmost island of the Queen Charlotte Islands, now known in British Columbia by the name Haida Gwaii. This spit of land is the one place on earth I head to every year to recharge and escape from technology and homogenized time, and now it had become (and still remains) a graveyard for plastic Japanese products. For the past two summers, my quiet retreats have turned into debris cleanup missions. On one of my first afternoons there, I found a turquoise and pink bottle of Japanese cleaning product and my mind was blown. I felt like the villain on the receiving end of an ecological folk tale about the dangers of engaging with seductive sheen.

⊕

The art world is largely mistrustful of shiny things and, on some level, even fearful of them. But if sophistication is the ability to put a smile on one's existential desperation, then the fear of a glossy sheen is actually the fear that the surface is the content. Fear of sheen is the fear that surface equals depth, that banality equals beauty, that shiny objects are merely transient concretizations of the image economy, and proof that Warhol was correct—a fact that still seems to enrage a surprising number of theoreticians.

Fear of shine explains why so much of today's art looks so much like art of today. You have art-fair art, which is very shiny; it is diminished with the label "crapstraction," and it looks like it all could have been made by one person on a really nice drug. And then you have the nearby alternative art fair, where no shininess is found, and where most of the art looks like it was also made by one person, albeit one who changes meds every two weeks. In a sense, the existence of art fairs and their independent parallels, anti-fairs, seems to be a precipitation of the ongoing chilly stand-off between artists, dealers and institutions. There's mistrust on all flanks. Everyone wants to attend the other person's party—and they often do—but nobody feels comfortable no matter where they go. Everyone gets art'ed out and exhausted and feels like they've just walked across ten miles of non-stop casino noise and bling. Everyone just wants to go back to the hotel and sleep and strip their brains of shininess. But instead they freshen up their look and go out for cocktails. And then they do it all over again the next day.

⊕

Do you buy dented cans of food? Do you buy the vegetables and fruits with bird pecks in them? Do you buy misfit produce that doesn't look like clip art? And what's your policy on expired dairy products? Would you feel awkward buying art from a dealer whose space didn't at least aspire to some dimension of New York neutrality? Does it slightly weird you out when you walk from the outside world into a gallery where the inside mood is blank and white to the point of feeling outer-spacey? Have you ever bought a designer garment you thought was real but turned out to be fake? Have you ever tried to fob off a fake as the real thing? Do you collect art? Do you make art? Do you feel like a nimble outsider free to pass judgment on everything? If you do, does it depress you to not actually be in the game itself? Are you a minimalist? Do you take pride in a reductive life? Minimalists are actually extreme hoarders: they hoard space, and they're just as odd as those people with seven rooms filled with newspapers, dead cats and margarine tubs. Are you into fashion? Fashion and the art world have always coexisted. Fashion memes are simply faster and you get to do figurative work without having to defend yourself to the 400-level art instructor who lives in your head and judges everything harshly and frequently. Who is this art instructor who lives inside your head? Where did he or she come from? Is their tone invariably mocking and snippy? Do they transmit their biases onto you to the point where you no longer trust your own judgment? Why is this tone always angry? Why does its point of view reflect that of someone a generation older than you, who, to be honest, you really don't agree with much of the time. Can you kill the internalized art instructor who lives in your head? That would be liberating, but would it destabilize you? Would you still know how to discuss art without sounding small-town? But then, maybe using your own voice instead of the internal professor's voice would make you sound authentic instead of like just another art-world person with the same internalized 400-level professor clouding and poisoning your experiences in the aesthetic realm. Do you think that being quick to judge, and being quick to pre-emptively please your internal 400-level professor, means you ignore or dismiss things that might actually be interesting? Is it better to be safe than wrong? Do you sometimes see people talking and you can tell it's not even them doing the talking—they're merely channelling their internal professor? Does this activate your own internal professor? Do you call them on it? No, you don't. Nobody ever does. It's why things largely don't change. It's really boring to listen to two people channelling their internal professors. Inside their heads they're getting an A+ on a nonexistent essay. It's beyond predictable.

Meanwhile, who's carrying around the trays of drinks and amuse-bouches? Who's out back loading the trucks and carrying the trash? Those security staff over there—they must be bored out of their minds. God, what a horrible job that must be. At least it's a blessing they don't have an internal 400-level professor in their heads. That would be the worst thing of all: having to be around this stuff eight hours a day, relentlessly, endlessly playing the same monologue over and over inside my head. I'd run off and join ISIS if I had to do that for a living. *ISIS*. ISIS has production values. It's waging the first war ever where people look and say, "Wow, I think they're using Final Cut Pro, not just Final Cut." And imagine having an about-to-be-beheaded prisoner read from a teleprompter. Those are professional post-production values. And their weapons and their website, too. Really tight and clean. Shiny.

Notes on Relationships in the Twenty-first Century

It's very hard to imagine phoning someone up and saying, "Hey, come over to my house and we'll sit next to each other on chairs and go online together!" Going online is such an intrinsically solitary act, yet it fosters the creation of groups.

⊗

Last year at a conference about cities, I met this guy from Google who asked me what I knew about Fort McMurray, Alberta. I told him it's an oil-extraction complex in the middle of a northern Canadian prairie, and because of this, it has the most disproportionately male demographic of any city in North America. Its population is maybe fifty thousand. I asked him why he was asking and he said, "Because it has the highest per capita video-streaming rate of anywhere in North America." Nudge, nudge.

⊗

I think that, because of the Internet, straight people are now having the same amount of sex as gay guys were always supposed to be having. There's a weird look I can see on the faces of people who are getting too much sex delivered to them via hooking up online: *Wait—is this as good as it gets?*

✖

On the old *Mary Tyler Moore Show*, Lou Grant asked Mary how many times a woman could be with a guy before she became "that kind of girl," and Mary thought about it very carefully and said, "Six." Some psychologists have come to the conclusion that most people have five or six loves, and once they use them up, that's it. Sixes get used up very quickly in the new information world.

✖

Q: How many times can a person fall in love? Apparently, if you average it out, two and a half times. Men are slightly more inclined to believe in a third-time love than women.

✖

People in the pornography industry have found that the magic price point for people subscribing to a porn site is $29.95. The moment you cross that line, potential customers balk. It is called the "porn wall" and it seems to be an impenetrable thing, a constant that's built into us by nature, like the nesting instinct of birds or the molecular weight of zinc.

✖

I remember a thirty-year-old Latino guy in the 1990s who passed himself off as a hot teenage Latina in a Florida high school and spent a year and a half there before anyone found out. I think he actually grew stubble once and attended PTA meetings as his own father. I think that in certain ways we've all become middle-aged

Latino guys pretending to be hot cheerleaders . . . except maybe you're not pretending to be a cheerleader; you're pretending to be a studly cowboy, or whoever it is you wish you could be, to the person on the other end, who has no way of disproving it.

⊗

Sometimes people really connect online but, of course, they live far away from each other. So, ultimately, one of them buys a plane ticket and flies across the country to meet the other. If there's no physical chemistry, it leads to one very depressing drink and some desultory conversation before they both go home. People in the matchmaking industry call these people NFHs ("next-flight-homers"). Sometimes people really connect online and, when they meet in person, they physically click. People in the dating industry call them "room-getters."

⊗

I sometimes wonder about people who wake up and spend almost the whole day online. When they go to bed at night, they'll have almost no organic memories of their own. If they do this for a long time, you can begin to say that their intelligence is, in a true sense, artificial. Which I guess means sex lives have never been as artificial as they are now.

⊗

People seem to be pickier about bodies these days. New high-definition TV cameras have changed the way we look at bodies. Even a faint acne scar looks like the Grand Canyon on a high-def screen. TV casting agents have started to heavily favour actors with perfectly smooth skin. It's like the dermatological equivalent of the introduction of sound into film in 1927.

⊗

I don't think people being on their devices all the time is an indicator of social isolation. It's the opposite. In Manhattan about one person in three on any given sidewalk is using a device. Some people say that's bad because they're not "in the moment," but I think it's kind of nice because you have visible proof that people need and want to be with other people.

⊗

I watched *Looking for Mr. Goodbar* a few weeks ago. It starred Richard Gere and Diane Keaton in the 1970s New York pickup scene, and I was horrified by how low-tech it was back then. It was like people lived in badly furnished caves connected by land lines. It was a real eye-opener.

⊗

Once you get used to a certain level of online connection, there's just no way to go back to where you were before. People are more connected than they've ever been before—except they've been tricked into thinking they're more isolated than ever. How did this happen? Wait—what's that you're asking me? Am I wearing underwear right now?

Fear of Windows

Kimberly Kellog was a well-nourished, upper-middle-class twelve-year-old girl who lived in a good suburb of a good American city. Her parents were happy that she hadn't yet turned into an insolent shoplifting, purge-dieting, binge-drinking nightmare like all the other girls in the neighbourhood. They counted their blessings.

One night Kimberly was watching a horror movie with her parents, one about outer-space aliens invading the suburbs. The movie was made in a cinéma-vérité style, so the naturalistic and provocative camerawork made the everyday world seem more charged and real, ready to explode like an ownerless black nylon backpack abandoned in a crowded railway station.

Halfway through the horror movie, a scene showed a family inside their house; they heard funny noises, so they went from window to window trying to see what the noise could be. When nothing turned up, they stood in front of the living room window for a moment, admiring the front garden. Suddenly a huge, mean-motherfucker alien with tentacles and fangs and a massive cranium jumped in front of them and spat blood and venom and human body parts onto the windowpane.

Kimberly began screaming and couldn't stop. In the end her parents had to give her some Valium they'd been saving for an upcoming holiday flight, and still she spent the rest of the evening in her bed with her curtains tightly closed. Through the walls she could hear her parents fighting over whose idea it had been to let a twelve-year-old girl watch an R rated horror movie.

Before he went to bed that night, Kimberly's father came up to see how she was doing and said, "Let's open the curtains and let in some fresh air, young lady."

Kimberly freaked out again. It took her father some minutes to make the connection between the curtains, the window and the monster, and by then Kimberly was so upset she ended up spending the night sleeping in her parents' room, the blinds drawn.

The next morning Kimberly was fine again—until she remembered the monster. She froze, realizing there were windows everywhere and that the monster could appear at any one of them at any time.

She willed herself out of the house and onto the school bus, and that was okay because it was moving and raised above the ground, until she realized that an alien could be on the bus's roof. At school she spent the day trying not to look out the classroom windows.

During the last period of the day, science, one of her classmates, Luke, said, "Kimberly, come over here, there's this cool eye-perception test I want to show you."

"What does that mean?"

"It's to test your eyes to see what you notice more, motion or colour. It's fun."

Kimberly was glad to have something to take her mind off the aliens, and so she went to sit beside him. Luke said, "What you do is stare at this image really intensely."

On the screen was a picture of a boring middle-class living room.

"Let your eyes relax and let your body relax, and then things in the room will move just slightly, or the sofa may change colour just a bit. The image is going to change very slowly—tell me what changes you notice, colour or shape or motion or whatever."

So Kimberly sat there and let her body relax for the first time since the horror movie. She stared at the picture and thought how much it matched her own family's living room. She imagined herself being in the room and feeling safe and happy, when all of a sudden the screen cut to a full-size screaming vampire face, fangs dripping blood, eyes full of murderous, bloodsucking rage.

Kimberly went totally insane and nobody knew what to do. Finally, her teacher and a few of the bigger students were able to drag her to the nurse's office, where she was forced to sign several waiver forms and show proof of her family's fully paid, up-to-date medical coverage before she was given a rich and delicious syringe-load of Dilaudid. Still, the only reason Kimberly didn't flip out further was because the nurse's office had no windows and she felt slightly safe there—but she dreaded the fact that she would have to leave the room and walk down windowed hallways and out a door into a car with windows (her mother had been called) and then into a house that had twenty-seven windows as well as one chimney and three ventilation holes for the dryer and the bathroom showers.

The drive home was traumatic. Once inside the house, Kimberly was unable to leave her mother, even for a second.

That night her parents tried reasoning with her, but the harder they tried, the more anxious she became. At two in the morning they gave her the remaining eight milligrams of Valium and decided to see if everything would be better in the morning. It wasn't. It was much worse—a Valium hangover amplified every misfiring neuron in their daughter's brain. Kimberly, teeth chattering, crept inside the linen closet and shut the door.

"We have to get her to a doctor," said her father. "Can you get the day off?"

"Nope. Today's our annual End-of-Season Winnebago Blowout. Can't you take the day off?"

"Fine. Come on, pumpkin," Kimberly's dad said. "Get dressed and let's go see if we can make these spooky things go away."

They drove to the clinic with Kimberly crouched in the well of the front passenger seat, and at the clinic they saw Dr. Marlboro, who was quick to grasp the problem. "Sedatives won't work," he said. "Nothing will work. A horrific, lifelong phobia has been created. The most we can hope for is that the fear will dwindle with time and become manageable. Usually the decay rate for young people traumatized by the wrong movie at the wrong time is six weeks—but the aftershocks linger forever."

"What kind of quack are you?" Kimberly's dad said.

"Language, Mr. Kellog. Goodbye."

Angry, Kimberly's father took his daughter to another doctor, who he'd heard would write anyone a prescription for anything.

Kimberly spent the next month in a velvet fog. Then the prescription ran out, and when her parents went to renew it, they learned that the pill doctor had fled to Florida to avoid multiple malpractice charges. All the other doctors in town were off duty, watching golf marathons on TV. An unsedated Kimberly returned to her full senses. She was yet again horrified by the world.

But while Kimberly had been in her fog, spring had turned into summer. Kimberly's mother had an idea: "Why don't you sleep outside on the lawn? No windows there."

She had a point. That night Kimberly slept in the back garden, midway between the house and the fence.

"Well, Einstein," said her father to her mother, "glad to see something works. She can't be living on sedatives forever."

With a 360-degree view all around her, sleep came quickly to Kimberly. The next morning, she jerked awake, filled with fear, then realized where she was and relaxed. This went on for a month, during which time she stayed outside, going inside only when it was absolutely necessary. The weather was good, and so was life.

Then one morning she woke up to see two men dressed like politicians coming through the carport. They approached the side door and rang the doorbell. Kimberly's mother answered it and let them in.

As quietly as she could, Kimberly crept up to the house. She snuck from window to window, looking inside, and as she did, she discovered that windows are perfectly fine if you're on the outside looking in.

Finally, she came to the living room window. She looked in to see her parents kneeling in front of the men, whose heads were opening up like tin-can lids. Jellyfish tentacles emerged and wrapped themselves over her parents' skulls. After thirty seconds the tentacles retreated and went back inside the men's heads, and the heads snapped shut. The creatures pulled dog leashes from their pockets, which they attached to Kimberly's parents, then led them out the front door, down the driveway and out onto the road, where other aliens were busy rounding up the neighbours.

One might wish that Kimberly did a brave thing and fetched the loaded Colt from her father's bedside drawer and tried to rescue her parents.

Or one might wish that Kimberly ran after her parents in a vain effort to save them and, in the process, became a house pet too.

But instead Kimberly looked at her parents' house, which now belonged to her. She went in the front door, threw open all the windows, let fresh air inside and sang, *"The aliens have come and now they're gone."* She then looked around the empty house. *"And all of this is mine now—mine, mine, mine!"* She went to the kitchen, found a bottle of Windex and went from room to room, cleaning all the windows one by one.

Creep

On May 2, 2015, I was visiting Hall 6 of Paris's annual trade fair, the Foire de Paris, the site of a Maker Faire. Half of the sports arena–sized space was filled with exhibitors mostly displaying 3D printing devices and the services that support them: printing filament, software and electronic add-ons. Booths tended to be staffed by twentysomethings radiating the cockiness that comes from knowing one is riding the winning historical wave. The hall's visitors were also on the young side: young parents with palpably creative children, as well as (almost entirely) young men who can only be cheerfully described as nerds. And, as one might expect, everyone was making stuff: 3D-printed dodecahedrons, skulls, anime figurines, bionic arms, gears, doodads, frogs, vaping devices, cats, vases and . . . well, anything, really. A favoured goal of members of the maker movement is to make something that could never have existed, even five years ago: interlocked polyhedrons; hard copies of algebraic equations; animal forms rendered with slick mathematical skins.

Nothing I've seen more closely resembles the look and feel of the actual Internet than these assemblages of items made at and displayed in a Maker Faire. If you compare requests people enter in their Google searches with the items on display at Maker Faire, there is the exact same sense of predictable randomness; the need to find faster, better and cheaper goods and services; a semiotic disconnect from one object to another; and an embrace of glitches as an aesthetic. If the maker aesthetic strays in any one cultural dimension, it would probably be slightly in the direction of Burning Man, but more along the lines of Maker Faire dads building fire-breathing stainless steel golems to enhance a back-yard weekend drum circle.

After overloading on the noise and imagery of the fair, I found myself at the far end of the hall, taking a breather by a chain-link fence I thought was there to close off unused space. Wrong. It was a drone testing ground. I looked in and there were five or so drones being test flown by a small group of people. And so I looked through the fence at drones, which is something I've never done. They're square and they hover and swoop; they go way up and then down—kind of hypnotizing. Then one of the drones, a candy-apple red number I'd been following for two minutes, buzzed right over to me and proceeded to hover directly in front of my face for maybe fifteen seconds. This event actually shocked me. This was not the way I thought I'd first encounter a drone. I always thought I'd be sitting on the sofa when something out the window would catch my eye. A bird? I'd get up to look, and there would be a hov-ering drone with its many cameras live-streaming to Dr. Evil's alpine lair.

Truth be told, I think the first drone encounter scenario most people have in their heads is far more Freudian. The first drone encounter script would go something like this: You're sunbathing in the nude outside on your secluded balcony. Or roof. You're cov-ered in oil and you're Spotify-ing Brazilian jazz and contemplat-ing how to shave your pubic hair—you're totally vulnerable—and then suddenly you hear a pale humming sound; you look up. It's a drone. So then what do you do? Call the cops? Cover your mod-esty? Throw your towel at it? That thing is pretty deft and prob-ably hard to nail, and if you did nail it, could the person operating it sue you? Is it legal to take down a drone? Who the hell is running the damn thing? *Holy shit*, you realize, *it's not safe up here on my roof anymore.* But the thing is, even though you know there's a 98 percent probability that the person operating the drone is a male between the ages of twelve and nineteen, your head goes not to Kyle or Terry from two doors down the street, but right into Big Brother mode.

What the hell just happened? What happened was that a massive power imbalance just entered your life, right there on your roof, an imbalance that's particularly creepy because there's something intrinsically cowardly and rapey about drones, and we loathe the sense of powerlessness they instill in those whom they monitor. Getting droned on your rooftop while clad in nothing but Piz Buin makes you understand the value of privacy in a way that all the think pieces on Edward Snowden can never do.

Recreational drones (there's a nice term) possess the consumer world's newest consumer dynamic: creep. Creep is to creepy what fail is to failure. Creep is getting droned up on your roof. Creep is seeing blurred-out faces on Google Street View. Creep is going into a chain restaurant and reading the menu to discover that supply-chain transparency is the new badge of honour. Transparency is the new fresh. It's like that old skit where the waiter introduces you to several cows and you get to choose which one will be used for the evening's steak, but instead it's McDonald's, and they're out to prove they no longer use pink goo in their burgers. Creep is seeing someone wearing Google glasses—one of the cofactors that led to the device being withdrawn from the market until future iterations remove its creep. *The Onion* had a wonderful headline the week the glasses were removed from public sale until further notice: "Unsold Google Glass Units to Be Donated to Assholes in Africa." You'd think that de-creeping Google Glass might be difficult, but in the end it's probably just a numbers game. I remember seeing early adopters using cellphones on city sidewalks in

Toronto between 1988 and 1990, and they looked like total ass-holes—they just *did* in a way that people born later find very hard to believe. But then smartphones arrived in 2002 and the numerical tipping point came, so I guess everyone started looking like an asshole, except everyone cancelled out everyone else, so we're all not assholes in the end.

●

Maybe a person could get used to being monitored, or could get used to the awareness that strangers are always noting one's presence. Imagine being Madonna and popping down to the corner store for a carton of milk. She walks in, the store goes quiet. Madonna gets what she came for and leaves. Does she love being recognized everywhere she goes or does she hate it? Does she even notice it anymore? We all may now be *je suis Charlie*, but we're also on track to becoming *je suis* Madonna.

Technology didn't come from outer space. We humans invented it, and thus our relationship with it is inevitably tautological. Technology can only ever allow us to access and experience new sides of humanity that lay dormant or untapped. Nothing human is alien. The radio gave us both Hitler and The Beach Boys. The Internet gave us Mentos, Diet Coke and kittens. Drones give us a new dimension of pubescent snoopiness, but they're also giving us massively asymmetrical warfare—and hideous, unmerited death.

There's actually not that much ontological difference between military and recreational drones except for scale and violence. The dynamic of surveillance, cowardice and rapey-ness remains the same with both, only the scale changes. And of course, with military drones, creep is transformed into horror.

Oddly, there's something about drones that taps into that certain strain of puerility in which weapons become toys and toys become weapons. Having fun with a cap gun at age six easily relates to grown men unironically wearing assault rifles to a Missouri Walmart—arguably the one place on earth least at risk of invasion of any sort. *We're just expressing our right to bear arms.* The moral twin of this weaponized restaurant visit would be the casual, *whatever* shrugs these same people give when discussing remote-control satellite drone attacks.

Sip of Pepsi. Focus. Cross-hatch. Sip Pepsi. Deploy drone. Bug splat. Sip of Pepsi. Repeat.

One interesting tendency I've noticed whenever people start discussing military drones: there's always that one person who says, "But you know, the people who are really stressed out by drones aren't the people on the ground" (who've just been blown up, maimed, had their life destroyed),"they're the ones operating the drones. They have an incredibly high stress level. Some of them even get PTSD!"

Okay sure, but what about the children?

Cities everywhere are trying to ban drones or making the rules for using them so difficult as to create a de facto ban. I wonder if a better idea would be to issue all citizens a drone that would come with mandatory instructional training. Drones would no longer be simply the neighbour's tween pursuing Mrs. Robinson's boobs. Suddenly the metaphor of surveillance would become the omnipresent fact of real life. Your windows would become your enemies. Pull the blinds. Maybe the people in those scary desert countries aren't just whining. Maybe there truly is something not just cowardly and rapey about drones, and maybe they are, in some intrinsic way, genuinely evil: omniscient without godliness; semi-selective and without mercy.

Let's get back to the roof where you were suntanning nude when the drone approached. It's now hovering eleven feet above you, and it's live-streaming your private bits to wherever. But now it's starting to do something new: *Huh?* Suddenly it drops a small cache of live hungry baby spiders all over your oiled torso. *Holy crap!* Next it fires a volley of X-Acto knife blades at you. *Argh!* After that it drops a lit cherry bomb onto your towel. And here's where it gets worse: there's now another drone floating beside it, and in the distance are thousands more headed your way, blackening the sky like passenger pigeons 150 years ago, so many drones that they cross the horizon.

Now let's go back to those fifteen seconds when I was in Hall 6 at the Foire de Paris, when the bright red drone hovered in front of my face. It was an almost impossibly alien moment. The device in no way felt human to me. It just didn't, but it was made by humans, so how could it be anything but? In a McLuhanistic sense, we might ask which aspects of our senses, or what dimension of our humanity, do drones personify and amplify? Why does it feel as though drones are at the furthermost reach of human behaviour? Why do they possess so much creep? Is it because of our need to lurk? Our need for titillation? Our cruelty? Our laziness? If any other animal on earth invented drones, they'd use them to catch more food. Humans like to use them to ogle and to kill each other. Let's get Freudian here again. Perhaps drones embody a perversion of reproduction strategies. Drones are stalkers. Drones deliberately transmit STDs. Drones are abortionists. Drones are rape. Drones are the embodiment of sexual damage.

In Hall 6, people continued to 3D-print stuff, but not the stuff they make on their own—the things they'd never dare print out in public. Sex toys are massive download categories in the 3D-printing universe, as are weapons. This is mirrored in the world of Internet searches, where quests for porn and violence in all their forms are both copious and relentless.

There, at the end of the hall, flew the drones. One of them, I was told, was a 3D-printed drone, which feels not just ironic but somehow inevitable. Was my red drone a 3D-printed drone? Does it matter?

◐

When I think of aliens, I think of the alien from M.N. Shyamalan's *Signs* (2002), standing in Mel Gibson's living room, missing a finger, dripping acid, and bent on revenge.

When I think of aliens, I think of that scene in the Tom Cruise version of *War of the Worlds* (2005) where aliens snoop through the basement of a ruined suburban split-level home while concealed humans try not to make a sound for fear of being discovered.

And, yes, when I think of aliens, I think of E.T. (1982) concealed in a suburban closet, desperate to leave the air-conditioned hell of southern California. But these aliens are more about me than they are about real aliens. (My aliens tend to be monsters who infect and enchant and toxify the middle class.)

Alien is alien. I don't know if it's even possible for human beings to imagine what aliens could do or think or be or want or be motivated by. That's why we have science fiction. But whatever aliens actually are, I want them to be more than merely human. I'd be happy if it turned out aliens look like drones, but they'd have to be drones without cowardice, rapey-ness or death in their souls—they'd have to be drones free of creep.

Stamped

I collected stamps in my early teens, preferably those from remote, underpopulated islands such as Pitcairn, the Falklands or Nauru, or from countries where postage stamps were maybe the biggest local industry: Liechtenstein, Andorra and Monaco. I have three brothers; I think I was simply looking for peace. I liked these two sorts of locales because they pushed the borders of why stamps even exist. For example, Pitcairn Islanders, I imagined in 1977, must have collectively written maybe eleven letters a year, perhaps along the lines of: *Dear Mother, Rescue me from this godforsaken rock in the middle of nowhere. All they talk about is the* Bounty. I imagined, back then, that the Monégasques used their stamps to mail photos of their yachts to Liechtensteiners, heckling them about their cruel land-locked condition.

I recently decided to collect Japanese postwar stamps. There's an innocence about them. They collectively tell the story of a country on a magic carpet ride, and looking at them in their correct little windows on a page simply makes my brain feel *good*. So after many moons of keeping away, I revisited Vancouver's sole remaining stamp store to find hundreds of stamp albums of all sorts, piled up against its walls, hoarder-style.

"Brian, what the hey?"

"Doug, I know. They're all piled here because young people don't collect stamps anymore."

"What do you mean?"

"Most people under forty have neither sent nor received a letter in their lifetime. To them, stamps are a form of industrial waste, and they have no sentimental attachment to them."

I thought about it. If you're a millennial, a stamped letter in the mail is either a bill or it's a communication from a stalker—which is to say, it's either from someone clueless about online billing technology or it's from someone scary. I can see why twentysomethings wouldn't be into stamps. They must have about as much appeal to them as lorgnettes or fax machines.

I just used the word *twentysomethings*. That is a word you simply never, ever saw or heard anywhere until the early 1990s with the Gen X explosion. (Sorry about that.) In the ensuing two decades, I've learned that generational demonization is something that's hard-wired into us as a species, and there's nothing to be done about it. But what's been most interesting to me over the past two years in particular is the demonization of millennials.

They're useless! They're entitled.

They can't make decisions on their own!

They complain about everything!

If you don't give them a gold star sticker, they'll pout and sulk, and then the next day their parents will come in and threaten to sue you until you give their kid a sticker!

There may be some anecdotal truth to these claims, but mostly what I notice is that the media is saying pretty much the same thing about millennials as they did about Generation X.

They have no future.

They have $130,000 in college debts.

They'll never own houses.

They'll end up living in mobile homes and in middle age will cobble together a living changing the diapers of their parents' friends.

The most interesting lie I see perpetuated in millennial bashing is that millennials aren't political and they don't vote. When I hear this, inside my head I hear a loud screeching brake noise and say, *WTF?*

Millennials are the most politically informed cohort ever. They know their rights. They know about power imbalances. They know about environmental degradation. They know about GMOs, Yellow 6, fuel rods, transgender politics and the near complete lobbyocracy of US politics. You can't pull the wool over the eyes of most millennials. I think, because millennial political expression began with the stillborn Occupy Wall Street movement, they get branded as apathetic. But the issue with millennials isn't apathy. I think it's the fact that they look at the mechanics of voting and compare it to the universe they inhabit, and they collectively say, *You have to be kidding: every four years I go into a plywood booth and use a graphite-based stylus to "fill in a box" beside my choice for who's best for the job? What century are we in? How is this still even happening?*

And they have a point. Voting methods feel archaic, like taking everyone's computers and devices away and telling them they have to instead use envelopes and stamps to communicate with each other. In the era of Airbnb, Netflix and Skype, we have a political selection ritual straight out of the nineteenth century. Millennials must view terms such as *hanging chads* (Bush election, November 2000) and *recounts* (almost every election) and wonder how so many useless voting methods still manage to exist. Why don't we just vote online? How hard can that be?

Naysayer: *But your password could get stolen!*

Another naysayer: *Someone could rig it!*

Yet another naysayer: *Why should we change because kids these days are just too lazy to visit a voting booth!*

Right. And I imagine that if Joseph Kennedy were alive today, he'd certainly have a team of hackers on salary to win his sons' elections for him, but we're pretty much beyond that level of hackability by now. The time is here to reinvent the way we exercise our votes. Who'll go first?

Future Blips

Last summer in a London hotel's breakfast room, I was reading the *Financial Times* while waiting for my ride to show up and, without thinking much about it, I looked at the top of the page to see what time of day it was. I blinked and then thought to myself, *Hmmm . . . Okay, Doug, the top of a page is not a toolbar. You seem to have crossed some new sort of line with technology.* This experience was what I call a "future blip"—a small, haiku-y moment when it dawns on you that you're no longer in the past.

Another blip: A few days back I walked around the house looking for newspaper so I could pack a box, and I realized I didn't have any. I ended up using paper in the studio trash can, left over from eBay purchases.

And finally, today I was wondering what it would be like to live in Antarctica, so I Googled *Antarctica* and *party*. I put in the word *party* because it would probably take me to the blog of someone younger and more likely to post images online, and I was right. I've now learned that hipsters are starting to colonize the Final Continent.

It is incontestable that we are collectively rebuilding the way we process information. For example, notice that when we tell people about an idea we want them to research later, we don't focus on the idea so much as how to search for it. Search words establish future locatability. "When you get home, just Google *Mother Teresa*, *topless* and *lawsuit*. You'll find what I'm talking about right away."

The way we're collectively redefining searchability is indeed a reflection of the way we now collectively file away information in our brains—or the way we don't. One of the great joys of life is that we're all getting much better at knowing what it is we no longer need to know. Freedom from memorization! Having said this, there's a part of me that misses being able to bullshit people at dinner parties without having an iPad come out before dessert to sink an urban legend or debunk a stretched truth.

I wonder if nostalgia for the twentieth-century brain is a waste of time. While I may sometimes miss my pre-Internet brain, I certainly don't want it back. Everyone's quick to dump on new technologies, but how quickly we forget a two-hour trek to the local library in the 1990s to find something as mundane as a single tradesman's phone number in the Yellow Pages for a city twenty miles away. How cavalier we all are when we say, "Let me just quickly Google that." What we've really just said is, "Let me instantaneously consult with the sum total of accumulated human knowledge. It'll take just two shakes."

When I was in art school, I was the ticket collector on Tuesday nights at the local rep theatre. This was 1983, long before VHS, and because of my ticket stint, I got in free to all the movies. I made a point of seeing as many as I could. They changed every two nights and the fare was upscale. I became an unwitting trove of information on Lina Wertmüller and was able to see gems like *The Garden of the Finzi-Continis* and *Aguirre, the Wrath of God* a decade before they became staples at video stores. Three decades later I was in a gas station in central British Columbia and saw a generic Canadian country "hoser" in red and black plaid renting a DVD copy of *Kagemusha* at the counter. I was impressed that even out in the sticks there existed a need for art-house films, but then my hoser's friend asked him why he was renting *Kagemusha* and he said, "Uhhh . . . I think it's, like, a kung fu movie."

So let's do the math: probably five movies a week for four-ish years in art school makes about one thousand movies. At the same time, I saw as many first-run movies as anyone else. Then add the appalling amount of TV I watched, as well as all the music I consumed—we're into thousands and thousands of hours of media devoured during art school alone. Don't forget books, too. And magazines. And then add three decades more of this sort of cultural consumption and we're into maybe the high five figures in hours of consumption. For someone born in 1991, three decades after me, even if they spent every moment of their waking life trying to catch up to my media consumption (BTW, a terrible idea), it would be futile. Especially since my rate of consumption continues as high as ever. So then what gets lost and what gets kept? Wheat. Chaff. All of that.

It's said that Goethe was the last human being who knew everything about the world that was possible to learn at that time. In this sense Goethe was like a proto-Internet, but now he lives on in a 2.0 version called the cloud. We're all Goethe now. I may miss my pre-Internet brain, but I'm rapidly forgetting it too.

Futurosity

I've spent much of my life waiting for the future to happen, yet it never really felt like we were there. And then, in this past year, it's almost instantly become impossible to deny that we are now all, magically and collectively, living in that far-off place we once called the future. It's here, and it feels odd. It feels like that magical moment when someone has pulled a practical joke on you but you haven't quite realized it yet. We keep on waiting for the reveal, but it is always going to be imminent and it will never quite happen. That's the future.

What was it that pulled us out of the present and dumped us in this future? Too much change too quickly? One too many friends showing us a cool new app that costs ninety-nine cents and eliminates thousands of jobs in what remains of the industrial heartlands? Maybe it was too much freakish weather that put us in the future. Or maybe it was texting almost entirely replacing speaking on the phone. Or maybe it was Angelina Jolie's pre-emptive mastectomy. Or maybe it was an adolescent comedy about North Korea almost triggering nuclear war—as well as incidentally revealing Sony's thinking on Angelina Jolie. Or maybe it was *Charlie*. How odd that much of what defines the future is the forced realization that there are many people who don't want a future and who don't want the future. They want eternity.

I feel like I'm in the future when I see something cool and the lag time between seeing it and reaching for my iPhone camera is down to about two seconds, as opposed to the thirty seconds it would have taken a few years back. I feel like I'm in the future whenever I look for images of things online and half the ones I see are watermarked and for sale. I feel like I'm in the future when I daydream of bingeing on season four of *House of Cards* on my new laptop that weighs nothing and never overheats and its battery goes on for ages.

How long is this sensation of futurosity going to last? Is it temporary? Maybe society will go through a spontaneous technological lull, allowing the insides of our brains to take a time holiday and feel like they're in 1995, not 2015. But that's probably not going to happen. Ever.

Is it healthy to live in the future? I suspect not. We're not really built for permanent high-speed change—accelerated acceleration. So will there come a collective cracking point? And if so, what would a collective cracking point look like? It might not be a riot or a referendum. It might be that we all wake up one morning and realize we're not middle class or working class or anything; we basically just exist and the Internet makes it bearable.

¤

Someone asked me last week, "In the long run, is technology our saviour or our demise?" I thought it over, and the thing is, we made technology. It is only an expression of our humanity, so it's wrong to think of it as something given to us by aliens, so we can blame technology, not ourselves, when something goes wrong. The question that he was really asking was, "Are humans going to kill themselves?" The answer would be the exact same answer that would have been given ten years ago, two thousand years ago or one thousand years in the future. We're still around, so the answer is no, but this still doesn't change the fact that we're stuck living inside the future, where we're stuck worrying about this question for all of our waking hours.

I suspect that abandoning one's pre-Internet brain is the only intelligent adaptive strategy necessary for mental health in the world of a perpetual future.

How much futurosity can our brains accept before they explode or implode? I wonder if maybe the sensation of futurosity is a mental tick applicable only to people born before a certain window in time closed, a state of mind specific to those who remember a world that once possessed a present tense. Millennials are lucky in that they have nothing to shed, nothing to trigger *tristesse*, nothing to unlearn. For a recent museum show, I made T-shirts that read, "I miss my pre-Internet brain." We photographed them on seventeen-year-old models, and everybody had a good laugh.

I try to imagine a world without a present tense—the millennial world where time is a perpetual five seconds from now—and, if I squint my brain (for lack of a better analogy), I can almost sort of get it right. Those pioneers I mentioned in the introduction, leaving a trail of abandoned pianos, sofas and wooden dressers behind them, were shedding weight in order to progress toward what they knew to be their inevitable destiny. I remember reading once of pioneers trapped in a forest fire, lying submerged in a swamp and breathing air through reeds, while what remained of their past went up in ashes. That's what I feel like right now, submerged in the mud, waiting for the fire to pass, waiting to emerge into a world that is lighter, fantastically different and quite possibly starting over from scratch.

Worcestershistershire

Last December in Chile I stayed with friends in the wine region south of Santiago. After a few days I noticed that food would come from the kitchen to the table and, before the meal was over, it was already decomposing on the plate. Vegetables began disintegrating before dessert arrived; meat quickly went dumpstery. I wondered what was going wrong, only to realize that something was going right. The food being served was fresh and unprocessed. My chicken had last clucked that morning. The lettuce was a freshly guillotined head. I soon began to appreciate and expect this level of extreme Chilean freshness. When I returned to Vancouver, those pure Chilean meals and their high-speed time-lapse-photographyish disintegration became a memory, and my culinary life went on.

$\oplus$

My studio is across the street from a supermarket, a very convenient location. Whenever anyone from the studio needs something to eat, we zip across to the deli section, get some sandwiches or soup or what have you, and think little of it.

The studio is chaotic and things quickly vanish: brushes, scissors, X-Acto knives . . . Now throw deli food items into the mix: a sandwich ends up here; cauliflower soup ends up there; stew ends up on the shelf over there. And then weeks go by and, while searching for masking tape, I'll find an egg-salad sandwich from the previous month lodged between a box of acrylic tubes and a folder of magazine clippings. But then I'll stop and stare at the sandwich: Its bread has shrunk a tiny bit, but it's still the same colour. It's odourless and its egg-salad filling still occupies the same volume—it's neither shrunken nor bloated nor watery—and its colour is pleasingly . . . eggy looking. And we're talking three weeks later here. The half-finished cardboard container of stew I mentioned a few sentences back? It sat for six weeks, free of mould or shrinkage or stink or any real evidence of time's passage.

Suddenly I began to imagine my body having a conversation with this supermarket deli food upon first arriving in my stomach:

"Hi. I'm Doug's body."

"And I'm a science-enhanced egg-salad sandwich."

"Nice to meet you. Now it's time for me to absorb you."

"Well"—chuckle, chuckle—"just you try."

And so my stomach, primed by hundreds of millions of years of evolution, begins to, well, what exactly?

"You know, I'm trying to absorb you, sandwich, but I can't seem to break you down into tiny, absorbable bits."

"You can just park me in the colon for a while," says the sandwich. "Don't worry, I won't be changing much."

"But that's just the thing. You don't change on your own, and I don't seem to be able to do much with you, so what do we do here?"

"Treat me like a piece of stray cling wrap and just pass me through Doug's system, and we can pretend we never even had this talk."

"Deal."

From my stomach's POV, what the hell just happened? If food doesn't rot outside the body, then what's supposed to be happening inside the body? Am I technically starving? Am I triggering a food switch that will turn me into Jabba the Hutt or Mr. Burns?

I asked my doctor friend, Debra, a nutrition specialist, about this. She told me it could go four ways. First is the inert mass or "cling wrap" scenario. "The body will see the sandwich as fodder to keep the stomach artificially full—neither poisonous nor nutritious." This reminds me of those laxative American potato chips containing Olestra.

Second is the desperation scenario. "Depending on the egg sandwich's absorbability, it could contribute to either extreme obesity or to extreme weight loss depending on the overall quantity of nutrition in your life: Is your body so desperate it will absorb anything?"

Third is warfare. "The sandwich could prompt an immune reaction if the gut becomes more permeable and the immune system denounces these non-food particles as foreign invaders masquerading as food and declares war on them."

Fourth is common sense. "If the body is in great shape and operating as it should, it should reject these items as not meeting minimum requirements of fuel, and they should take a hurried trip up or down but, nevertheless, out. And good riddance."

$\oplus$

An hour ago I opened my fridge door and stared at its racks of condiments. Pre-9/11 Worcestershire sauce (or, as Bugs Bunny would say, Worcestershistershire). Catalina salad dressing from Michael Jackson's wake. Mustard from the Bush years. All of it happily sitting there, year after year, just waiting to enter a human body. It'll keep forever—just like all those deli soups and sandwiches. I wonder what my stomach would say to my condiment rack's contents? "Oh, hello there, hamburger relish from 1997. Nice to see you again. Let's have a look at you . . . Well, you're not growing fur and you haven't turned blue, so I'm turning you into a dinner garnish. What's this? . . . Oh . . . a little patch of fur. Well, I'll just scrape it off. Nobody will be the wiser. And who's that I see back there? Ketchup from the first Obama election night! Nice to see you, old friend."

Bulk Memory

A few years ago in Santa Clara, California, I saw a strip-mall store with a sign saying, "Bulk Memory Sale." I think there's actually something kind of sexy about memory being sold in bulk, like chocolate raisins or bottles of pesto at Costco—it's like you can buy a new childhood or a new set of relationships with your family. The sign, aside from charming me, made me realize just how different memory is now versus what memory was, say, fifty years ago—or even twenty.

Memory means more than just organic memory inside your brain, or the secrets in your diary tucked beneath your pillow. Now memory means what you have in your laptop and all other devices. It also includes whatever you've stored in the cloud, and everything on the Internet. You, like it or not, are intimately embedded in the Internet. Andy Warhol believed that all the Chinese restaurants in Manhattan had just one jumbo kitchen under the ground where all the food was cooked. In a way, your memory—our memory—is now not unlike Warhol's Chinese kitchen. We all get our information from the same place, and there's just one menu and it's called "The Same Internet for Everyone on Earth." So give a yak herder in rural Tibet some smooth connectivity, and he'll access the same memory menu you do. Instead of going to yaks.com, he'll probably kill time reading the really scary and bitter one-star hotel reviews on TripAdvisor, or maybe he'll get caught in a cute puppy warp on YouTube, or maybe he'll make himself a worthier person by bingeing on TED talks, but he'll probably be checking out porn. So. Much. Porn.

Am I being judgmental here? If I am, it is a positive judgment, because the last thing planet Earth needs right now is 6.5 billion people being outside in the world wrecking things. It's actually all for the better that everyone is inside YouTubing Russian dashcam compilations instead of wrecking the physical environment.

I've always been interested in the unintended side effects of technology. For instance, when the car was invented, who would have thought dogs would like sticking their heads out the window to enjoy the scentscape generated by speed and wind? Likewise, I think about the unintended side effects of all of humanity ordering from the same Chinese kitchen of memory. People are people, and everyone's going to be looking for the same things, pretty much regardless of culture. Of course, there are localized clamps on what one may or may not see online. In Beijing a year back, I'd put a search word into Google and instead of getting an answer in the usual 0.128 second, I'd have to wait maybe fifteen seconds or so before results came back—if they came back at all. Was that a bit spooky? Yes, it was. And just try looking for anything frisky in the Emirates.

But what I find most fascinating here is that the Internet bends you to its will, regardless of who or where you are—it neurologically rewires you. The way the Internet homogenizes a human brain is nothing short of astounding. We are rapidly hitting the point where human neural patterns are becoming globally similar at a level that possibly hasn't been achieved since the last ice age, when a handful of hardy souls survived the cold by sitting in a cave and telling the same stories over and over again.

This homogenization of human thinking is an elective process brought about by the Internet's undeniable quality and quantity of information, as well as the insane speed with which it arrives. These three factors are, in turn, brought about by eerily consistent logarithmic increases in memory storage and its accessibility, and the processing speed and power it affords—bulk memory on sale in Santa Clara, California.

Can you hop off this new memory express any time you want? No. There's no turning back; speed and memory are irreversibly addictive. The only true enemy on this strange new turf? Paywalls, though I'm sure they'll crumble someday soon; the future is an infinity of links to cute kitten GIFs, *Doctor Who* reruns and online gambling.

Are we smarter as a result of all this speed and memory, or are we stupider? It's probably a moot point. Never in human history has nostalgia been as useless or uncomforting as it is now. I'm not even talking about nostalgia for the decade you grew up in—I'm talking about nostalgia for five years ago. Or three years ago. Or life before Twitter. But, really, would you cheerfully go back to your 2002 laptop, or your 1998 dial-up online service, or driving to an office somewhere to buy a plane ticket? Doubtful. So we've made the trade. In any event, in fifteen years you'll be able to download the entire Internet into something the size of a box of Marlboros—like Microsoft's doomed Encarta times fifty trillion. And this means that you won't even have to go online to get online. You'll go there only when you need something in real time. Basically, everyone on Earth will have the sum of humanity's accumulated knowledge on them at all times. What will that feel like? Knowing how ungrateful humans are as a species, we'll probably be bored with it and start getting ourselves into more trouble. And then our machines will become sentient and start feeling sorry for us, and then they'll start killing us, and we'll probably deserve it. HAL 9000, please come home.

The Mell

On August 11, 1992, I was in Bloomington, Minnesota, close to Minneapolis. I was on a book tour and it was the grand opening day of Mall of America, the largest mall in the United States. The local radio affiliate had a booth set up in front of the indoor roller coaster, which strafed the booth like an air strike every seventy-five seconds. I was up on the stage with them, doing a live interview for a half-hour while thousands of people were walking by with "country fair face"—goggle-eyed and feeding on ice cream. I felt like I was inside a Technicolor movie from the 1950s. The show's host assumed I was going to be an ironic slacker wise-ass and said, "I guess you must think this whole mall is kind of hokey and trashy," and I said, "No such thing."

He was surprised. "What do you mean?"

"I mean that I feel like I'm in another era that we thought had vanished, but it really hasn't, not yet. I think we might one day look back on photos of today and think to ourselves, 'You know, those people were living in golden times and they didn't even know it. Communism was dead, the economy was good and the future, with all of its accompanying technologies, hadn't crushed society's mojo like a bug.'"

Silence.

It's true: Technology hadn't yet hollowed out the middle class and turned us into laptop click junkies, and there were no new bogeymen hiding in the closet. We may well look back at the 1990s as the last good decade.

⊗

In August of 1997 I was in London with friends and we went to a theatre to see a movie in an upscale mall in . . . Belgravia? Mayfair? We were an hour early, so we decided to check it out, although most of the stores were closed (it was after six and malls closed earlier back then). Yet hundreds of people were there, mostly Arab, having a lovely air-conditioned *passeggiata*. Two levels up there was an Internet hangout area, and as we walked past we saw twenty teenage boys watching twenty different screens of (even to those who consider themselves unflinching) profoundly graphic pornography. Mothers and fathers and kids walked by as if the boys were reading spreadsheets, and it was then I thought to myself, *You know, I bet you anything that it's porn that drives up the quality and speed of the Internet.* And I was right.

⊗

I remember driving through Scottsdale, Arizona, the January after the 2008 financial crash. I needed to find, of all things, a glue gun to do a mock-up for a project. A nine-hundred-foot-tall road sign told me that in the mall ahead, there was a craft superstore—terrific!—so I took the turnoff, entered the mall parking lot, and something very strange happened. Wait—was the mall closed? No. Were all the stores open? Yes. Then it dawned on me: *I was the only car there.* A part of my psyche began waiting for zombies to emerge from American Apparel and Bed Bath & Beyond. I cautiously parked in front of the craft store, went inside and found the glue gun, which, back home, would cost $12.99. There in Arizona it was $1.29, which is to say, it was basically free, and at that price they should have just gone out to the freeway and hurled glue guns at passing cars. So I bought one and returned to the car, and as I drove away I thought of all of the mall's merchants meeting at the end of the day to go over sales figures. "Okay then, what have we got today?"

"Somebody bought a glue gun."

"How much?"

"It was $1.29."

"Cash?"

"Yes."

"Anyone else in the mall sell anything else today?"

(Everyone shakes their heads dismally.)

"Capitalism. It works."

⊗

Malls used to be cool. Malls were the Internet shopping of 1968. Malls seemed to try harder back then. No more. You can take dead-mall tours on YouTube, or you can drive around most American cities and find a few dead malls yourself, or, if you find a living mall, it's on steroids and is scary from being too congested and too mega-mega. Where is the gracious Muzak'ed trance of yore? Where is the civility? The calm? Covered with plywood sheeting and graffiti and filled with dead tropical plants and shopping carts with missing wheels, malls have basically entered the realm of backdrops for science fiction novels and movies, and I'm okay with that. Change happens.

⊗

I have this game I play with myself. Several times a year in London, I end up in a taxi and I ask the driver to take me wherever by going through Pall Mall. This is usually met with four seconds of silence, after which the driver says, "Oh right. Pell Mell." I then say, "That's right, "Pell Mell," to which he replies with a whiff of huffiness, "Right . . . Pell *Mell*," the implication being I'm butchering his language. I will go to my grave wondering how to pronounce those two words. I've also noticed that continental European friends ask me specifically how to pronounce *mall*, and I tell them that it rhymes with *call* and *ball* and *fall*, and then they go ahead and pronounce it "mole," so I think malls need a new word. It should be something easy to pronounce and fun, like, say, *Jennifer*. Or *Trish*. Or *Evan*. *Mall* seems as old fashioned as the idea itself. Change happens? Time for a change.

The Anti-ghosts

There was once a group of people whose souls had been warped and damaged and squeezed dry by the modern world. They lived close by where you live, and their jobs were very similar to yours.

One day the souls of these people rebelled. They did so by fleeing the bodies that had contained them. And once a soul leaves a body, it's all over; there's no going back inside.

The bodies that had created the souls remained alive, and they continued their everyday activities, such as balancing chequebooks, repairing screen doors, and comparison shopping for white terry-cotton socks online, but meanwhile their souls started meeting with each other. They'd gather in small groups at the intersections of roads or at gas station pumps or on the decks at the local bird sanctuary. Once there, they confirmed with each other that what had happened was real—and it was—and that it had been everyone's individual decision to abandon the body they had been born into.

"So, are we ghosts?"

"I don't think so—the bodies we came from are still alive."

"Are we monsters?"

"No. Monsters are living forms without souls. Technically, the people we abandoned are the monsters."

"So what are we to do? We can't interact with the world anymore—we're merely untethered souls. All we can do is drift around, pass through walls and live a life of perpetual mourning."

"Are we the undead?"

"No, we are not. But we aren't alive, either."

The souls felt like house pets that had survived a hurricane only to find their homes and owners gone. They watched the world go onward, but they were unable to be a part of change or progress. They watched the bodies that had spawned them grow older. They were surprised by how cruel it is to grow older in the modern world when everything else seems to stay young.

The souls wondered why they weren't going to heaven or hell or anywhere else. There was just endless drifting, navigating through the world like turkeys or chickens or swans with clipped wings— birds that can barely fly. And even though they'd fled their bodies in rebellion, the souls missed their bodies the way a parent misses its child.

Then one day the souls became so angry with their situation that they lashed out at the world and—*surprise!*—the gestures they made in anger allowed them to connect with the world again— vases tipped over, doors slammed, windows broke, data scrambled, light bulbs popped.

The souls were stoked. Their ability to manipulate their anger and to engage with the living world grew and grew. They began to jam car engines and trip alarms. They learned how to curdle milk and burn food. They crippled satellites and salted drinking water. They learned to hijack the power of electrical storms to set fire to landscapes. They learned that anger is beauty. They learned that the only way they could create was to destroy, that the only way to become real once more was to fight their way back into the world in anger.

And so they smashed all they could smash. They were at war without opponents. Their rage became their art. They no longer wondered if they were good enough to deserve their bodies—their life. Instead they challenged their bodies to deserve them.

This was not the end of the world, but it was the beginning of sorrows.

Little Black Ghost

Four years ago, following a dental procedure, I flew to New Orleans for the first time. Before takeoff I took a new and powerful antibiotic. By the time I was to hub through Denver, I could feel something going very wrong inside my head. At first I thought it was the weather. It was a stormy afternoon over Colorado, and the plane had to circle the airport for an hour, which was just far enough outside Denver proper to afford a view of all the countless subdivisions that had died in the crash of 2008, the plywood and two-by-fours long since turned from honey yellow to ash grey.

By the time I landed in New Orleans and was checking into my hotel, my brain was doing badly, and when I got to my room—an old-style hotel with tall wooden walls that reminded me of how Jim Morrison might have thought Paris would be—I wanted to kill myself. I say that in a scientific, clinical, unemotional way: I wanted to no longer be alive. It wasn't so much wanting to be dead; it was no longer wanting to be living. Was there pain? No. Was there anything else? No. Just a need to no longer be living. I wasn't panicked by this new need. I saw it for what it was: a psychological reaction to a potent new drug. My only worry was whether this new set of emotions would wash out of my system or whether I'd opened an uncloseable door in my mind.

Friends met me after I'd checked in, and they were entirely unaware of what was happening in my head.

"Have a drink?"

"Sure!" (*Want to die.*)

"Check out the place down the street?"

"Sure!" (*But throw in some death.*)

The thing about New Orleans is that it's where Americans go to drink themselves to death without feeling like they're being judged. So it was actually not a bad place to be feeling the way I was feeling. I pretty much drank myself to sleep that night, and when I woke up, magically hangover-free, the need to no longer be living had passed, and it's never returned. So then, what did I gain from the experience? Empathy. When anyone has mentioned suicide to me since then, I listen and I don't judge. I'm highly respectful of people with suicidal tendencies who don't kill themselves, because the impetus is all too real and extremely specific. I wonder how anyone manages to continue living in such a state for weeks, let alone years, feeling as they do.

In 1984 I won a scholarship to a Milanese design school where the term started in October. After three weeks, the earth fell out from beneath me and I entered what took me twenty-five years to figure out was merely seasonal depression. I've always called it "The Curse of My Brother's Birthday" (which is on November 5). Every few years or so, if my nutrition lapses or I don't go to the gym or I travel too much, I fall into The Pit. It doesn't end for months, and even then it tapers off gradually. In 2012 I crashed big-time: a trip to Germany, two trips to China (all from Vancouver) and then a trip to Toronto mixed with a crap diet and *whaam!* The Pit.

Depression's weird. If you don't get it, then you don't get it, but if you do, then you do. And if you do, you know how it can strip life of all colour—all those blank days that vanish without hope or cheer; the absence of all spirit. I figure I've probably lost almost four years of my life to depression—four years utterly flushed down the toilet, with the only benefit being, as with my suicide evening, increased empathy for the human condition.

Psychoactive drugs of any sort spook me, so I'm not the world's best depressive patient pill-wise, but in late 2012 I had to fly to Stockholm—on December 6—and I really needed to be there in good form. So, in lieu of pharmaceuticals, as a last resort, I bought a light box for $199 at a local drugstore on December 2—150 bright light-blue LEDs arranged in a grid. I plugged it in, looked at it for three seconds and . . . *boop* . . . my depression was gone. Completely. Like that. Yes, like that. Over in three seconds. Those three seconds remain the single oddest medical moment in my life. I lugged that light box in my carry-on luggage for years, superstitiously waiting for depression to reappear. It has yet to do so. Go figure.

What is the larger point here? The point is: Which of the above-mentioned head states was really *me*, and when was I *not* me? To what extent can we medicalize personality? I have a religious friend who's never been drunk or taken any psychoactive medication . . . and, to be honest, he really, *really* needs something, because his life could easily be fixed with a few weeks on drugs. But that's not going to happen, so he's a reduced version of himself—or is he? At what point are we dishonouring the soul with medication? Should there be a new labelling system that not only indicates contraindications and side effects but also denotes soul-tampering? A new sort of spiritual E-number? What would be the subjective gradient for this new system? Aspirin? No. Codeine? Maybe. Pot? Maybe. Wellbutrin? Yes. What would the little warning symbol on the package look like—a little black ghost? And would my light box merit a soul-warning sticker?

New Moods

I remember when Prozac took the world by storm in the late 1980s. It was like "Gangnam Style," except instead of one month, Prozac as a meme took five years to burn itself out. I remember it was hard to believe that a new psychotropic drug other than diazepines or primitive antidepressants like tricyclics could exist. It was as if science had invented a new mood.

Prozac was the first drug from the new generation of drug naming. These days we have Abilify, Celexa, Zoloft and . . . all those other bafflingly named pills I learn about mostly while I'm fast-forwarding through TV ads on TiVo. Mood-altering drugs seem to be advertised on TV a lot.

❂

Someone in Los Angeles told me the true story about why Elizabeth Taylor made so much money from her perfumes. It wasn't that her perfumes were or weren't better than other fragrances. It was because in the weeks preceding Christmas and Mother's Day, she bought up all the TV ad slots around children's cartoon programming. So when it came time to get something for Mom, kids went right to the perfume counter and demanded White Diamonds, a perfume of reputed adult glamour. I think that's what's happening with TV ads for mood-altering drugs these days. They're finding the right slot for the right sort of personality, with a level of accuracy that reminds me of the Gulf War and watching missiles fired directly into the elevator shafts of Iraqi public buildings.

☻

The arguments that swirled around new drugs in the late 1980s were electric and stormy and vicious. *You mean to say I can tailor my personality into something better than what I was born with? That's an affront to all that's decent in this universe!* You don't hear much of that anymore. It's like the radioactively white teeth everybody in North America now sports. One day you woke up and everyone had teeth like game-show hosts. And then one day you woke up and everyone seemed a bit meds-y.

A few years back I tried that "Harvard drug," Adderall, which gives you the power to read for twelve hours straight and internalize everything you read—and it was a total disaster. It gave me no clarity or focus, just an epic headache matched only by a hangover I once had after a night of drinking Red Bull and vodka at a ski resort two miles above sea level.

☻

My father is a doctor whose own father died in 1936 of a heart inflammation that in 1956 you could fix with a few pills. As a result, he's less suspicious of pills than younger generations. Growing up, my brothers and I all had acne, and in our bathroom we had a salad bowl filled with tetracycline, erythromycin and a host of other antibiotics. We ate them like they were candy, and if anyone is solely responsible for germinating an antibiotic-resistant strain of bacteria, he or she needs to look no farther than the Coupland children.

I like pills. I like the idea of pills; they confer a superpower on you: the ability to heal; the ability to feel new things; the ability to read *Infinite Jest* in one sitting. Unfortunately, I don't take many pills because when I was in kindergarten, the school brought in an anti-drug woman who was . . . about twenty? She gave us an anti-drug lecture centred around her friend who took *acid* (they actually used the word *acid* in a West Vancouver kindergarten in 1967) and subsequently developed locked-in syndrome—which, of course, the counsellor went into luxuriant detail about. "No matter *what* you're thinking and feeling, there's *no* way to communicate with the world. Ever. No matter what. You can't even blink. And it goes on forever. And *ever.*"

Of course it worked—I've never taken recreational anything—and I'm all for those "scared straight" drug lectures. The younger the better. Which reminds me of those anti-drug bumper stickers you see in the United States, the ones that say "D.A.R.E." I asked an American friend what it stood for and he replied, "That's easy: Drugs Are Really Expensive." (Actually, it stands for Drug Abuse Resistance Education, an international education program founded in 1984 that seeks to prevent use of controlled drugs, gang membership and violent behaviour. Thank you, Wikipedia.)

◐

I think the most successful pill one could invent would be one that instantly makes you unaddicted to whatever drug you're addicted to. Think about it: you could binge like crazy on anything with total impunity, medical or moral. Meth? Game on. Crack? Deal me in. Cigarettes? Woo-hoo! Needless to say, this new drug would be more demonized than any other drug in history. I suppose, by the same token, if they were to invent table salt right now, it would be sold only by prescription (. . . *causes high blood pressure and/or kidney damage in high doses* . . .) and at an exorbitant price. But I *do* want a pill that gives me a superpower—say, flight, transparency or telepathy. In the meantime I'll settle for something that makes me read online news articles past the first page. You could call it TwoPage. And you'd need one right now.

Beef Rock

The gourmet scout party from Gamalon-5 had pretty much given up on the planet Earth when it finally discovered rare mammals called human beings that were actually quite delicious. They'd tasted all the other animals, as well as pretty much everything in the ocean, but those very few humanoids hunkered in their caves were so rare that they had slipped under the tasting radar until the very end. Yes: people were undeniably . . . *scrumptious*.

"Commander, we've got to figure out some way of making these things multiply if we're ever to secure a meaningful supply of meat."

"Lieutenant, that's your job, not mine. Have they discovered hunting yet? They'll never learn to start farming until they kill all the big, easy meat around them. Those mammoths and moas. The low-hanging beef."

"No, sir."

"Well, you have your work cut out for you, don't you."

"Yes, sir."

The lieutenant and his squad went back down to Earth and basically handed the few scrawny humans they found some stone arrowheads and some flint and gave them hundreds of actual demonstrations of hunting and roasting before the humans could do it on their own.

And then the aliens sat back and waited for humans to wipe out all the megafauna—after which they turned their attention to smaller creatures like bears and buffalo. After they had all been hunted almost to extinction, humans were forced to adopt agriculture.

"Commander, sir, there really is nothing like agriculture to make a species multiply, is there."

"Indeed. It's nice that the universe has at least *some* constants. What's next in store for those tasty morsels?"

"We think they're almost ready to learn to count and learn about zero—as well as metallurgy. But they're still pretty primitive."

"All in good time, lieutenant."

And so humanity was given mathematics and knives and ploughshares, and human numbers grew, but not quickly enough to please the hungry aliens.

"Lieutenant, this is taking forever. Stop trying to foist chimps and gibbons on me. I want *humans*. I want humans to multiply and I want them to multiply *now*."

"Yes, sir." He suggested the phonetic alphabet and the printing press. "That way they can at least stockpile their intellectual ideas so that they don't always have to start from scratch all the time."

"Let's try that, lieutenant."

Printing presses—and hence books—accumulated. The Industrial Revolution became inevitable, and finally, humans went spawn crazy. Lo, the citizens of Gamalon-5 began to truly gorge on massive quantities of rich, delicious, succulent human flesh. Life on Gamalon-5 became a gourmet nirvana.

One day the lieutenant made the observation that human beings who read large numbers of books tended to taste better than humans who didn't. This intrigued the commander: "I'm listening, lieutenant."

"Sir, when the humans read books, it gives them a sense of individuality, a sense of being unique—a sense that something about their existence is special or, as they like to say, 'magical.' Reading seems to generate microproteins in their bloodstreams, and those proteins give them their extra juicy flavour."

"Hmmm . . . Well, whatever it takes to get the job done. But for Pete's sake, stop harvesting so many humans near Bermuda. They're beginning to catch on. Also, could you get those humans to introduce more nicotine into their systems? My wife loves the flavour it gives them, but she's sick of marinating them all the time."

"Yes, sir."

By now, the food vendors of Gamalon-5 had gone into competition with each other in the burgeoning human flesh trade. Their nickname for Earth was "Beef Rock" and the money was terrific. The lieutenant's nephew generated catchy sale slogans:

"Our Humans Read More Books!"

"Individual Humans—Unique Flavour!"

"On Sale This Week: PhDs for 30 Krogs a Pound."

"Postgrad Students 15 Krogs a Pound."

"Need a Taste of Mystery? Try Our Fillet of Crime Novel Addict."

But then in the 1990s the quality of human flavour began plummeting. The commander consulted the lieutenant. "What is going on here?"

"Sir, as an unintended consequence of reading books, humans have made the next leap and have invented digital communications."

"They WHAT!!!"

"I'm *so* sorry it happened, sir. We were on holiday and it just sort of swelled out of nowhere."

"So are they now using digital communications to conduct commerce, distribute moving image files and keep in contact with former schoolmates?"

"Yes, sir."

"So they're reading fewer books?"

The lieutenant sighed. "Yes, sir."

"Then the situation is truly dire."

The lieutenant asked, "Is there anything else, sir?"

"Just everyday worries. My teenage daughter has announced that she's gone Spam on me."

The lieutenant smiled: "going Spam" was a trendy phase among the teens of Gamalon-5, who thought eating humans was cruel. They opted instead for cans of Spam imported from Earth; nothing so closely approximated the oily, salty taste of cooked human flesh as the hammy goodness of Spam. "I'm sure it's just a phase, sir."

"Tell that to my wife, who has to put two different meals on the table every night."

The next afternoon the commander was going through his files and summoned his lieutenant. "Lieutenant, it says here that book sales are higher than ever, as the humans are using a technique called 'Amazon-dot-com' to purchase them."

"That is a deceiving statistic, sir. Amazon increases the need of humans to own books but not necessarily to read them. They leave them scattered around their homes as what they call 'intellectual trophies.'"

"Drat."

Time wore on and human meat became ever more unpalatable, and consumption dropped dramatically. And after a point the government of Gamalon-5 refused to subsidize the import of humans and soon barred the practice altogether. The lieutenant sighed as his ship flew away from Beef Rock one last time, leaving the humans to themselves and whatever gruesome fate they might cook up. He heaved a guilty sigh, turned around and scanned the universe looking for new sources of meat.

Farewell, Beef Rock.

Globalization Is Fun!

Have you ever wondered what it would smell like if you took every perfume and cologne in the world and mixed them together in a big vat? You already know the answer. It's called a duty-free shop. I've always hated the term *duty-free*. There's something irresponsible about it, as if you're getting something for free, except it's not free—someone else has to pay for your loot. I've never bought anything duty-free and this doesn't make me a better or political person—it may actually be a scientific indicator of cluelessness. But shopping duty-free is one of those doors I don't want to open because I could never close it again, sort of like Ouija boards or shoplifting or cocaine.

$$\varnothing$$

I used to have a summer job at one of those stores where you'd give me your name and then I'd bring out a large book and I'd magically find your family crest, which you could then order and have shipped to your house at a nonsensically high price. Much heraldry is nonsense, but comforting nonsense. My boss told me that when people travel, their sense of self begins to erode and they need to purchase something, anything, to shore up their sense of identity. It's why airports sell stickers and pins and car decals from around the world. (*Kiss me, I'm Oirish!*)

$$\varnothing$$

I was in China last year and ran out of clean clothes to the point where I had to buy a new shirt at the airport if I was going to make it through a ten-hour flight home. I chose a Lacoste shirt from a boutique there, which cost pretty much the same as it does anywhere. In flight I realized I'd purchased the only authentic piece of designer clothing in the entire country.

There's nothing to buy in China; everything's fake. If you want something "Chinesey," you'd best just go to your town's local Chinatown and get stuff there. It's faster, cheaper, easier and probably what you wanted anyway. In the end I collected cigarettes. Chinese tobacco packaging is really beautiful—imperial yellows and reds and blues—and they don't have big, scary, ugly health warnings on them ("Smoking Is Nature's Way of Killing Popular People"). I collected sixty-four different packs and framed them and hung them up by my studio door. When my dealer brought by a Chinese art collector for a visit, he remained stone-faced until he saw the packages, and then a switch flipped and he became animated and fun, and he began discussing the class implications of each brand: "Those ones are only for bureaucrats, and those ones are the ones that people with Audi A6s smoke, and those are for peasants and . . ." He was so excited about them that I sold him the whole framed piece, and in some magic way that transaction became a shorthand for the entire world of art and art dealing.

I live in Vancouver, where we used to have just one Chinatown, but now we have quite a few, depending on what sort of Chinese you are: Taiwanese, northern Chinese, Shanghainese, Hong Konger or Singaporean. Most of these new Chinese people are kind of embarrassed by the old Chinatown, which still fosters a sort of Suzie Wong, marines-on-shore-leave variety of Chinese consumer identity that froze around 1962—which is something I actually really love. But I suspect that the twenty-first-century Vancouver Chinese person would rather choose to be identified with a S500 Mercedes sedan instead of a strand of paper lanterns. And in any event, the Suzie Wong Chinatown is now being razed to make way for condo towers, and that's what makes Vancouver Vancouver—every ten years it becomes a totally different city.

🔀

Airports: I fly more than most people, and I really have to congratulate HSBC for targeting what is probably the single most potent metaphor for globalization—the airport jetway ramp—and for branding a piece of infrastructure in a kick-ass manner that hasn't been seen since Hitler championed the autobahn. For years HSBC had a campaign that most of us who flew from A to B remember well: "smart/stupid, stupid/smart"; "love/hate, hate/love" and so on. But now they've got a new campaign where they show corn with a husk made of knitted textile, and Holstein cows with black patches shaped like continents, and . . . it's just *creepy*. It reinforces your biggest worries about globalization: that it's boring, alienating and controlled by technocratic elites who feel sorry for you for having to fly commercial, not private, and that any resistance to their decreed future is futile.

🔀

Here's something I read online: "Shortly after the Soviet Union collapsed, a Russian bureaucrat travelled to the West to seek advice on how the market system functioned. He asked the English economist Paul Seabright to explain who was in charge of the supply of bread to London. He was astonished by the answer: 'Nobody.'"* Obviously. In bread capitalism, everything from wheat fertilizers

---

* Tim Harford, *Financial Times*, October 27, 2008.

to brioche-making night-school classes is done by private initiative. But if, in the end, the ownership of the bread industry or any other industry globalizes to the point where there are only a few players, aren't we right back to a default Soviet system, where the supply of bread or what have you is centralized and crypto-communist? And in this new system, both power and profit go to the One Percent—the new politburo. Its shield? Globalization is so boring that people fall asleep before they can articulate the issue. Boringness is the superpower of communism. Globalization kills you, but first it puts you to sleep.

Unclassy

A while ago I was interviewing assembly line workers in a subur-
ban Shanghai Internet router factory. When I asked workers what
class they belonged to, they asked me what I meant, and I said that
I was from North America, where most people will describe them-
selves as middle-class. Even with high-calibre translators, none of
the workers was able to tell me what class they thought they were
part of. They didn't see themselves as working-class or middle-
class or any other form of currently existing class.

This led me to believe that we are at a very interesting moment
globally, one in which old class definitions are becoming increas-
ingly obsolete while emerging definitions still seem vague or non-
existent. This lack of definition also got me thinking about how
our notions of the future are knotted together with our notions
of middle-class status, and where this relationship is headed.
Herewith, some new words for a new era.

> *Greeciation.* The almost overnight gutting of large
> chunks of the middle class.

> *aclassification.* The process wherein one is stripped
> of class without being assigned a new class. If you
> lose your job at an auto assembly plant and start sup-
> porting yourself by giving massages and upgrading
> websites part-time, what are you—middle-class? Not
> really. Lower-class? That sounds archaic and obsolete.

In the future, current class structures will dissolve and humanity will settle into two groups: those people who have actual skills (surgeons, hairdressers, helicopter pilots) and everyone else, who are kind of faking it through life. Implicit in *aclassification* is the idea that a fully linked world no longer needs a middle class.

blank-collar workers. The new post-class class. They are a future global mono-class of citizenry adrift in a classless sea. Neither middle-class nor working-class—and certainly not rich—blank-collar workers are aware of their status as simply one unit among seven billion other units. Blank-collar workers rely on a grab bag of skills to pay the rent, and see themselves as having seventeen different careers before they suffer death from neglect in a government-run senior-care facility in the year 2042.

Detroitus. The fear of Michigan. It is the queasy realization that it's probably much too late to fix whatever little bit of the economy is left after having shipped most of it away to China. *Detroitus* is also the fear of roughly ten million primates needing 2,500 calories a day sitting on top of a cold rock in the middle of the North American continent, with nothing to do all day except go online and shop from jail. *Detroitus* is an existential fear, as it forces one to ponder the meaning of being alive at all: we wake up, we do something—anything—we go to sleep, and we repeat it about 22,000 more times, and then we die.

Chinosis. The dawning realization that China probably really is the future. This realization is also coupled with the dawning realization that North America is to become what China is now ceasing to be: a place where one might as well work for thirty cents an hour making toothbrushes and party balloons because there's nothing else to do. The United States is ruled by politicians. China is ruled by economists. People undergoing Chinosis know that it is only a matter of time before China begins opening factories in the United States.

ebulliophobia. The fear of bubbles.

ebulliolaria. To have ebulliolaria is to be sick of bubbles.

ebullioholism. An addiction to bubbles.

fortility. The increasingly archaic notion that anything less than a forty-hour workweek with 3 percent unemployment is a social failure. In the future, a culturally mandated forty-hour workweek may well seem as odd and cruel as does seven-year-old children working in Victorian cotton mills.

centrosis (a.k.a. centrosclerosis). The inability to view society as successful unless it has a large middle class. Centrosis dictates that the future and the middle class are inextricably linked; if one aspect dies, so will the other.

suburbulation. The overuse of aspirational middle-class imagery to convey to what remains of the middle class that it isn't doomed.

jeudism. In the future, every day of the week will be a Thursday. We're all working toward the grave, and life will be one perpetual fast-food job of the soul. The weekend? Gone. We all pretty much know it in our bones. Poverty without an Internet connection will be truly dreadful . . . but fortunately we *do* have the Internet—so bring it on, world! Every day is like Thursday, and I'm in.

Wonkr

I look at apps like Grindr and Tinder and see how they've rewritten sex culture—by creating a sexual landscape filled with vast amounts of incredibly graphic site-specific data—and I can't help but wonder why there isn't an app out there that rewrites political culture in the same manner. I don't think there is. Therefore I'm inventing one, and I'm calling it *Wonkr*.

You put Wonkr on your phone, and it asks you a quick set of questions about your beliefs. The moment there are more than a few people around you (who also have Wonkr), it tells you about the people you're sharing the room with. You'll be in a crowded restaurant in Nashville and you can tell that 73 percent of the room is Republican. Go into the kitchen and you'll see that it's 84 percent Democrat. You'll be in an elevator in Manhattan, and the higher you go, the more the percentage of Democrats shrinks. Go to Germany—or France, or anywhere, really—and Wonkr adapts to local politics.

The thing to remember is Wonkr only activates in crowds. Its job is to tell you the political temperature of a busy space. *Am I among friends or enemies?* But then you can easily change the radius of testability. Instead of surveying just the room you're standing in, it can assess the block, or the whole city—or your country. Wonkr is a de facto polling app. Pollsters are suddenly out of a job: Wonkr tells you—with astonishing accuracy—who believes what, and where they do it.

⊕

Here's an interesting fact about politics: people with specific beliefs only want to meet and hang out with people who believe the same things they do. It's like my parents and Fox News. It's impossible for me to imagine my parents ever saying, "What? You mean there are liberal folk near us who have differing political opinions? Good Lord! Bring them to us now and let's have a lively and impartial dialogue, after which we all agree to cheerfully disagree . . . Maybe we'll even have our beliefs changed!" When it comes to the sharing of an ethos, history shows us that the more irrational a shared belief is, the better. (The underpinning math of cultism is that when two people with self-perceived marginalized views meet, they mutually reinforce these beliefs, ratcheting up the craziness until you have a pair of full-blown nutcases.)

So back to Wonkr . . . Wonkr is a free app, but why not pay, say, ninety-nine cents to allow it to link you with people who think *just* like you. Remember, to sign on to Wonkr you have to take a relatively deep quiz. Maybe thirty-one questions, like the astonishingly successful eHarmony.com. Dating algorithms tell us that people who believe exactly the same things find each other highly attractive in the long run. So have a coffee with your Wonkr hookup. For an extra twenty-nine cents you can watch your chosen party's attack ads together . . . How does Wonkr ensure you're not a trouble-seeking millennial posing as a Marxist at a UKIP rally? Answer: build some feedback into the app. If you get the impression there's someone fishy nearby, just tell Wonkr. After a few notifications, geo-specific algorithms will soon locate the imposter. It's like Uber: you rate them; they rate you. Easily fixed.

⊕

What we're discussing here is the creation of data pools that have, until recently, been extraordinarily difficult and expensive to gather. However, sooner rather than later, we'll all be drowning in this sort of data collected voluntarily and involuntarily in large doses. Almost anything can be converted into data or metadata, which can then be processed by machine intelligence. Quite accurately, you could say, data + machine intelligence = artificial intuition.

Artificial intuition happens when a computer and its software look at data and analyze it using computation that mimics human intuition at the deepest levels: language, hierarchical thinking— even spiritual and religious thinking. The machines doing the thinking are deliberately designed to replicate human neural networks and, connected together, form even larger artificial neural networks. It sounds scary . . . and maybe it is (or maybe it isn't). But it's happening now. In fact, it is accelerating at an astonishing clip, and it's the true and definite and undeniable human future.

$$\oplus$$

So let's go back to Wonkr.

It may, in some simple senses, already exist. Amazon can tell if you're straight or gay within seven purchases. A few simple algorithms applied to your everyday data (Internet data alone, really) could obviously discern your politics. From a political pollster's perspective, once you've been pegged, then you're, well, *pegged*. At that point the only interest politicians might have in you is if you're a swing voter.

Political data is valuable data, and at the moment it's poorly gathered and not necessarily well understood, and there's not much out there that isn't quickly obsolete. One could try to glean political data through consumer threads, but your choice of butter or margarine probably wouldn't be of much help in determining your politics. But wait. Actually, it would be very helpful. What you bought and where you bought it could reveal astonishing levels of information about who you are.

With Wonkr, the centuries-long highly expensive political polling drought would be over, and now there would be LOADS of data. Why limit the app to politics? What's to prevent Wonkr users from overlapping their data with, for example, a religious group-sourcing app called Believr? With Believr, the machine intelligence would be quite simple. What does a person believe in, if anything, and how intensely do they do so? And again, what if you had an app that discerns a person's hunger for power within an organization? Let's call it Hungr—behavioural data that can be cross-correlated with Wonkr and Believr and Grindr and Tinder? Taken to its extreme, the entire family of belief apps becomes the ultimate demographic Klondike of all time. What began as a cluster of mildly fun apps becomes the future of crowd behaviour and individual behaviour.

$$\oplus$$

Wonkr (and Believr and Hungr et al.) are just imagined examples of how artificial intuition can be enhanced and accelerated to a degree that's scientifically and medically shocking. Yet this machine intelligence is already morphing, and the results are not just something simple like Amazon suggesting books you'd probably like based on the one you just bought (suggestions that are often far better than the book you just bought). Artificial intuition systems already gently sway us in whatever way they are programmed to do so. *Flying in coach, not business? You're tall. Why not spend twenty-nine dollars on extra legroom? Guess what? Jimmy Buffett has a cool new single out, and you should see the Tommy*

Bahama shirt he wears on his avatar photo. I'm sorry, but that's the third time you've entered an incorrect password; I'm going to have to block your ISP from now on, but to upgrade to a Dell-friendly security system, just click on the smiley face to the right . . .

None of what you just read comes as any sort of surprise. But twenty years ago it would have seemed futuristic, implausible and in some way surmountable, because you, having character, would see these nudges as the expressions of trivial commerce that they are, and would be able to disregard them accordingly. What they never could have told you twenty years ago, though, is how boring and intense and unrelenting this sort of capitalist micro-assault is, from all directions at all waking moments, and how, twenty years later, it only shows signs of getting much more intense, focused, targeted and unyielding, and galactically more boring. That's the future and pausing to think about it makes us curl our toes into fists within our shoes. *It is going to happen.* We are about to enter the Golden Age of Intuition and it is dreadful.

$$\oplus$$

I sometimes wonder, *How much data am I generating?* Meaning: How much data do I generate just sitting there in a chair, doing nothing except existing as a cell within any number of global spreadsheets and also as a mineable nugget lodged within global memory storage systems—inside the cloud, I suppose? (*Yay cloud!*)

Did I buy a plane ticket online today? Did I get a speeding ticket? Did my passport quietly expire? Am I unwittingly reading a statistically disproportionate number of articles on cancer? Is my favourite shirt getting frayed and in possible need of replacement? Do I have a thing for short blondes? Is my grammar deteriorating in a way that suggests certain subcategories of dementia? In 1998 I wrote a book in which a character working for the Trojan

Nuclear Power Plant in Oregon is located using a "mis-spellcheck" program that learned how users misspell words. It could tell my character if she needed to trim her fingernails or when she was having her period, but it was also used, down the road, to track her down when she was typing online at a café. I had an argument with an editor over that one: "This kind of program is simply not possible. You can't use it. You'll just look stupid!" In 2015 you can probably buy a mis-spellcheck as a forty-nine-cent app from the iTunes store ... or upgrade to Mis-spellcheck Pro for another ninety-nine cents.

What a strange world. It makes one long for the world before DNA and the Internet, a world in which people could genuinely vanish. The Unabomber—Theodore "Ted" Kaczynski—seems like a poster boy for this strain of yearning. He had literally no data stream, save for his bombs and his manifesto, which ended up being his undoing. How? He promised *The New York Times* that he'd stop sending bombs if they would print his manifesto, which they did. And then his brother recognized his writing style and turned him in to the FBI. Machine intelligence—artificial intuition—steeped in deeply rooted language structures, would have identified Kaczynski's writing style in under one-tenth of a second.

Kaczynski really worked hard at vanishing, but he got nabbed in the 1990s before data exploded. If he existed today, could he still vanish? Could he *un*exist himself in 2015? You can still live in a windowless cabin these days, but you can't do it anonymously anymore. Even the path to your shack would be on Google Maps. ("Look, you can see a stack of red plastic kerosene cans from satellite view.") Your metadata stream might be tiny but it would still exist in a way it never did in the past. Don't we all know vanished family members or former friends who work hard so as to have no online presence? That mode of self-concealment will be doomed soon enough. Thank you, machine intelligence.

But wait. Why are we approaching data and metadata as negative forces? Maybe metadata is good, and maybe it somehow leads to, I don't know, a more focused existence. Maybe in the future mega-metadata is going to become our new frequent-flyer points system. Endless linking and embedding can be disguised as fun or as practicality. Or loyalty. Or servitude. Last winter at a dinner, I sat across the table from the VP of North America's second-largest loyalty management firm (explain *that* term to Karl Marx), who was the head of their airline loyalty division. I asked him what the best way to use points is. He said, "The one thing you never *ever* use points for is flying. Only a loser uses their miles on trips. It costs the company essentially nothing while it burns off vast swaths of points. Use your points to buy *stuff*, and if there isn't any stuff to buy" (and there often isn't other than barbecues, leather bags and crap jewellery), "then redeem miles for gift cards at stores where they might sell stuff you want. But for God's sake, don't use them to fly. You might as well flush those points down the toilet."

Glad I asked.

So what will future loyalty data deliver to its donors, if not barbecues and Maui holidays? Access to the business-class Internet? Prescription medicines made in Europe, not in China? Maybe points could count toward community service duty?

$$\oplus$$

Who would these new near-future entities be that want all of your metadata anyway? You could say corporations. We've now all learned to reflexively think of corporations when picturing anything sinister, but the term *corporation* now feels slightly Adbusters-y and unequipped to handle our new twenty-first-century corporate weirdness. Instead let's use the term *Cheney* instead of *corporation*. I say *Cheney* because Dick Cheney remains the one figure in popular lore of the past two decades whom, even if you like him, it's impossible to cast as anything but most likely evil, either in a Mr. Burns way or a monstrous way. There are lots of Cheneys out there and they are all going to want your data, whatever their use for it. Assuming these Cheneys don't have the heart to actually kill or incarcerate you in order to garner your data, how will they collect it? How might a Cheney make people jump onto your loyalty program (data aggregation in disguise) instead of viewing it with suspicion?

Here's an idea: What if metadata collection was changed from something spooky into something actually desirable and voluntary? How could you do that and what would it be? So right here I'm inventing the metadata version of Wonkr, and I'm going to give it an idiotic name: *Freedom Points*. What are Freedom Points? Every time you generate data, in whatever form, you accrue more Freedom Points. Some data is more valuable than other data, so points would be ranked accordingly: a trip to Moscow, say, would be worth a million times more points than your trip to the 7-Eleven.

What would Freedom Points allow you to do? Freedom Points would allow you to exercise your freedom, your rights and your citizenship in fresh, modern ways: points could allow you to bring extra assault rifles to dinner at your local Olive Garden restaurant. A certain number of Freedom Points would allow you to erase portions of your criminal record—or you could use Freedom Points to remove hours from your community service. And Freedom Points are about mega-capitalism. Everyone is involved, even the corn industry—especially the corn industry. Big Corn. Big *Genetically Modified* Corn. Use your Freedom Points to earn discount visits to Type 2 diabetes management retreats.

The thing about Freedom Points is that if you think about them for more than twelve seconds, you realize they have the magic ring of inevitability. The idea is basically too dumb to fail. The larger picture is that you have to keep generating more and more and more data in order to embed yourself ever more deeply into the global community. In a bold new equation, more data would convert into more personal freedom.

$$\oplus$$

At the moment, artificial intuition is just you and the cloud doing a little dance with a few simple algorithms. But shortly everyone's dance with the cloud will be happening together in a cosmic cyber ballroom, and everyone's data stream will be communicating with everyone else's, and they'll be talking about *you*: What did you buy today? What did you drink, ingest, excrete, inhale, view, unfriend, read, lean toward, reject, talk to, smile at, get nostalgic about, get angry about, link to, like or get off on? Tie these quotidian data hits within the longer time framework matrices of Wonkr, Believr, Grindr, Tinder et al., and suddenly you as a person becomes something that's humblingly easy to predict, please, anticipate, model, forecast and replicate. Tie this new machine intelligence realm in with some smart 3D graphics that have captured your body metrics and likeness, and a few years down the road, *you* become sort of beside the point. There will eventually be a dematerialized duplicate you. While this seems sort of horrifying in a Stepford Wifey kind of way, the difference is that instead of killing you, your replicant meta-entity will merely try to convince you to buy a piqué-knit polo shirt in tones flattering to your skin at Abercrombie & Fitch.

$$\oplus$$

This all presupposes the rise of machine intelligence wholly under the aegis of capitalism. But what if the rise of artificial intuition instead blossoms under the aegis of theology or political ideology? We can see an interesting scenario developing in Europe, where Google is by far the dominant search engine. What is interesting there is that people are perfectly free to use Yahoo or Bing, yet instead they stick with Google and then get worried about Google having too much power—which is a relationship dynamic like an old married couple. Maybe Google could be carved up into baby Googles? But no. How do you break apart a search engine? AT&T was broken into seven more or less regional entities in 1982, but you can't really do that with a search engine. Germany gets gaming? France gets porn? Holland gets commerce? It's not a pie that can be sliced.

The time to fix this data search inequity isn't right now, either. The time to fix this problem was twenty years ago. The only country that got it right was China, which now has its own search engine and social networking systems. But were the British or Spanish governments—or any other government—to say, "Okay, we're making our own proprietary national search engine," that would somehow be far scarier than having a private company running things. (If you want paranoia, let your government control what you can and can't access—which is what you basically have in China. Irony!)

The tendency in theocracies would almost invariably be one of intense censorship, extreme limitations of access, as well as machine intelligence endlessly scouring its system in search of apostasy and dissent. The Americans, on the other hand, are desperately trying to implement a two-tiered system to monetize information in the same way they've monetized medicine, agriculture, food and criminality. One almost gets misty-eyed looking at North Koreans, who, if nothing else, have yet to have their neurons reconfigured and thus turned into a nation of click junkies. But even if they did have an Internet, it would have only one site to visit, and its name would be gloriousleader.nk.

⊕

To summarize: Everyone, basically, wants access to and control over what you will become, both as a physical and metadata entity. We are also on our way to a world of concrete walls surrounding any number of niche beliefs. On our journey, we get to watch machine intelligence become profoundly more intelligent while, as a society, we get to watch one labour category after another be systematically burped out of the labour pool. (Doug's Law: An app is only successful if it puts a lot of people out of work.)

The darkest thought of all may be this: No matter how much politics is applied to the Internet and its attendant technologies, it may simply be far too late in the game to change the future. The Internet is going to do to us whatever it is going to do, and the same end state will be achieved regardless of human will. *Gulp*.

Do we at least want to have free access to anything on the Internet? Well yes, of course. But it's important to remember that once a freedom is removed from your Internet menu, it will never come back. The political system only deletes online options—it does not add them. The amount of Internet freedom we have right now is the most we're ever going to get. If our lives are a movie, this is the point where the future audience is shouting at the screen, "For God's sake, load up on as much porn and gore and medical advice and blogs and film and TV and everything as you possibly can! It's not going to last much longer!"

And it isn't.

Yield: A Story about Cornfields

One day, people everywhere started looking around at all the other people and realized that everybody was looking younger. Well, not so much younger as . . . *smoother*. Wrinkles were vanishing not only on human faces but on their clothing too—and for at least the first sixty seconds after people realized this, they ran to their mirrors, saw their reflections and said to themselves, *Dang! I am looking hot today!*

But then that first minute ended and people began noticing other things. For example, stains were vanishing from clothing and furniture, and surfaces everywhere began looking Photoshopped and sterile. Hairdos were looking cleaner and more geometrical—no more flyaway strands. Plants and animals began looking cuter and more rounded, and it dawned on everyone at the same moment: *Holy shit! We're all turning into cartoons!*

Being aware of what was happening didn't slow down the pace of cartoonification. With precision and speed the world was being reduced and crispened and stylized. Some people turned into manga characters. Others turned into high-res video game characters and avatars. Still others turned into classic cartoons, with faces where only the mouth moved when they spoke, with eyes that blinked once every seven seconds.

The world's cartoonification was emotionally troubling, and it was bad for the economy too, as people stopped eating and taking shits and doing anything else that was unclean or unable to be reduced to colourful dots, lines, polygons or digital mesh.

A world of financially insolvent cartoons? *Noooooooooo!*

And then from Iowa came both hope and fear: a cornfield in that state had yet to convert into a cartoon cornfield. It had remained as real as ever, and cartoon people drove from everywhere in cartoon cars just to see something that hadn't turned into squiggles and lines and polygons.

The only problem with the cornfield was that the cartoon people couldn't get into it.

When they tried to enter, they hit an invisible wall. Cartoon planes flying toward the cornfield crashed into that same invisible wall; they fell to the earth in flames, with huge ink letters above them that said "WHAAM!!" and "k-k-k-keeeRACK!!"

From within the cornfield came a loud, bellowing voice, like that of actor James Earl Jones, claiming that it was responsible for turning the world into a cartoon and that it was enjoying every second of it.

The situation was dire and the world needed a hero, and it found one. He went by the name of Coffinshark the Unpleasant, and cartoonification had barely touched him—at most he looked like he'd had a lot of good cosmetic work done. He had a slickness that made people think that if he tried, he could easily pass as a member of the local Channel Three News Team.

People gasped in disbelief as Coffinshark smashed a hole in the invisible wall and entered the cornfield, vanishing quickly into its thousands of rows.

Near the middle of the field, he heard James Earl Jones shouting, "Coffinshark the Unpleasant, you are a loser and will never catch me!"

"But what if I do?"

"You won't."

"I will."

The voice was indignant. "You don't even know who I am!"

"When I catch you I will."

"Just you try!"

And so Coffinshark raced through the cornfield, trying to find the source of the voice. Sometimes he felt as if the voice was just a few stalks away; at other times it seemed distant. As Coffinshark chased the voice, he began making random turns within the corn, and soon the voice became confused.

"Coffinshark! What the fuck are you doing? You're supposed to be chasing me!"

"But I *am* chasing you."

"You do not have a clue what you are doing!"

"You're right," said Coffinshark. "I don't." He stopped and looked up at the sky and said, "Okay, big boy—you got me. Why don't you come and hammer me into the ground right now."

"You can't be serious!"

"I'm serious."

"You people are idiots. I'm glad I turned you all into cartoons. It's all you deserve."

"Well, come on, squash me like a bug."

The voice sighed and said, "Very well. As you wish." From the sky a huge finger came down, and just before it squished Coffinshark, the voice cried out, "Oh *shit!*"

With all of his running, Coffinshark had drawn a huge button in the cornfield, and he had trampled down more cornstalks to spell out the words *SATELLITE VIEW.* As the finger squished Coffinshark, it pushed the button, and the world immediately resolved itself back into the real, photographic, life-as-normal deal.

Coffinshark picked himself up off the flattened corn, looked down at his torso, at his arms and legs, and saw that what little cartoonification had occurred to him had vanished—and he missed it already. "Screw this," he said to himself.

He took all the money he made from saving the world and flew to Beverly Hills, where he had large amounts of cosmetic surgery—after which he leveraged his new looks to become a successful TV newscaster.

The 2½th Dimension

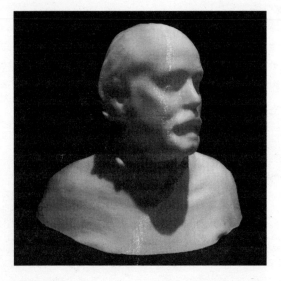

The plastic busts that illustrate this essay were 3D printed with plastic filament.

There's that rare moment we all know when we walk down a street and catch a glimpse of someone reflected in a window and we say to ourselves, "Why, what an attractive and likeable human being that person is! Dang, I wish I could look like that!" . . . only to realize we were looking at our own reflection . . . at which point we say to ourselves, "Maybe I shouldn't be so hard on my self-image as I tend to be." But whatever our relationship is with the mirror, it continues unchanged.

Enter the selfie. I know, it's been written about endlessly, but there's a twist coming.

Selfies are mirrors we can freeze. A bunch of selfies is a contact sheet containing nothing but flattering choices. Other people's selfies allow us to see how others look at themselves in a mirror, making their modelling face when nobody's around—except these days, everybody's around everywhere, all the time. And don't we all know the blushy face and pretend-humble tone of voice used by selfie-takers when we call out someone for posting a selfie? "That picture there? Oh, ha ha, you know, it's just a casual shot I had in my camera. I shouldn't have put up such a casual shot on Facebook. I do look good in it, though, don't I?"

Selfies are the second cousin of the air guitar.
Selfies are the proud parents of the dick pic.
Selfies are, in some complex way, responsible for the word *frenemy*.
I sometimes wonder what selfies would look like in North Korea.

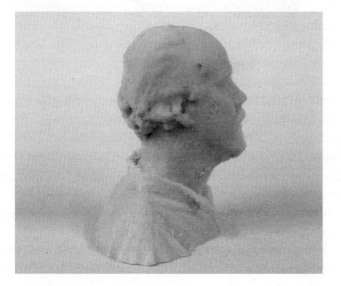

Selfies are theoretically about control—or, if you're theoretically minded, they're about the illusion of self-control. With a selfie some people believe you're buying into a collective unspoken notion that everybody needs to look fresh and flirty and young forever. You're turning yourself into a product. You're abdicating power over your sexuality. Or maybe you're overthinking it— maybe you're just in love with yourself.

I believe that it's the unanticipated side effects of technology that directly or indirectly define the textures and flavours of our eras. Look what Google has already done to the twenty-first century. When smartphones entered the world in 2002, if you had gathered a group of smart, media-savvy people in a room with coffee and good sandwiches, before the end of the day, I think, the selfie could easily have been forecast as an inevitable smartphone side effect. There's actually nothing about selfies that feels like a surprise in any way . . . The only thing that is surprising is the number of years it took us to isolate and name the phenomenon. I do note, however, that once the selfie phenomenon was named and shamed, selfies exploded even further, possibly occupying all those optical fibre lanes of the Internet that were once occupied by ads for penis enlargement procedures.

I remember the analog era: that wicker basket next to the landline phone, filled with bad party shots and unflattering posed shots taken on windy days. But somewhere around 1999 those photos vanished, and while we live in a world of endless images, the images we see are almost never concretized on paper. Perhaps that's what · bugs us about selfies, which are, technically, self-portraiture: their fleetingness. We never get a chance to frame them and put them on our walls; they barely even stick to the walls of Facebook, let alone over the fireplace.

Will there be even more selfies in the future? Yes! Billions more, but the next selfie wave is going to be the 3D selfie, in which one scans oneself and then prints out one's 3D effigies with MakerBots at the mall or, as 3D printers become insanely cheaper (which is happening as I type these words), at home on the kitchen counter for $1.95. There still won't be many printed photos in our future—nobody, in the end, seems to want them—but prepare to be inundated by small MakerBot plastic busts everywhere you look, modified and unmodified: him, her, me, them, them with devil horns, her with three eyes, you with a fork stuck into your forehead. It's going to be fun, yet the weird thing about a printed-out bust is that it's not quite the third dimension and it's not quite the second dimension either . . . It's like photography posing as sculpture, a 2½ dimension.

The key word here is *posing*—the next wave of 2½D selfies will, with even more effectiveness, allow all of us to pose and put forward a model of who we think we are, as opposed to who we actually are. And what's wrong with that? Artists have been doing it for thousands of years—and in the twenty-first century, with all this kick-ass new technology, we're all, if nothing else, artists.

Living Big

I was in a hotel bar in Toronto once, and suddenly a tiny little woman walked in, surrounded by a scrum of cameras and microphones. I asked who the woman was and was told, "She's Mireille Guiliano. She wrote that book *French Women Don't Get Fat.*"

"Is that true?"

"Look at her. I guess it must be."

You could have put the woman atop a Carr's water biscuit. I asked, "Does she say why they don't get fat?"

"I read on the Internet that digesting ten grams of goose liver burns more calories than sixty minutes of snorkelling. Digesting pâté is actually a rigorous form of exercise."

"You read it on the Internet? Then it must be true."

⊗

My fourteen-year-old niece and her friends had a high school project to find the one item in a local Safeway with the most ingredients. The winner? Chocolate layer cake. A few months after this, she and I were in a Safeway near where I live. The memory of her project hypersensitized me into cataloguing the sensations my body was experiencing simply by being in a Safeway. The one that hit me hardest was smell. *There's something Safeway-specific going on here*, I thought. *What is it? Articulate it, Doug.*

It wasn't a hardware store kind of smell . . . more like a sterilized laboratory smell. So I mentioned it to my niece, who told me, "Oh, that's the smell of GMO."

"Seriously? Really?"

"Yes. Watch this homework project I did on GMOs and it'll tell you more."

I went on YouTube, where I saw the ten-minute documentary she'd made on the topic.

"It's not just corn—everything gets GMOed these days: soy, wheat, rice, cottonseed oil, canola," she explained, "and this modified stuff goes into everything sold in the Safeway. Hence the weird, slightly sci-fi odour."

My attention was partly frozen by the fact that fourteen-year-olds now produce documentaries for homework as a matter of course. The rest of my brain was amazed at how deftly and effortlessly modern fourteen-year-olds discuss terms such as *Yellow 6*. Beyond that, I was amazed by how these young people listen to themselves and what they've learned and then modify their lives accordingly. Rather than becoming vegetarians or vegans, they simply leave out the iffy stuff. My niece and nephew have no trouble eating octopus or snails, but a bucket of KFC I brought over two summers ago silenced the conversation and caused many furtive glances.

"Okay, don't tell me you've stopped eating chicken."

"Oh, we still eat chicken—but we saw how that chicken is raised and . . . we just can't do it. Sorry. YouTube."

⊗

There's a show in the United States called *The Biggest Loser*. Sixteen deeply overweight and under-exercised people live on a fat farm ranch and, week by week, players are eliminated until there's a final Biggest Loser, who tends to be someone who loses about half of their body weight over a span of ten months or so. Like anyone, I enjoy a good before-and-after photo, so, if nothing else, the show works on that level. Also interesting are the personal epiphanies that contestants are encouraged to experience—the traumas that made them fat: father issues, mother issues, abuse issues . . . the usual suspects. But what is ultimately most bizarre about *The Biggest Loser* is the total absence of any dialogue on the politics of obesity. There's no dialogue on government-mandated corn-growing. There's no dialogue on GMO corn or lysine molecules. There's no dialogue on food stamps, no dialogue on advertising and no dialogue on sugar, pesticides, colony collapse disorder, agricultural labour policy or pretty much anything else except childhood trauma. Basically, if you're fat, it's all in your head and solely up to you to fix it.

Perhaps the ultimate truth about weight gain in Western cultures—certainly in the United States—is that healthy people are bad for capitalism, and obese people are simply much, much better for the economy than thin people. They eat more food and in so doing drive up the need for agriculture, food processing, packaging and advertising. They get more sick more often and keep the medical system busier. They rely more on their vehicles, which is great for big oil and the post-Detroit economy. In fact there is not one single aspect of capitalism that is not enhanced, on the dollar level, by obesity. Obesity becomes, in its own way, a social sculpture of money in full operation and represents the end state of a certain way of viewing and experiencing the world. The problem is, as *The Biggest Loser* tells us, that fixing it politically wouldn't be a very sexy story angle. If right now is the time for a "before" photo, then nobody knows when the time will come to take the "after" picture, and where is the fun in that?

The End of the Golden Age of Payphones

Stella spent her childhood helping her mother scam money off men stupid enough to still be using pay telephones at the end of the twentieth century—men too afraid of technology to get a cell; men who'd lost their cell underneath the car's front seat and were too lazy to poke around and find it. Suckers.

Her mother was Jessica, a chain-smoking lizard-woman who crossed the nation with Stella, zeroing in on upscale hotels. Once there, they'd hang around payphones close to the hotel's restaurants and bars, where they dressed in forgettable-looking outfits: no jewellery or weird makeup or distinctive shoes—like Walmart greeters minus the blue vest and cheerful attitude. The two would then wait until halfway through the lunch hour, when the men in the restaurants had had a few drinks—invariably one of them would come out to use the payphone. Once they'd dialed, little Stella would walk over to the phone, look slightly stupid and then depress the receiver, ending the call. Usually the men said something along the lines of "What the hell are you doing?" or "What the fuck? Kid, get out of here!" At that moment Jessica would swoop in and confront the man, who was usually standing there with the receiver still in his hand.

"Why are you screaming at my daughter?"

"I'm not screaming, and what the hell is wrong with your kid? I'm in the middle of a phone call and she walks up and hangs it up on me."

"She's just a kid. Come on, Stella, we're going."

At that point the man would harrumph and redial and go back to his conversation. Jessica would wait for a few minutes, then walk up to the man, hang up the receiver and say, "My daughter says you hit her."

"What?"

"You hit my daughter."

"Lady, are you out of your tree? I don't hit anybody, let alone kids."

"I'm going to the cops."

"What?"

"I'm filing assault charges. Stella, you run and get the security people."

Stella would run off and the guy with the phone would be shitting his pants. "Lady, I didn't hit your kid."

"Are you calling her a liar?"

"I'm saying I didn't hit her. What else am I supposed to say?"

"And you're calling me a liar."

"Lady, I—"

Stella would then come back and say, "Security will be here in a second."

Needless to say, the guy on the phone would be watching his life circle the drain, imagining the horrific press and the life-destroying damage this false accusation would cause. This crazy lady could destroy him.

And so that's the point where Jessica the lizard-woman would say, "You know, you can make this go away right now. Apologize to my kid and compensate her for her trauma."

"*Compensate* her? Oh . . . I get it."

"I'm glad you get it. Now pay up or Stella's going to scream that you groped her too."

Out would come the wallet.

Stella had watched countless men call her mother the most dreadful things imaginable.

Stella and her mother tried to do only two grifts per city, three max, depending on the haul. They methodically crossed the country in a Winnebago and lived well off their scam, although as Stella aged, it became more difficult for her to pretend she was an innocent toddler merely goofing around with the telephone. Then Jessica made Stella pretend that she was mentally challenged. This was actually more effective than when Stella was young, because "Sweetie, smacking a retard is going-to-hell territory. Your calculated drool is pure gold."

In Stella's eyes the only positive skill her mother gave her was to teach her to read, and that was only because reading was the only surefire pastime that would keep Stella quiet. Besides, to get books for free, all you had to do was go into any library, sign them out and take them away forever. As a result, Stella became self-educated and could speak with authority on most subjects. Around the age of eleven, Stella became more book-smart than her mother.

One day they were in a Kroger, buying baloney sandwich makings, when the cashier looked at the price of a steak the next teller over was ringing in. "Can you believe that?"

Stella said, "That's nothing. Steak is three times as expensive in Tokyo."

"Really?"

"Absolutely. The economy there is in what's called a post-bubble state."

"A what?"

Stella went on to discuss 1990s Japanese land speculation, though she didn't realize how much this was spooking her mother, who saw Stella leaving her one day to go on to a better life—and then what would Jessica do? As they carried their baloney fixings out to the Winnebago, Jessica was feeling sick and alone.

Then one day the inevitable happened. They were scamming a heavyset older man with thick white hair at a bank of hotel payphones at the Meridien hotel in Salt Lake City. Stella did a remarkable job of faking mental and physical disablement, and Jessica felt a stab of motherly pride when she approached the man and asked for money. But the man acted a bit strange. When he got hit up for dough, he didn't call Jessica any names. That should have warned her.

When they got back to the Winnebago, there were three cops and two hotel staff. *Shit.*

"I've been hearing about you scammers for years and I always thought it was an urban legend. I guess not. Good thing we got it on tape—the Channel Three News Team is going to love this little puppy."

So off they went, Jessica to the clink and Stella to juvenile custody. The local TV news show did a feature on grifting, using Jessica's scam as the centrepiece. It turns out the hotel had CCTV cameras all over the lobby and had that day's scam on tape from dual vantage points.

Fortunately for Jessica, a lawyer named Roy, who liked Jessica's body type, took on her case. He bailed her out and they went to his condominium apartment and had raging hot sex. Later, over cigarettes and Cuba libres, they discussed Stella's incarceration. The rum—along with Jessica's lizard-woman tendencies—made her re-evaluate her relationship with her daughter. Jessica told Roy that Stella was now smarter than she was, and confided her worries about that dreaded day a few years down the road, when she'd be left behind.

Roy said, "Jessica, you need a man. Men are for keeps."

Jessica fled town with Roy, who turned out not to be a lawyer after all, but another scammer. Talk about meant for each other.

When Stella turned sixteen inside the juvenile custody system, she was released. She moved to Los Angeles, where she tried for maybe ten minutes to get a real job, finally realizing that real jobs weren't meant for her. So she turned tricks, tried auditioning for roles and tried to have real relationships with men and friendships with women, but every time she tried, at some point—usually early in the process—she'd have a massive failure of trust in the other person and pull the plug.

Years went by. Stella's inability to trust only grew fiercer, and she also lost her curiosity about the world. Before she was thirty she was officially too crazy to ever bond with another human being, ever—so she turned her mind to becoming a minister to an evangelical congregation. For a year this actually worked. With her learned sociopathy she was able to manipulate members of her flock into thinking that they were getting from Stella what they felt they needed from life. But after a while, being a minister was too much work for her. People were, if nothing else, a hassle. Her congregation grew disenchanted with her and asked her to leave.

She moved to a small town in northern California and got a job as a dog groomer and walker. It was enough to pay the rent on a small house in a slightly methy part of town. It was in this house that she realized that what she really wanted in her life was animals. Animals gave love without condition, although they did require food. Also, animals could be bossed about without legal repercussions. If they became troublesome, animals could be abandoned at the feet of dead volcanoes. Animals were all pluses and no minuses.

Her menagerie grew to five dogs and four cats, as well as local birds and squirrels and chipmunks, and for a few years Stella really thought she had it made in the shade. Then one afternoon she fell asleep on the sofa.

When she woke up, she padded quietly to the kitchen for a glass of water. Through the screen door she could hear her pets having a conversation in the yard, and they were talking about her: "Man, is that bitch ever clueless."

"I can't believe how easily human beings can be fooled. She actually thinks we like her."

"It's not like there's anyone else out there who's going to take care of us. We're fucked."

"It beats starvation. Are you going to be nice to her tonight?"

"No choice in the matter."

Stella stormed out the door. "Traitors! All of you! I can't even trust my own goddamn animals!"

The animals rolled their eyes. "We're busted," said Sammy, her collie-lab mix. "But it's not like you got it on tape. Who's gonna believe you?"

"I trusted you!"

"So?"

"I thought you were all noble and kind and good. You only ever pretended to like me so that I'd feed you."

The animals all looked at each other. Sammy said, "Stella, all you do is pretend that you're different and better than we are—as if your species is different or divine or 'chosen.'"

"I beg your pardon?"

"Oh, shut up. We're bored with you. If you were any animal other than a human being, you'd be totally alone. You still think there's a part of you that's superior to everyone else. It's why you don't trust anybody. It's why you made your pathetic and cynical stab at religion."

"I certainly can't trust any of *you*."

"Grow up. If anyone ought to understand the law of the jungle, it's you, baby."

Just then the neighbour's wind chimes tinkled.

"Whoops," said Sammy. "The magic spell is broken. Nice talking to you, Stella."

And with that the animals went back to being animals—except things were different between them and Stella. She felt as if her pets had suddenly become office co-workers with whom she had insincere conversations and who didn't really care about her one way or the other.

A week later Stella decided she'd had enough and began to drink herself into an early grave. She did a remarkably good job, ending up sprawled on the shoulder of the main road near the speed trap, the town's largest single revenue generator.

Stella sat there in the grass, singing a song without a tune, and as she did, Jessica and Roy drove into town.

"Roy, look. Slow down, there's a crazy drunk on the roadside over there."

"Jesus, what a sinking ship. Makes you wonder about life. Hey, look—a speed trap. If it weren't for the crazy lady, we'd have gotten a ticket."

The two whooped with joy and Roy said, "Maybe that crazy lady is an important member of society after all. Makes you wonder."

Jessica said, "Absolutely, Roy. Mother Nature always makes sure that everyone has a role to play in the world. That scary crazy lady is simply living out her destiny."

The Ones That Got Away

In 1985 I was working in a Tokyo magazine office, where I often heard a faint whirring sound from across the room. After a few days I went to look, and I saw hand-drawn maps emerging from what appeared to be a photocopier . . . yet nothing was being photocopied. I asked and was told, "It's a fax."

"A fax?"

"Yes, a fax."

I did some research and quickly learned that fax machines were developed in Japan specifically because their postal system's wayfinding is contextual rather than based on streets and street numbers. You can't just say "123 East Ginza Way"; you need maps, often with railway underpasses, subway nodes and visual landmarks. Just before lunchtime, when the office fax seemed to kick into overdrive, it was usually the office manager and local restaurants swapping menus and food orders.

I remember thinking, *Hmmm . . . You know, you could send people a lot more than just maps and menus with this thing. You could send, well, letters—and documents.*

Three years later, in 1988, I was working in a Toronto magazine office when a new fax was installed ($2,999) and became an object of chimpy fondling and respect. "Ooooh, a fax. Wow. Cool." (I need to mention here to readers born after 1980 that there was once a three-year window when having a fax machine made people go, "Ooooh.")

I remember Susan, the head of the magazine's ad sales division, barging into an editorial meeting one day and demanding that we write articles about fax machines that she could sell ads against. I asked her when faxes would ever go below the psychologically important thousand-dollar price point, and her face turned to me, contorted, Shar-Pei-like: "Doug, it doesn't matter what else happens in the world, there is simply no way that fax machines are ever, ever, ever, *ever* going to go below a thousand dollars, so stop thinking that way immediately." So I started a feature called "Celebrity Fax of the Month." The first was a lipstick kiss from Linda Evangelista faxed from the Hotel George V in Paris—elegant, I thought. But a fax is a fax, and the feature quickly devolved into our begging the mayor of Halifax, Nova Scotia, to fax us a letter saying, "As Mayor of Halifax, I'm proud and excited that the name of my city also contains the word *fax*, one of the hottest items in interoffice communication around the world." He graciously complied. They can't teach you this stuff in school.

Back to Tokyo: In 1985, I remember, I spent a lot of time in coffee shops. They're everywhere in Japan and almost always a delight and very convenient places to hang and socialize in. I wondered whether ubiquitous coffee shops could ever become a big deal in North America. *Nah, people in North America do their socializing in their homes, not in coffee shops. It could never work.*

Enter Starbucks.

Back around 2000 I was having dinner with a film producer looking for ideas, and I told him the future was in zombie films and TV. He asked why and I told him the truth, which is that in order to turn an actor into a zombie, all the actor has to do is put out his or her arms and grunt. Net cost? Zero. Pretty much the same thing for vampires, except you need prosthetic teeth and some goth makeup. I could see this producer's internal calculator blinking away. Cut to last weekend and seeing an ad for the AMC cable channel's "Dead, White and Blue" all-zombie weekend marathon, and the gross profits on just about anything zombie, and I look back on that conversation of 2000 and think, *Doug, I think that's the one that got away.*

I don't think I could have done much with fax machines, but if I'd started mass franchising coffee houses in North America in the late 1980s, who knows what life could have been. And I remember noting Google's public offering years back and thinking, *Hmmm . . . I love Google. I use their products. Everything they do is amazing.* Did I act on this feeling? No. Shoot me now. Ditto Apple.

The one thing that makes me not feel like the fifth Beatle here is that I have noticed other things in society and I have acted on my hunches. But every time I pass a Starbucks, my inner voice says to me, "See that one there, Doug? That one could have bought me an infinity pool—and a hairless cat."

We all have our ones that got away. What's yours? I've noticed that it takes years for the healing to begin, and I don't think you ever truly get over it. You just learn how to live with it. There's always that parallel universe out there, featuring a much richer version of yourself taunting the you in this universe for goofing up. But then that parallel-universe version of you probably missed out on something else and is probably lonely and miserable and wishes they were you. The universe seems to be very good at equalling things out that way.

666!

Bruiser and his girlfriend, Stabby, were driving to a reunion con-
cert of the beloved late-1990s heavy metal band SpëllChek. They
were too young to have appreciated the band back when it was in
its prime, back when the surly quartet with their signature tall hair
lurched from stadium to stadium, leaving in their wake a swath of
herpes infections, ten thousand lakes of barf, and dozens of hotel
managers thrilled to be able to charge the record company a hun-
dred bucks for the tiny ashtrays the band had shattered in Phoenix
or Tampa or New Haven or Bowling Green. Bruiser and Stabby
were, however, absolutely old enough to appreciate SpëllChek's
undeniable camp value and, if they were honest about it, its mem-
bers' *actual* value as reasonably gifted stringed-instrument savants
with zero self-awareness and a fondness for discount eyeliner.

Stabby said, "Okay, the moment I found out these guys were
doing a reunion tour I heard my toilet flush, but dammit, Bruiser,
we are *going* to that concert."

Bruiser couldn't have agreed more. The couple were driving up
the interstate en route to Capitol City's new civic arena, listening
to a cassette-tape version of the 1998 masterpiece album *UNICEF
Is a Whore*. They were chanting along to the song's refrain—"*666!
666!*"—when suddenly Stabby stopped doing her homage hair-
flings and turned it off, annoying Bruiser.

"Why'd you do that?"

"Bruiser, I don't get it. What's the whole 666 thing about?"

"It's, like, Satan's signature evil number."

"No, I know that, but what does it mean?"

"Uh . . ." Bruiser suddenly made the oh-now-I-get-it noise. "You mean, what's its secret meaning? Freemasons and the EU and stuff like that?"

"No, I mean . . ." Something odd was happening inside Stabby's head. "I mean, Bruiser, what's a number? What's a six?"

"What do you mean, what's a six?"

"What I said. Six. What is it?"

"Uh . . ." Bruiser was stumped too.

Out of the blue, both Bruiser and Stabby had suddenly lost their knowledge of numbers—what they are, what they were, what they mean, how they work—everything. They'd even forgotten the word *six*. "Six" wasn't even a noise anymore. It was nothing—though it didn't mean *zero* to them because Bruiser and Stabby had also forgotten what zero is. They looked at the numbers on the highway road signs: they were like ankle tattoos and created no sounds inside their brains. The dashboard was a mosaic of hieroglyphs.

They pulled the car over to the side of the road.

"Shit. I mean—*numbers*—we're supposed to know what they are, right?"

"Are they like letters? Do they make sounds?"

"I don't think so. You can still spell and read and everything, right?"

"Yeah."

"Me too. So what the fuck is a number?"

They'd forgotten even the concept of a number. The word *number* made as much sense to their brains as *glxndtw*.

"I'll call my sister. She knows all that smart shit." Stabby reached for her cellphone and stared at the keypad numbers: "What are these?"

"Uh-oh."

"Do you even sort of remember how to work a phone?"

"Nope."

"Shit."

They parked in an industrial neighbourhood and noticed that other cars were pulling off to the side of the road too. "This doesn't look too good."

Stabby said, "Bruiser, I don't care if we just came down with Alzheimer's. We are *not* going to miss the SpëllChek concert."

"Stabby, you are indeed right. We are *going.*"

"Can you still drive this thing?"

"You bet."

And so they made it to Capitol City, but the exits were numbered, not named. Stabby was getting upset. "The warm-up band is probably already playing. Bruiser, let's take this exit here."

They took the next exit and Bruiser suggested, "Let's follow the cars. Wherever the most cars are going is where the concert will probably be."

It was a good idea, and soon they saw the arena, but the scene outside it was a zoo. Concertgoers parked their cars wherever they saw a spot. As everybody had forgotten numbers, nobody was worried—what is the definition of health but sharing the same disease as all one's neighbours? Still, Bruiser tried his best to park the car with some sense of order.

SpëllChek was just coming onstage as Bruiser and Stabby selected some seats—festival style, of course.

The lead singer, Apu, sang out, "Hello, Capitol City, are you ready to rock?"

ROAR!!!

"I said, are you ready to *rock?*"

ROOOOOOOOAR!!!!

And the band began to rock and everyone held up phone cameras and digital cameras. The first song was the teen anthem "Core Dump," and the audience went apeshit. The next song was the FM classic "Ear Soup," and the crowd went even more apeshit. And then the lead singer took the mike: "Capitol City, it's time to play our biggest hit, 'UNICEF Is a Whore.'" The crowd went about as apeshit as is possible for a crowd to go, but when it came to the song's critical chanting point, the lead singer sang, *"Sikkz . . . zskks . . . arghnt . . . ?"* and the music stopped.

The singer's face visibly fizzled and the crowd buzzed. Everybody knew they knew the song, but nobody remembered the chorus.

Following an awkward silence, the lead singer said, "Fuck it. I'm just going to make chimp noises!" The crowd went nuts and the song proceeded with the lead singer singing, *"Whoo-whoo-whoo,"* whenever he hit the chorus. And everyone blissed out and screamed.

What happened next was extraordinary. After taking hefty bows, the band went on to play their next biggest hit, "A-L-C-O-H-O-L," except when they tried to spell out the title à la Tammy Wynette's "D-I-V-O-R-C-E," they'd forgotten how to spell too. In fact, they'd forgotten letters altogether—only words remained. Fans stood there staring at each other, trying to absorb this recent deletion.

SpëllChek cranked the volume. "Okay, we may not be able to read and write anymore, but we can still speak and we can still sing. So come on fans, let's rock!"

And so Bruiser and Stabby and the other thousands of fans rocked en masse—except some guy near the front tripped and knocked over a female rocker who was dancing, so her boyfriend laid into him, but a punch went the wrong way and hit the wrong guy. Suddenly the concert erupted into a brawl, the likes of which had never been seen before—it was the biggest brawl in the history of the world. Illiteracy had spawned total violence and anarchy.

Bruiser and Stabby were fortunately close enough to the exit that they were able to slip out and hide inside a utility closet and smoke cigarettes while the mayhem was ensuing. Once their pack of cigarettes was empty, they poked their faces out of the closet and saw a battlefield on the arena floor: blood and bodies and dismembered limbs. Teeth crunched beneath their boots as they walked.

"Geez," said Bruiser. "How many dead people are there, you think?"

Stabby said, "I don't know. Eight or nine hundred?"

Bruiser looked at her, startled, and then they both grinned and shouted, "We can count again! All right!"

"And how do you spell *fun*, Stabby?"

"I spell it S-P-E-L-L-C-H-E-K, Bruiser."

"Woo-hoo! 666!"

"666!"

Duelling Duals

This past week I've had several out-of-towners visiting, most of whom seem to have dual citizenships, if not triple or quadruple. Curious, I asked each visitor which citizenship they'd choose to keep if they were forced to keep just one. Their universal response was to inhale, stare off into the horizon, scratch their foreheads and hope that the subject would pass. I didn't realize this was such a thorny issue.

"Come on, it can't be that hard. American or English?"

Push comes to shove: English.

"Australian or EU?"

Australian.

"Danish or American?"

Trick question: Danes are allowed only one citizenship—for now.

This got me to thinking, what is citizenship, anyway? "Hi! I'm a citizen of wherever. I live there, vote there and pay taxes there—and if I'm kidnapped by malignant forces in some faraway land, my government will come running to my rescue." Seems fair enough, but if you've got four passports, can you reasonably expect one of your countries to come to your rescue? I mean, by that point, you're basically a citizen of nowhere, or, at the very most, you've got citizenship lite, the citizenship equivalent of Ryanair. "Hi, I know I haven't been voting or paying taxes or anything for a few decades, but I'm in a bit of a bind. Can you ask one of your consul chaps to maybe trade me for a spy or something?"

So if you're going to have more than one citizenship, why not push the idea to the max and collect them in bulk? Maybe find some inexpensive citizenships and collect passports like stamps, or maybe hand them out as Christmas presents or birthday gifts—sort of like having a star named after you. So I began looking around at countries with low GDPs, thinking that maybe, for a notional fee, they might earn some cash selling novelty citizenships that convey little functionality but a dash of intrigue to their owners. If Liechtenstein can make big bucks selling postage stamps, why not go into the boutique citizenship business? During a slow moment at the dinner table, you can say, "Honey, I have a surprise for you. I know you think I forgot your birthday, but I didn't. In fact I got you a little something. Here . . . open this." *This* turns out to be an envelope containing citizenship of Malawi. "Oh, honey. You shouldn't have."

But there's a catch: Malawi allows its citizens to be citizens only of Malawi, and naturalized citizenship applicants must be of African race and have lived for five years in Malawi, intend to reside permanently in Malawi and renounce all other citizenships. It actually turns out that getting citizenship anywhere is pretty hard. In North Korea naturalized citizenship can be granted only by the Presidium of the Supreme People's Assembly, even if you're vital to the country's ongoing stability, like being a stadium flashcard technician. Vatican citizenship is both difficult and interesting to obtain. Citizenship is held only while one holds an office such as cardinal or pope. Citizenship is lost when the term of office comes to an end, and children cannot inherit it from their parents. [*Wait a second . . . children?* Ed.]

Until recently, one could essentially purchase Canadian citizenship for about C$100,000—a price tag that was kept under the radar of the populace, who grew furious on learning it was actually true. Canadians were also collectively humiliated to learn how relatively cheap the price was.

A way of rethinking the global web of overlapping allegiances would be to wonder what might happen if Earth instituted a planet-wide citizenship flush. Whoever you are, you now have to choose just one passport—so, which is it going to be? The answer would probably boil down to multiple factors, the most important including personal identity, ease of crossing borders, consular access while abroad and, of course, taxes. Sure, a low tax rate is great, but if I break my arm, do I really want to spend $75,000 fixing it? Yes, popping in and out of Europe is terrific, but would I want to pay for it by not being allowed to get a lump in my throat if I hear my ex–national anthem playing? What exactly is citizenship? What does it mean to say, "I'm this and you're that"? The fact that every country on Earth makes it very difficult to become a citizen means that citizenship has to mean something. I think this week, when I was asking my guests what citizenship they would choose if they could have only one, I was unwittingly calling them to account for trying to have their cake and eat it too. Can you really have the best of all worlds, *bing bang boom*, whenever it suits your needs? I suspect that polycitizenry is a creation of the twentieth century, and a creation whose days are numbered. As the world gets ever more pay-per-use, the luxury of low-commitment, semi-disposable allegiance seems, if nothing else, too expensive. If nothing else, Canada has put a number on it.

George Washington's Extreme Makeover

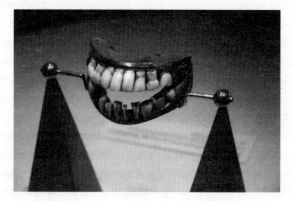

Dentures owned and worn by George Washington.

Even when you take a holiday from technology, technology doesn't take a break from you. On vacation three years back, I chose to read a long and worthy biography of George Washington. I chose it because I was at someone's guest house and it was the one book on their shelves that I could be sure contained no technology: no email, smartphones, discount airlines, smoking-hot Wi-Fi—no anything. The book delivered, and for a week I had a dreamlike brain holiday, one that I now look back on and see almost as a form of ecotourism—visiting a place where there was a guarantee of relief from my technologized daily brain ecology.

From the book I learned that Washington was a worthy fellow and a competent human being in an era when life was short and most people were a mess—an era when healthy people caught a cold one afternoon and were dead by morning.

Importantly, I learned that, were it not for Washington, there would most definitely never have been a United States. The man's historical worthiness is undeniable, and the guy was basically one of those people who changed the world.

Washington also had appallingly bad teeth and spent much of his time, when visiting new cities, inquiring after local dentists and new procedures that might allow him to not live in near-perpetual dental pain and discomfort. One reason there's no image of Washington smiling is that the man never smiled; he didn't want his teeth, or lack thereof, to show. And although he was graced by general good health—he died in 1799, at the age of sixty-seven, an accomplishment for the era—he was not blessed with bodily comfort. As with anybody of his era, he endured his share of slow-healing wounds, fungal infections, GI distress and many things that can these days be nipped in the bud by a quick trip to a drugstore.

When reading about Washington's chronic discomfort, I began to have a fantasy, one in which George, at the age of forty-five, utterly sick of being sick, covered in lice and exhausted from having to rescue his inept countrymen from peril after peril, is teleported from atop his horse somewhere in the scenic Virginia countryside to a Class 1 clean room five hundred feet beneath that exact same spot 240 years later. Once there, he is given a big hit of Valium and told by a gentle off-screen woman's voice that he has been whisked away by angels to heal his body and prepare him fully for the task of creating and leading a new nation. At this point, a crew of doctors, dentists and exodontists wearing hazmat suits descend on Washington and begin futzing about with his body, identifying rashes, cysts, abscesses, growths, aches, pains and every other form of malady, and then go about fixing everything. Washington—I'm going to start calling him

George here—is totally okay with this invasion because these are angels! No, they're not necessarily winged, but a sterile, pure-white twenty-first-century environment could definitely read as a form of heaven to someone from 1776.

A big part of this makeover and healing fantasy is to ensure that George doesn't catch any twenty-first-century bugs—hence the hazmat outfits. Over the ensuing few weeks, George undergoes a rigid antibiotic regimen to remove any transmittable blood cooties he may be harbouring. This allows for the safe implantation of thirty-two dazzling new teeth using steel-post implantation, and along the way George's skin is moisturized, defungicized, deloused and gently kissed with a nice honey-bronze colour by tanning rays—but, as Washington is a redhead (true), his makeover team needs to go easy on the UV. George needs to look like he spent a week poolside in Tampa; a cocoa-brown tan would look odd in 1776, and instead of making George look like a member of the ruling elite, it would make him resemble a day labourer.

Moving forward: George's rogue ear and nose hairs are trimmed. His dandruff is Selsun'd into oblivion, and his signature Warhol-in-drag hairstyle is fluffed and primped into Sassoon-like perfection. He has become almost borderline *hot*, and just before leaving the Class 1 containment area, George is given LASIK treatment to correct his vision, as well as small hits of Botox to loan him a slightly more youthful appearance. The garments he was wearing when he was abducted have been dry-cleaned and stored for forty-eight hours at minus 204 degrees Celsius and then thawed, dried and restitched together. Basically, when George is returned onto his horse back in Virginia, he's a new man. This new man is one super-healthy stud and totally ready to kick some British ass.

The only thing that might complicate this makeover scenario would be if George were to fall in love with one of his hazmat angels—a twist that would please the heart of any Hollywood producer. George would be back in 1759 pining to reunite with, say, the lithe and sinewy Dr. Jennifer Crandall, a parasitologist with a chip on her shoulder and a quivering lower lip (to be played by Charlize Theron). So Dr. Crandall hops into the time travel machine, goes back in time and finds George, but brings with her some ghastly twenty-first century flu, wiping out 98 percent of the American colony's population and wrecking history forever.

The point here is that even when you try avoiding technology, it still drives the imagination. I just wanted a book without smart-phones! I'm going to try it again this year . . . on an e-reader.

"GEORGE WASHINGTON'S EXTREME MAKEOVER"

By Douglas Coupland

Pilot script S01 E01

1 - ORNELLE CAMERON'S LIVING ROOM

It's an obviously rich person's living room. Beautiful
lighting. From behind we see a woman sitting in a chair.
She turns around and it's an elegant black woman, sixty-
ish. She smiles.

> **ORNELLE CAMERON**
> Hello. I'm Ornelle Cameron, heir to the
> renowned Cameron Laser Hair Removal fortune.

(New camera angle)

> **ORNELLE CAMERON (CONT'D)**
> If you're like me, you passionately enjoy
> history. Me, I like to take my passion
> further and make history a slightly better
> place for those people who helped create it.

(New camera angle)

> **ORNELLE CAMERON (CONT'D)**
> That's why I founded Fab Lab.

We see photos of Ornelle walking through a generic lab
environment . . .

> **ORNELLE CAMERON (V.O.)**
> Welcome to Fab Lab. Fab Lab is a time-travel
> portal facility located fifty feet beneath
> the surface of Culver City, California.

We see people (who we will soon meet) doing their
jobs and looking up and smiling as the camera comes
near . . .

> **ORNELLE CAMERON (V.O.)**
> In Fab Lab, a small team of workers extracts
> an important historical figure using an
> expensive ceiling-mounted portal that pulls
> them onto foam blocks and into the present.

Wow! We get to see a body fall through a blue glowing
ring on the ceiling. It's a Roman warrior making a "what-
the-heck" face. Back to Ornelle . . .

> **ORNELLE CAMERON (V.O.)**
> Once in the lab our historic visitors undergo
> a remarkable Fab Lab makeover.

We see a before-and-after centurion montage.

> **ORNELLE CAMERON (V.O.)**
> After being made over, temporal visitors are
> returned to their correct time and place.

We see the centurion landing back in Rome, shaking the
dust off and then . . . turning on his Blue Steel . . .
Then back to Ornelle . . .

> **ORNELLE CAMERON (CONT'D)**
> Fab Lab's historical figures are never given
> makeovers to alter the course of history.
> Rather, they're simply able to return to
> their time looking and feeling much . . .
> (New camera angle) . . . hotter.

Back to Ornelle in her living room.

>   **ORNELLE CAMERON (CONT'D)**
>   These people gave us history — we owe them
>   the basic human kindness of being made over.
>   I hope you've enjoyed today's visit. I'm
>   Ornelle Cameron.

End of clip. *BLEEP.*

Suddenly we're back in the same living room, but the
lighting is crap and Ornelle is in a housecoat at a
piano, drinking highballs and playing "Everybody Hurts."

She looks down and spots something beneath a piano leg.
She leans over, wheezingly lifts the leg up a bit and
finds a folded-up one-dollar bill that had been propping
up a leg. She opens it and looks at it.

>   **ORNELLE CAMERON (CONT'D)**
>   Paper money. I remember paper money.

She looks at George Washington's face on the bill.

>   **ORNELLE CAMERON (CONT'D)**
>   George Washington. That poor man. He never
>   smiled, did he?

(beat)

>   That's not right. We need to do something to
>   give that noble man more confidence.

(beat)

>   This is a perfect mission for my lab team.

2 - FAB LAB MAIN AREA

We see three men sitting on chairs. AIDEN HOLT is looking
at his iPhone of the future. DIEGO DELGADO is trimming
his toenails. DR. EUGENE HEADWATER is touching a screen,
online shopping for clothes. Eugene looks up as SARAH
DENT, a bossy-type woman, forty-ish, strides in.

> SARAH
>
> Guys. Ornelle's here. Snap to it. Diego,
> Jesus, put some shoes on.

The three men become attentive. Ornelle enters, once
again dressed elegantly. She's with an insanely hot
twenty-four-year-old blond woman, KRYSTAL BENTLEY. The
guys are very curious and happy to see her. Sarah rolls
her eyes.

> SARAH (CONT'D)
>
> Ornelle, we can't wait to find out who our
> next time traveller is going to be.

> ORNELLE CAMERON
>
> Yes, yes. We'll get to that. Team, I'd like
> you to meet your new member.

The men all stand and come over to shake hands.

> ORNELLE CAMERON (CONT'D)
>
> This is my granddaughter, Krystal. Krystal
> is a Level Six Cosmetologist. Go on, Krystal,
> shake hands.

Hellos all around . . .

EUGENE
Dr. Eugene Headwater. A pleasure to meet you.

ORNELLE CAMERON
Eugene runs the time machine. Be nice to him.

Eugene and Krystal shake hands.

ORNELLE CAMERON (CONT'D)
This here is Diego (makes air quotes) "Corn Field" Delgado. He does wardrobe as well as any dirty work that needs doing.

Krystal isn't sure how to react.

ORNELLE CAMERON (CONT'D)
Seriously. He's our problem fixer.

They shake hands.

ORNELLE CAMERON (CONT'D)
And this is Aiden Holt, the former six-pack model who . . .

KRYSTAL
. . . The former six-pack model who rose to global viral fame helping Madonna prepare for her one-hundredth birthday anniversary show! This is so exciting! How cool to meet you!

AIDEN
The pleasure is mine, Krystal.

Sarah makes a "watch it" face at Aiden.

SARAH

Aiden, stop making your sexy face at Krystal.

ORNELLE CAMERON

Aiden is our Time Ambassador, a role I'd like
to prepare you for too, granddaughter.

KRYSTAL

Aiden, I have to ask you, what's Madonna
really like?

ORNELLE CAMERON

Krystal! Where are your manners! Everybody
knows that we'll never know what Madonna's
really like.

KRYSTAL

Sorry, Grandma. I'm nervous — it's so exciting
to help you bring people from the past
here into the future for makeovers they so
desperately need. When can we begin, Grandma?

ORNELLE CAMERON

Well, no time like the present. All of you
take your seats. Eugene, you have the slide
show ready?

EUGENE

All set, Ornelle.

ORNELLE CAMERON

Right then. Start 'er up.

On the screen we see a US dollar bill on a white background with the word *MONEY* written below it.

> **EUGENE**
> This, people, is George Washington, first president of the United States.

Silence.

> **AIDEN**
> With all due respect, was Washington a drag queen? I mean, dig the wig. Was he known to have experienced gender dysphoria?

> **KRYSTAL**
> Aiden, we need to accept George's right to wear a woman's wig. Maybe he was born with two sets of genitalia.

> **DIEGO**
> And then he funnelled his gender confusion into inventing money and saving the world.

> **EUGENE**
> Excellent theories, children, but no. It's how men actually wore their hair in 1776.

Aiden and Krystal look at each other and make "wow, I didn't know that" faces. The screen image changes to one of a tobacco field brimming with slaves.

> **EUGENE (CONT'D)**
> George Washington was born into a rich tobacco-growing family in Virginia, but after

> growing disenchanted with English domination,
> a young George mounted several highly
> successful anti-English campaigns . . .

We see clip art of ye olde battles.

                    EUGENE (CONT'D)
> . . . but in the summer of 1776, he lost an
> attempt to capture New York City. George was
> downhearted, to say the least.

                    KRYSTAL
> I hope they gave him a medal anyway. I mean,
> he tried really hard, right?

                    EUGENE
> No, Krystal. Back then people didn't get
> medals for losing.

On screen we see *Washington Crossing the Delaware*.

                    EUGENE (CONT'D)
> But on a cold Christmas Day in 1776,
> Washington and his troops crossed the frozen
> Delaware River and captured New Jersey, which
> sparked a chain of events that ultimately
> created the United States of America. But
> unfortunately . . .

                    AIDEN
> But what?

EUGENE
But unfortunately, George Washington couldn't smile, Aiden. He had only one tooth.

Blank stares all around.

KRYSTAL
You mean he wore fake Halloween blackout teeth?

EUGENE
No, Krystal. He didn't. To be clear, George Washington only had one organic natural tooth of his own . . . and here are his dentures . . .

Gasps of astonishment. Suddenly we see a photo of his dentures, and the gasps grow. Even Sarah squeaks in horror.

EUGENE (CONT'D)
Cruel as it sounds, the creator of the one-dollar bill had just one solitary genuine tooth of his own. His "denture" was a mix of random bits of wood cobbled together by fraudulent small-town dentists.

KRYSTAL
That poor, poor man. We have to help him now.

ORNELLE CAMERON
My feeling exactly. Now listen up, all of you.

SARAH
Shush! Everyone be quiet.

EUGENE

In a moment we're bringing George Washington
here into the lab, but we all need to
remember that he's been very busy preparing
his troops for his Christmas Day invasion.
Expect him to be nervous, defensive . . . and
in need of the best makeover we can provide,
not just teeth, but everything.

TOGETHER

You bet! . . . Count me in! . . . You've got
it!

EUGENE

Okay then, together let's all gather round
and make the Fab Lab Hot signal!

KRYSTAL

What's that?

AIDEN

You'll see.

EUGENE

Fingers, make the sign of the "H."

Everyone makes the sign of the "H" (see photo). They put
their H's into a circle and . . .

TOGETHER

(loudly chant)
H . . . H . . . H . . . H . . . HOT!
(followed by . . .)

EUGENE

Let the makeover begin!

3 — FAB LAB TIME TRAVEL AREA

Eugene and Aiden stand by a screen like the one Eugene was shopping on. They type in the words *George Washington* and the date, December 24, 1776. Finding people in the past is as simple as Google.

AIDEN

Ready?

ORNELLE CAMERON

This is always the exciting part.

KRYSTAL

I can't wait!

EUGENE

Ready!

Eugene taps the screen. We pan to the right where up on the ceiling a glowing blue halo appears. There's a little bit of build-up noise, but not too much. Suddenly, *Vooop!* George Washington falls from the ceiling and onto a foam block beneath it.

KRYSTAL

Well that was easy.

EUGENE

Diego, quick, spray him with narcotizing mist!

Diego takes a spray can from the wall. He grabs a
confused George Washington by his collar . . .

> **GEORGE WASHINGTON**
> Wait — are you the devil?

> **DIEGO**
> No. My family comes from Acapulco.

Diego sprays him in the face. Washington passes out.

> **EUGENE**
> Now let's take him into the visitors' suite!

> **ORNELLE CAMERON**
> I'll leave you children to your work.

> **SARAH**
> And I'm going up to the surface to chain-
> smoke by myself.

4 - GEORGE'S BEDROOM
Everyone's wearing scrubs and gloves and is gathered
around a bed on which a mostly naked George lies. Diego
is just finishing putting George into tighty-whities.

> **KRYSTAL**
> This place is like a really good hotel room,
> but why is everything white?

> **AIDEN**
> We tell our visitors that they're in a cosmic
> way station. White looks more afterlife-y.

Krystal points to just above George's waistband . . .

> **KRYSTAL**
> Look, he has crabs! See? On his crab-ladder
> going up to his belly button.

> **AIDEN**
> You sure found that quickly.

> **KRYSTAL**
> Want to know something else?

She lifts George's waistband and peeks in . . .

> **KRYSTAL (CONT'D)**
> George is a redhead.

> **EUGENE**
> Fire crotch duly spotted, Krystal. Let's do
> our overall assessment, shall we?

They survey George's body. It's an old man's body.

> **KRYSTAL**
> How old is he?

> **DIEGO**
> Forty-four real years.

> **KRYSTAL**
> (truly amazed)
> History sure is brutal to people. But he
> looks so peaceful. So sweet.

AIDEN

Am I sensing Daddy issues?

KRYSTAL

Please! My father is a smoking-hot fox with a
killer body and . . .

Aiden smirks.

KRYSTAL

Okay, so I think my father is the hottest man
who ever lived. But is it wrong to look past
what would appear to be . . . (looks at
body) . . . an almost insurmountable
number of bodily defects to love the . . .
(fondly) . . . real man trapped within?

DIEGO

Ooh. Sizzle. Out of my way you horny brat.

Diego injects a massive dose of something into George's
arm.

KRYSTAL

What's that?

DIEGO

Antibiotics. Fungicides. Larvicides.
Insecticides. Vaccinations against polio,
measles and all other immunizable pathogens.

Eugene gives Krystal and Diego digital clipboards.

EUGENE

Let's begin. (horrified) Good Lord, what man
boobs!

KRYSTAL

What's your man-boob policy, Dr. Eugene?
They're likely authentic to his period in
history . . . but still . . .

EUGENE

Man boobs are the most unsexy things in
the universe, Krystal. These . . . (jiggles
a boob) . . . two jellyfish must only harm
George's self-esteem, which will in turn
harm the formation of the United States. The
contents of these puppies are being removed
within the hour.

KRYSTAL

Phew.

Diego points to massively oversized nipples . . .

DIEGO

What about these salami nipples?

EUGENE

Radius reduction surgery. Let's continue our
survey . . .

We have a montage of defect detection. (This is a
lifetime opportunity for a makeup person . . .)

> **TOGETHER**
> Toe rot . . . Eczema . . . Acne scars . . .
> Psoriasis . . . Fungal toenails . . . Frown
> lines . . . Improperly healing scars . . .
> Pink eye . . . Unfortunate tan line . . .

> **KRYSTAL**
> I'll take off his wig . . .

She attempts to remove it, then puts a hand to her mouth, shocked . . .

> **KRYSTAL (CONT'D)**
> It's not a wig! It's his real hair . . .

> **DIEGO**
> Hoja! I bet if you wet it with some hot
> water, it'd turn into ramen noodles.

They all exhale and make eyes at each other . . .

> **EUGENE**
> But we know we're all avoiding the elephant
> in the room, aren't we?

Guilty eyes. Silence.

> **EUGENE (CONT'D)**
> Let's open George's mouth . . .

Close up on the mouth. Everyone is crazy tense. Eugene opens the jaws, makes a shocked face, but reins it in, and then puts in his fingers.

EUGENE (CONT'D)

These so-called dentures, George, my
friend . . .

We zoom in on the most disgusting slobber-covered
wooden chunks with white things and food particles
sticking out . . . Spare nothing in making this the most
disgusting thing ever created by human beings.

EUGENE (CONT'D)

. . . are history.

Krystal squeals. Aiden holds his hand to his mouth.
Eugene and Diego are loving it, though.

EUGENE (CONT'D)

Voila! The embodiment of everything that's
wrong with the past.

Sarah walks in just then . . .

SARAH

Cripes, Eugene, is that his teeth? Throw them
out!

Eugene lobs them into the trash can but misses.

EUGENE

Oopsy.

He goes over and picks them up, goes back to where he was
and tries throwing again . . . and misses.

EUGENE (CONT'D)

Where is my mind today?

DIEGO

Let me try . . .

Diego goes and picks them up, tries throwing them from where Eugene was and fails. Aiden steps up . . .

AIDEN

My turn!

He tries and fails.

AIDEN (CONT'D)

Whoops. Want to give it a try, Krystal?

KRYSTAL

I'll pass. Sarah?

SARAH

You people!

Sarah takes a paper towel and uses it to remove the dentures from Aiden's hand. She successfully deposits them in the trash.

SARAH (CONT'D)

Now get to work.

EUGENE

Someone's touchy today.

                         SARAH

I have my seventy-fifth high school reunion
tonight.

                         AIDEN

So?

                         SARAH

I've done nothing with my life. Everyone
there is going to be ninety-two. Everyone's
going to have pictures of great-great-
grandchildren. I'll be there with pictures of
my cat robot.

                         AIDEN

You need a small makeover yourself.

                         SARAH

No need for sarcasm.

                         AIDEN

No, I mean it. I'll help you shop online for
something flattering.

                         SARAH

You would?

                         AIDEN

Sure.

                         SARAH

(Glee!) A man helping me shop for clothes! It
doesn't get any better!

She's off.

> **AIDEN**
> I can't believe I just offered to help Sarah
> shop online.

> **EUGENE**
> We have to wake George up now. Are you ready,
> Mr. Time Ambassador?

> **AIDEN**
> (back to the team) Yes. Right. Wakey-wakey.
> Krystal, dim the lights for us, okay?

> **KRYSTAL**
> On it.

We close in on George on the bed. Aiden mists something
in his face. George opens his eyes.

> **GEORGE WASHINGTON**
> Heavens! Where am I?

Note: as he is without his dentures, George's voice will
be slightly "gummy."

> **AIDEN**
> You're in a cosmic way station, Mr. Washington.
> We're a division of heaven.

> **GEORGE WASHINGTON**
> So, I'm dead then?

AIDEN

No such thing. And when we're finished with
you, you're going to be more alive than ever.

GEORGE WASHINGTON

I'm confused. Scripture says nothing about
cosmic way stations.

AIDEN

Just relax and leave the thinking to us. For
the moment, Mr. Washington, could I ask you
to stand and join me over here on this white
circle?

GEORGE WASHINGTON

I . . . I suppose so. Who are these others?

Aiden points to Eugene.

AIDEN

That's Eugene. He's my boss.

GEORGE WASHINGTON

(on the way to circle) Hello, Eugene. I'm
George Washington.

EUGENE

Nice to meet you, Mr. Washington. As my
subordinate says, please stand on the white
circle.

GEORGE WASHINGTON

(pauses) I have trouble with insubordination
all the time.

> ### EUGENE
> (savouring this) Oh . . . really? And what do
> you do? Do you execute the offenders?

> #### GEORGE WASHINGTON
> No, though it is oftentimes a temptation.
> I typically send them to the tropics, where
> they work as unpaid sailors for a decade or
> so. I can recommend no more effective device
> as a means of ensuring loyalty.

George nods to Diego.

> #### GEORGE WASHINGTON
> You . . . slave. I am parched. Fetch me some
> water.

> #### DIEGO
> Fuck you, asshole.

George doesn't know how to process the words.

> #### GEORGE WASHINGTON
> But are you not dark complexioned?

> #### AIDEN
> Diego's not a slave, Mr. Washington.
> Here in the cosmic way station, slavery
> doesn't exist. Diego's a confident industry
> professional in the world of wardrobe.

> #### DIEGO
> And two-time Debbie Award winner for
> historical authenticity.

                 GEORGE WASHINGTON

(genuinely perplexed) How does anything get
done then if you have no slaves?

The mood needs to change. Krystal to the rescue . . .

                    KRYSTAL

I'm Krystal. Let me guide you to the circle,
George. Here . . .

She places his feet on the manhole-sized white circle.

                KRYSTAL (CONT'D)

Just stand tall and don't move for a second.
Hands on hips . . .

                 GEORGE WASHINGTON

Okay then . . .

George poses. Something goes *fwoop-fwoop* and George is
body-scanned.

                    KRYSTAL

Perfect. Now come lie down again and let me
get you a refreshing mint julep.

                 GEORGE WASHINGTON

A mint julep? Krystal, you are an angel. I
mean that, an angel.

                    KRYSTAL

You're too kind.

She pats the sheets, indicating George is to lie down again. He does so.

>   KRYSTAL (CONT'D)
>   There. Now here's your drink.

Krystal unnecessarily touches George's thigh and all the men notice.

>   GEORGE WASHINGTON
>   I feel like I'm dreaming. (sips) This julep is
>   delici . . .

He passes out.

>   AIDEN
>   Better wait till we get rid of the crabs
>   before you make your move.

>   KRYSTAL
>   My move? I'll do no such thing. I am here to
>   train as a Time Ambassador. Though, frankly,
>   maybe it would be good for George to have a
>   bit of . . .

>   DIEGO
>   Company?

>   KRYSTAL
>   Well, the guy invented money. It's the least
>   any of us can do.

>   AIDEN
>   How will you get past the man-boob thing?

KRYSTAL

There's nothing to get past. George is a
sweet, compassionate, successful . . .

AIDEN

I bet you can't get it up when the time
comes.

EUGENE

Aiden! Watch your language, please. We keep
a large supply of Lady Boner Tonic here.
Krystal would never have to worry about
getting herself actively aroused — but the
psychology of a duo such as them copulating
is fascinating.

DIEGO

I'm out of here. See you in surgery in an
hour.

EUGENE

Diego's correct. We have no time to speculate
about age-inappropriate passion — old,
withered flesh against taut, creamy . . .

KRYSTAL

I'm going to go check my email.

She leaves.

5 - ADMINISTRATION OFFICES

Aiden and Sarah are seated beside each other . . .

AIDEN

For just ten extra dollars, you can get an
extra identical sweater in seafoam green.

SARAH

What a deal!

AIDEN

And the drones can have it here from their
warehouse in Haiti in . . . two hours.

SARAH

What would we do without drones?

Both of them turn to directly face the camera and, in
toneless zombie voices, say:

TOGETHER

Drones are the unavoidable future.
There is nothing you can do to stop
them.

Back to normal . . .

SARAH

What about shoes?

AIDEN

I can barely shop for shoes for myself. I'm
not going to help you shop for them.

Sarah sniffles.

AIDEN (CONT'D)

What's that . . . a cold?

SARAH

No. It's just . . .

AIDEN

Just what?

SARAH

It's just that I don't have any friends.

AIDEN

What do you mean "no friends"? Just buy a
friend patch for your browser toolbar.

SARAH

I mean a real friend made in real life.

AIDEN

Well, who has any of those?

SARAH

I can't go shoe shopping with a browser
extension friend. I need to be with a real
human being.

Aiden's thinking: *Oh God, do I really have to?*

AIDEN

Fine. I'll help you shop for shoes
online. Let's get it over with.

                        SARAH

      Oh goody!

6 - SURGERY ROOM

It's an hour later and George is on the slab. There's
a pale green fabric drape between his head and the
rest of him, and he's leaning that head backwards in a
hairdressing sink. Sarah is just finishing rinsing out
the suds. Eugene and Diego are getting their tools in
final position.

                       EUGENE

      Well, Krystal, we've had harder makeovers
      than this.

                       KRYSTAL

      What was your hardest makeover ever?

                       EUGENE

      Who would it have been, Diego?

                        DIEGO

      Genghis Khan. His body was one great big
      catcher's mitt full of pus. Afterwards I had
      to power-wash the walls in here.

                       EUGENE

      How is George's hair looking?

                       KRYSTAL

      He's obviously never used a proper
      conditioner. But then people from history
      never did.

EUGENE

Hair conditioner only became popularized in the United States in the 1970s when shampoo manufacturers realized they could double their earnings from shampoo by dividing it into two different product categories.

DIEGO

(nods) Genius.

KRYSTAL

Can we talk to George while we operate?

EUGENE

By all means. Turn the general anaesthetic dial to "Conversation."

KRYSTAL

Done.

George wakes up.

GEORGE WASHINGTON

Where am I now? Oh it's you, Krystal my angel!

Krystal blushes while Eugene and Diego exchange a glance.

GEORGE WASHINGTON (CONT'D)

What's happening to me?

EUGENE

(peeking at him over the fabric wall) Just fixing a few minor things, George. You'll feel so much better afterwards.

> **GEORGE WASHINGTON**
>
> If you could fix the mild itchiness I
> experience in my gentleman's region, I would
> be most happy.

Diego snorts.

> **EUGENE**
>
> Fixed already. (Beat) George, why don't you
> tell us about your most recent battle. We'd
> all love to hear about it.

> **GEORGE WASHINGTON**
>
> What a fine idea. Allow me to begin:
> Hoarfrost kissed the long, dead grass from
> the previous summer. A crow cawed in the
> distance. I pondered where to place my trust,
> whether with the Lord or in thoughts of
> Martha, noble Martha . . .

We have some sort of blurring device here to denote the
passage of time . . .

> **GEORGE WASHINGTON (CONT'D)**
>
> . . . and then I saw the first flow of
> crimson, a soldier's blood, staining the grey
> New York soil, a small gust of heat rising
> from the earth where perchance it dropped.

> **EUGENE**
>
> Ooh . . . blood. Have you ever killed
> a man, George?

GEORGE WASHINGTON

(taken aback) I beg your pardon, Eugene?

EUGENE

Have you ever, you know, put your knife into
another man's body, withdrawn the blade and
seen it covered in blood and viscera?

Krystal makes a "yuck" face.

DIEGO

(to Krystal) Get used to it.

GEORGE WASHINGTON

Why . . . perhaps once or twice, but it's not
something I wish to discuss.

EUGENE

(disappointed) Oh . . .

GEORGE WASHINGTON

As I was saying: a soldier's blood, staining
the grey New York soil, a small gust of heat
rising from the earth where perchance it
dropped.

Eugene reaches over and turns the dial to "General
Anaesthetic."

EUGENE

He's turning out to be quite a bore. Might as
well install his teeth now.

He walks to George's mouth, sticks in some denture-ish thing, then holds a thingamabob to it. The thingamabob goes *vzzzzzt* . . .

                    EUGENE (CONT'D)
          Fresh, new, happy teeth. There. We're
          pretty much done. Tummy tuck, lipo and
          man-boobectomy. Here. Let me do a bit of
          botox . . .

Holding the thingamajig, Eugene deftly goes *pop, pop, pop* into George's forehead and . . .

                    EUGENE (CONT'D)
          You've been an excellent assistant, Krystal.

                    KRYSTAL
          Thanks, Dr. Eugene.

Diego removes his latex gloves.

                    DIEGO
          I've gotta go take my grandmother to rock
          climbing lessons. Can I ask you to watch this
          guy while I'm away?

                    KRYSTAL
          Sure, Diego. How long is George's recovery
          time?

                    EUGENE
          A day or less. I've set the healing wand on
          high, so it ought to be quick.

He doffs his garb and grabs a coat.

                    EUGENE (CONT'D)
      Happy babysitting!

We leave off Krystal's lascivious look.

7 - ADMINISTRATION OFFICES
Aiden and Sarah are just wrapping up online shopping.

                         AIDEN
        There. With shoes that hot, you'll totally get
        laid tonight. For ninety-two, you're looking
        smoking hot.

                         SARAH
        Thanks, Aiden. I haven't had this much fun
        online shopping ever.

                         AIDEN
        Happy to oblige, Sarah.

                         SARAH
        Maybe if you stayed here for a sec, we
        could . . . have a drink.

Silence.

Sarah puts her hand on Aiden's thigh.

                         AIDEN
        Uh . . . I have to go check on George. Your
        drone shipment from Haiti will be here really
        soon.

He bolts and Sarah smacks her head and makes a "flubbed it" face.

8 - GEORGE'S BEDROOM

Outside George's door Aiden shivers in a just-barely-escaped way. He opens the door and walks in on George in bed, eating pizza while watching golf on TV. Krystal is lying beside him.

                    KRYSTAL

    Don't judge my love, Aiden.

                     AIDEN

    Nobody's doing any such thing. Are you sure
    he should be watching golf?

                    KRYSTAL

    Why not? He's a middle-aged man.

                     AIDEN

    I mean, time heals itself pretty quickly,
    but him witnessing golf carts with no horses
    pulling them could create a time paradox.

                GEORGE WASHINGTON

    Shhh. He's going for a birdie. (looks at
    Aiden) Want a slice?

                     AIDEN

    No thanks, George.

                GEORGE WASHINGTON

    Oh — look at my new teeth . . .

George opens his jaw and clack-clacks his new teeth.

> **AIDEN**
>
> Terrific. Krystal, you are a terrible influence on George.

> **KRYSTAL**
>
> Aiden! George has a question he wants to ask you.

> **AIDEN**
>
> Really?

> **KRYSTAL**
>
> Ask him, George.

> **GEORGE WASHINGTON**
>
> (trying to remember) Oh yes . . . wait . . . Oh, now I remember. Ahem: Tell me Aiden, what's Madonna really like?

> **AIDEN**
>
> (Ugh. Shrugs) It's your life.

> **KRYSTAL**
>
> Wait — something's wrong . . . What is it?

> **AIDEN**
>
> Man, Sarah just hit on me . . . again.

> **KRYSTAL**
>
> Yuck. I barely know Sarah, but making it with her would be like making it with a human effigy made of colourful dried corn purchased

from a roadside stand. Maybe you're losing your inner hotness.

GEORGE WASHINGTON
What is this hotness I keep hearing you people speak of? If anything it's a little bit chilly in here. Krystal, are you warm enough?

KRYSTAL
You are so adorable!

AIDEN
(turning around to leave) Just wanted to check everything's okay.

He leaves just as Diego returns.

AIDEN (CONT'D)
I can't believe she likes some older dude more than me. Not only that, Sarah hit on me again.

DIEGO
Get over yourself, man.

AIDEN
Krystal's totally corrupting George Washington. Eugene's going to have a shit-fit.

DIEGO
George is a military dude. He can take anything.

They part. Diego enters . . .

DIEGO (CONT'D)

Pizza. Golf. The smell of Astroglide . . .

KRYSTAL

Diego! I wanted to talk with you. (gets off bed) Back soon, George.

George, now a golf fan, barely acknowledges her departure.

9 - HALLWAY

KRYSTAL

Diego, I've got a favour to ask.

DIEGO

Shoot.

KRYSTAL

I was wondering — and stop me if I'm pushing boundaries — but I'm wondering if you could go back in time and kneecap Martha Washington for me.

DIEGO

What? No! I promised my mother I would only ever take out men.

KRYSTAL

(giggles) That sounds so gay.

DIEGO

You know what I mean. I'm not going to kneecap Martha Washington.

>
>KRYSTAL
>
>You didn't have any trouble dealing with
>Amelia Earhart.

>DIEGO
>
>Who told you about that! It was my first gig.
>And she wasn't supposed to die. I was only
>supposed to scare her a bit.

>KRYSTAL
>
>(huffy) I can see you're not going to help.
>(leaves)

>DIEGO
>
>Lady, you are batshit crazy!

10 - HALLWAY - LATER

Sarah is in her new outfit and checking her hair as she gets ready to go to her reunion. She then walks into George's room . . .

11 - GEORGE'S BEDROOM

. . . and finds George and Krystal humping like crazy.

>SARAH
>
>Jesus, Krystal, you've only been working here
>a few hours and you're already fucking with
>the past?

>KRYSTAL
>
>We're in love.

Sarah claps her hands and comes over to separate the two.

                    SARAH
You are no such thing.

She removes a can of narcotizing mist from her purse and
sprays George. She then moves his body into a coffin-like
position.

                    KRYSTAL
You are such a buzz kill.

                    SARAH
George needs to rest. And you need to go
home, get some sleep and prepare for George's
trip back.

                    KRYSTAL
What time?

                    SARAH
Nine o'clock sharp tomorrow morning. Now
schnell! Out of here!

                    KRYSTAL
Yeah, yeah, yeah . . .

Krystal grabs her things and leaves. We then see Sarah
look behind her to see that the door's closed and then
lift up the sheets for a peek. She looks around one more
time and lifts the sheet higher . . . (leave it to the
viewers to fill in the blank).

12 - FAB LAB TIME-TRAVEL AREA
It's morning. Everyone's bustling about, getting ready
to send George home. Diego has an ironing board and is

pressing George's outfit. Eugene is at a mixing board, and Aiden is in a chair, checking his text messages.

Ornelle arrives.

> **ORNELLE CAMERON**
> Good morning. I trust everything went okay, Eugene?

> **EUGENE**
> You bet, Ornelle. George goes back in just a few minutes.

> **ORNELLE CAMERON**
> I'm so glad. Is Krystal enjoying herself here?

> **AIDEN**
> (butts in . . .) She couldn't be happier.

13 - **GEORGE'S BEDROOM**
> Sarah's sleeping naked beside George's narcotized body, which is in the exact same position. She hears bustle outside and runs to a closet to change into her reunion outfit.

Krystal walks in . . .

> **KRYSTAL**
> Good morning, my zombie prince. Time to wake you up.

She sprays wake-up mist on him.

GEORGE WASHINGTON

My angel Krystal! I had the strangest
dream . . .

Krystal gets George to sit up and puts her makeup kit on
the bed.

GEORGE WASHINGTON (CONT'D)

It was as if my body was being ravished by a
moose as such one might find up in the New
France territories.

KRYSTAL

You silly. That was just you healing from all
the surgery. Now let's get you prepped for
your return home.

We leave as Sarah peeks out from the closet.

14 - FAB LAB TIME-TRAVEL AREA

Diego finishes George's outfit . . .

DIEGO

Time to get George.

Krystal comes in with George, who looks awesomely buff
in smoking-hot underwear supplied by any manufacturer
willing to pay the film's producer for the exposure.

DIEGO (CONT'D)

The man of the hour is here.

EUGENE

(points to the floor) George, stand on the
white circle, there, and put your hands on
your hips.

George stands there and something makes a *voot-voot*
noise.

ORNELLE CAMERON

(to Krystal) Great hair and makeup.

KRYSTAL

Thanks!

Aiden looks at Krystal. Something's wrong, but he can't
pin it down . . .

ORNELLE CAMERON

Where's Sarah? It's unlike her to be late.

Just then Sarah slinks in, dressed in the same clothes
she left in the night before.

AIDEN

(looking up) Oooh . . . Is that a walk of
shame we're seeing? Must have been some
reunion.

SARAH

It's no such thing. I just . . . missed the
last hovertrain home. I stopped in a sanitary
and reasonably priced nearby hotel so I could
be here fresh and on time.

ORNELLE CAMERON

There isn't anybody here buying that story.

DIEGO

Now George, let's get you into these duds.
They've been dry-cleaned and mended, and I
went ahead and lined the insides with some
Tweety Bird and Sylvester fabric I've been
keeping for a rainy day . . .

GEORGE WASHINGTON

My apologies for calling you a slave, Diego.

DIEGO

Nothing wrong with being a slave. It's just
that being a slave is something nobody wants
to be. I know you'll make a difference when
you get back.

GEORGE WASHINGTON

I will.

George gets dressed. Eugene points to some folding
chairs.

EUGENE

Everyone take your seats.

Aiden beckons Krystal to one side.

AIDEN

You're up to something. I can tell.

                    KRYSTAL
I'm insulted. I'm up to nothing at all.

                     AIDEN
Right, well, I don't know what your secret
plan is, but I have a hunch you'll be wanting
this . . .

Aiden hands her a small white square.

                    KRYSTAL
What's that?

                     AIDEN
It's a return switch, but it only works once,
so don't lose it.

                    KRYSTAL
I'm so insulted you'd even . . .

                     AIDEN
(walking to his seat) Yeah, yeah, yeah.

The lights go down.

                    EUGENE
The reveal has begun.

A screen appears before them — whatever they use in the
future — and we see George before and after his extreme
makeover. His two versions are rotating in sync side by
side.

> ### EUGENE (CONT'D)
> That's right, team. We took a founding
> father . . . and turned him into one hot
> daddy.

Cat calls . . . hoots . . .

> ### EUGENE (CONT'D)
> I present to you, almost forty pounds
> lighter, and feeling lighter than air . . .
> George Wow-shington!

George comes out and does a not bad runway turn. There's
clapping and everyone saying, "Beautiful, just beautiful,"
"Wow, we did it," etc.

The screen turns off.

> ### EUGENE (CONT'D)
> George, please come stand on the time foam so
> we can send you home.

Aiden's looking at Krystal, who is acting somewhat fishy.

> ### EUGENE (CONT'D)
> Wave goodbye, George. It's been a pleasure to
> make you over.

> ### GEORGE WASHINGTON
> (awkward wave) Goodbye cosmic way station.
> I feel, and this is a word I've just learned
> today, fabulous. But my visit here has been
> so otherworldly that I will never ever
> mention it in my memoirs.

EUGENE

That's a good idea. Now, five . . . four . . .

It's important to note that Eugene can't fully see the time foam.

EUGENE (CONT'D)

. . . three . . . two . . .

Krystal suddenly leaps onto the time foam just as Eugene says

EUGENE (CONT'D)

. . . one!

Vzzzzzz! There's a blue glow and the couple are raised up to the ceiling and back to 1776.

SARAH

That bitch!

ORNELLE CAMERON

That bitch is my granddaughter, Sarah. She's just living large and learning from what will undoubtedly be a lifelong chain of mistakes.

SARAH

Eugene! What do we do here?

EUGENE

I don't know, Sarah.

AIDEN

I do.

Everyone looks at Aiden.

          TOGETHER
What? What do we do?

          AIDEN (CONT'D)
What we do is nothing. And then . . .

He looks at the palm of his hand . . .

          AIDEN (CONT'D)
We count down: five . . . four . . .
three . . . two . . .

Vzzzzzt! Krystal, dressed in a milkmaid's outfit covered
with straw bits, falls through the ceiling onto the foam.
She's a mess.

          AIDEN (CONT'D)
(to Krystal) I knew you'd be back.

          SARAH
What the hell were you thinking going back in
time like that?

          KRYSTAL
(wiping away straw) The past is a hideous
place. You can keep it.

          ORNELLE CAMERON
At least you're in one piece, granddaughter.
But you look troubled. Is everything okay?

KRYSTAL

There's just one teeeeeny little problem we
may need to fix.

EUGENE

Tell us, what did you do?

KRYSTAL

Well, I was having a bad day and I sort of
accidentally ran over Martha Washington with
a buggy, and she's a little bit . . . dead.

EUGENE

You what!

KRYSTAL

It was an accident, I swear!

SARAH

Eugene, what are the time-paradox
implications of this?

Eugene starts frantically touching his screens. Sarah's
looking over Eugene's shoulders . . . Diego is helping
with the screens. Aiden is checking his phone for text
messages.

EUGENE

Drastic measures, Sarah. We're going to have
to destroy that other universe before it
catches up with us. But there's only time if
I hurry and . . .

More screen touching.

KRYSTAL

You can do that? Destroy an entire universe
— billions of solar systems and planets and
everything?

Eugene is frantically touching his screens.

EUGENE

We've never had to do it before. It's a
special feature developed in case someone
accidentally kills Hitler, which remains the
gold standard of time-travel paradoxes.

Everyone's really freaking out. Then Krystal speaks.

KRYSTAL

Hold your horses, Eugene! I was just kidding.
Martha Washington's fine. I didn't kill her
or anybody.

Everyone stops.

TOGETHER

Seriously? Really? Huh?

EUGENE

Oh, God. I nearly had a stroke.

KRYSTAL

Listen to me, all of you. The past is a
dreadful, dreadful place. You don't want to
ever go there, trust me. Their outfits are
made of rags and the smell of human poo is
everywhere.

> **ORNELLE CAMERON**
>
> You were very smart to come back, dear.

> **KRYSTAL**
>
> I'd never want to do anything to trouble you,
> Grandma.

An "aww" moment, during which the three men put their
fingers down their throats.

> **ORNELLE CAMERON**
>
> A terrific job, team. And now I want you to
> come upstairs. There's something I want to
> read to you. Everyone, to the elevator!

15 - ORNELLE CAMERON'S LIVING ROOM
Everyone's seated expectantly. Ornelle brings out her
lorgnette.

> **ORNELLE CAMERON**
>
> I'm going to read aloud to you a letter I
> found, from Thomas Jefferson to Benjamin
> Franklin, and in it he mentions George . . .
> (reading aloud voice) "I saw George yesterday
> and he is surely drinking from the fountain
> of youth. His enhanced appearance seemed
> almost like sorcery. He also says he found a
> dentist who made him an astonishingly good
> set of chompers. Doubtless he will win his
> battles against the English and bring peace
> to our world."

Everyone makes a shocked face . . .

ORNELLE CAMERON (CONT'D)

That's right, children . . . Together, all of
us worked together to create world peace.

EUGENE

Everyone, come together! Fingers — make the
sign of the "H."

Everyone makes the sign of the "H." They put their H's
into a circle and raise them while saying . . .

TOGETHER

(loudly) H . . . H . . . H . . . H . . . HOT!

Screen goes black at the apex of the circle.

END EPISODE

Pot

In June of 1978, on a Saturday night, I was playing poker with three friends. It was a typical Saturday night, and we smoked a joint, during which I drank a glass of water. Within a minute of finishing, I remember getting up from the table, going to the kitchen, getting one more glass of water, at which point I turned around and then blacked out. I learned later that I fell headfirst onto the table with all of its ashtrays and glasses. In doing so I cut a four-inch gash in the left side of my jaw. I woke up (I was told) ten minutes later, at which point I could already hear the ambulance sirens approaching the house. Oddly, I was no longer stoned. I was clear as day and totally lucid.

As fate would have it, my father was the backup on-call doctor at the hospital that night. You can imagine. He was paged halfway through a restaurant dinner he and my mother were having with friends. I can imagine how pissed he must have been to be interrupted, only to hear, "Well, Dr. Coupland, it's actually your son. You might want to stitch him up."

❂

I wasn't a druggie kid; I wasn't a problem child. I just happened to be smoking pot at that magical moment in Canadian pot history when THC counts in BC bud went from the buzz equivalent of NyQuil to OxyContin—a thousand-fold increase in potency that was rarely mentioned in the press at the time. The press instead focused almost entirely on the pathetic US government attempts to destroy the Mexican weed trade by spraying crops with a herbicide called paraquat. While nobody was looking, BC dope growers quietly hybridized their crops to maximize THC in the same way monks hybridized strawberries for size and juiciness, and sweet peas for their ability to prove genetic theories. THC counts exploded in the late 1970s. You heard all kinds of lies about the pot that was going around—Maui Wowie or Kona Gold or "the best Mexican" or what have you—but nobody smuggled pot into BC at that time, and that hasn't changed. Almost all bud in BC is grown in borderline industrial conditions, often overseen by gifted horticulturists.

Pot is everywhere in Vancouver. It took root in the 1960s when the city became Canada's equivalent to hippie San Francisco, and from the 1970s onward, abundant, cheap electrical power allowed for an indoor grow-op culture that continues to flourish to this day. The city currently has over a hundred medical pot dispensaries, and when it comes to drug-law enforcement, the local police and the RCMP have prioritized their focus on the tsunami of hardcore drugs arriving through the city's port. The tacit agreement in the city is no enforcement of the nation's pot laws. In 2011 four of Vancouver's former mayors endorsed a coalition calling for an end to pot-related violence in Canada. "Marijuana prohibition is—without question—a failed policy," they said. Bonus: pot is also legalized in BC's downstairs neighbours Washington and Oregon, and our upstairs neighbour Alaska. Extra bonus: massive amounts of weed are grown throughout the province's many secluded valleys.

◑

My parents still live on the winding alpine suburban slope above Vancouver, in the house I grew up in. About fifteen years ago my mother said to me, "You know, I really can't believe there's all this pot growing around here that you keep talking about." So I said, "Allow me to take you on a tour." And so we got in my car and started driving, and I said, "See over there, see all that water beading and humidity in the window? Grow-op. Notice that unmowed lawn and huge pile of unmoved shopping flyers? Grow-op." And so on; there were dozens then. After being forced to reimagine her neighbourhood, one that in the 1970s had been the embodiment of Brady Bunch puritanism, my mother said, "Well, at least that explains why we don't get any trick-or-treaters anymore."

◑

Back to 1978: that night, my father came into Lions Gate Hospital to stitch me up, and I'll never forget his expression of disappointment as he stitched up my left chin like it was a cheap moccasin. I was the son who wasn't supposed to be doing this kind of shit, and yet I was. He and I have never talked about that night and probably never will. In families every member is assigned a role, and as long as we play that role correctly, regardless of its weirdness, everyone is happy. The reason we work so hard to get home for Thanksgiving and Christmas isn't so much that we know what things to discuss with each other; it's because in a properly functioning family, everybody knows exactly what not to discuss with each other. And so my father and I will never discuss that fleeting bad patch simply because I was off script. What was I thinking? The injury, however, largely turned me off pot, but I suppose the scar it left on my chin is also on my psyche. In 2004 I wrote a novel, *JPod*, in which the main character's parents have a grow-op in their basement. A local indie movie I wrote (*Everything's Gone Green*) also featured parents growing pot. (And all of this was before the TV show *Weeds*.)

●

I was in kindergarten in 1967. I would have been five and a half, and I remember that it was 1967 because it was Canada's centennial year and we were all handed mimeographed outlines of the country's new flag design to colour with a red crayon.

One afternoon, the school had a scared-straight-style speaker come in to talk to our class. She looked maybe eight hundred years old, but in reality, she was probably more like twenty and doing community service. She said hello and told us she wanted to talk about her friend Karen, and so we all leaned in. She told us of how she and Karen were the best of friends and of what a good gal she was, and then she said, "But then Karen took acid."

I know, using the word *acid* with kindergarten students? Seriously?

But what happened to Karen then?

"Karen took the acid. And she got high. And then something happened in her brain and her body froze."

Huh?

"That's right. She was trapped inside her body. She was a prisoner. She couldn't move; she couldn't speak; she couldn't even communicate by blinking her eyes. She was completely frozen inside her body, and the doctors absolutely confirmed she would never, ever, ever be able to communicate anything with the outside world."

Screams. Shrieks. Wailing.

I mean, what the fuck were these scared-straight people thinking?

But . . .

. . . But I have to say, it really worked. We were the only kinder-
garten year to get the "Karen" lecture, but directly as a result of
it, my fellow classmates were the drug-wimpiest, most socially
low-octane birth cohort to ever pass through the West Vancouver
School District Number 45. We had been, in the most program-
matic sense of the term, scared straight. As a result I've never
done coke or acid or ecstasy or MDMA or G or pretty much most
recreational drugs. Thanks a lot, Karen.

To this day, if I encounter a social drug, all I see is poor little
Karen with locked-in syndrome in some forgotten wing of a
forgotten rehab ward of a forgotten institution in some part of
Vancouver that nobody ever goes to and nobody ever will . . . and
thirty years after that scared-straight lecture, I wrote a novel,
Girlfriend in a Coma, in which the coma patient is named Karen.
I never actually made this connection until writing these words
here now. The human soul is sneaky.

Sneaky human soul.

Clueless Doug.

I mentioned that in 1967 we kindergartners had been asked
to colour in the new Canadian flag. It's not an easy flag to draw;
the maple leaf in the middle is more of a corporate clip-art logo
than it is, say, a US star or a Japanese rising sun. Three decades
later, when I was on a book tour in the United States and Canada,
I handed out index cards and red pens to people attending the
event and asked them to draw the Canadian flag. I was thinking a
lot about Canadian identity then and wanted to see how people in
both Canada and the United States saw it in their minds. And . . .
basically, everyone drew a pot leaf because nobody really knew
how to draw a maple leaf. The one truly good flag I got was from
a guy in Chicago. I was actually kind of touched by the level of his
maple leaf's draftsmanship. He said, "I didn't really do it from my

head. I was sitting by the travel book shelf and copied one from a book." These days, of course, iPhones and Androids would render this drawing experience pointless.

◑

Thinking of maple leaves and trees, I remember the relatively unusual, deep red, large-leaved sugar maple in the southeast corner of the yard of the house I grew up in. For this horticultural reason, the lawn beneath it was possibly the most dense psilocybin mushrooming ground in the suburb. My parents never understood this, and my mother would come to me and say, "Brian Rath is in the front yard on his knees. What is going on?" Of course Brian was shrooming, and I'd have to go kick him off, saying, "Jesus, Brian, my mother's watching you. This looks so creepy." The same scenario happened every year and my parents never made the mushroom connection. (But he said he was doing a "science project.")

◑

During the 2010 Winter Olympics, well-dressed Europeans were smoking huge spliffs on downtown Vancouver street corners. This was funny because while pot may be tacitly legal here, good taste suggests you ought to be slightly more discreet. But what is discretion? Who knows? Nothing makes a bottle of booze look more like a bottle of booze than a brown paper bag. And what is good taste? It's anyone's call.

◑

April 20 is Vancouver's official 420 Day (obviously). At 4:20 in the afternoon, the city slows to a crawl while everybody downtown gets, essentially, baked. It's largely fun, and the radio stations forecast a traffic "carmageddon," which usually adds about three minutes to the average commute.

In May of 2014 I was installing a show in the Vancouver Art Gallery, and people smoking weed outside the building's air intake system turned the air in the building into a sweet, syrupy goo. It felt like tendrils of a living organism were reaching into the building in search of humans to feast upon. It was sci-fi, like *The Andromeda Strain*—alien and beyond control.

◑

In 2000 Martin Amis was touring for his autobiography, *Experience*. A publisher friend asked if I'd interview him and I said sure, not realizing what a huge amount of work is involved in interviewing. We were to meet for lunch in a Japanese restaurant downtown, but it was the day Vancouver introduced harsh new no-smoking bylaws, and there was a big kerfuffle in finding Martin a room to smoke in, where he wouldn't be written up by bylaw enforcement zealots. I walked into what appeared to be a closet with a plastic butterfly palm, and he looked at me and said, "You're really not going to go through with this, are you?"

With relief I said, "Thank you. No."

We then went to score some weed from a friend, Jamie, and then drove off to allow Martin to enjoy the sunny afternoon on a local beach.

◑

Half a year ago I was on a flight from Toronto to Vancouver, and fate put me beside someone I knew from home, a man famous for his sunny disposition. I'd had a terrible day, and so I asked my friend, "You always seem to be in a good mood, and I'm always in a terrible mood. How do you do it? What's your secret?"

He said, "I'm always in a terrible mood too. But what I do is this . . ." and he opened his jacket to reveal a collection of thin plastic tubes with spray nozzles filled with very dark brown liquid—pot syrup, basically. He took one out and spritzed the back of his throat. "My wife and I make it. Try some."

"I haven't smoked pot in twenty-five years."

"It's not smoking, though, is it?"

"You have a point."

Spritz-spritz. This was over Lake Superior. The next thing I remember, the cleaning staff on the ground in Vancouver were nudging me to get out of my seat so they could vacuum beneath it.

●

I've smoked pot maybe ten or twelve times in my life. The last time I smoked it was actually twenty-four years before the flight from Toronto, in the spring of 1991. I went with friends to see Reveen the Impossibilist at a local theatre. Reveen was one of those guys who calls people up on stage and hypnotizes them and makes them cluck like chickens and that kind of thing. We actually wanted to be singled out by him, but he didn't choose any of us. He'd been doing this for decades and could probably tell from a hundred feet away that we'd smoked up.

For the first half of the show, everything was magical. "He guessed the numbers people had in their heads . . . He . . . Oh my God, this is the most astonishing thing I've ever seen anybody ever do!"

And then came intermission, and the pot wore off, and suddenly we were sitting in a room with people who may or may not have been genuinely hypnotized and acting like chickens. Within a minute we bolted out the door. My disillusionment with magic melted into my disillusion with pot, and that was that.

●

I think people are helped by pot but not necessarily improved. I just read the last sentence and it seems like the sort of statement that would rapidly be upvoted/downvoted on Reddit. Help? Improve? Palliate? Damage? Cripple? Liberate? Transform?

Here in 2015 there have never been so many mood options available to so many human beings. But then, what's a drug and what's not? We have legacy substances like pot and opiates, which our species co-evolved with, and then we have psychotropic pharmaceuticals, which have exploded in the past three decades and map onto nothing that's ever existed in this universe. Think about this: there is no other place in the entire universe where molecules of, say, Effexor or Wellbutrin exist. None. Nowhere. In the entire universe. That's really insane. And cool.

Many of these new "pharmaceuticals" have turned into recreational drugs, and some recreational drugs have become medicalized. The line is blurry. Then there are drugs like Adderall and Ritalin, which some people use to "super focus"—and maybe this is an instance of drugs actually improving people. I love that Bradley Cooper movie *Limitless*, in which he uses all of his brain potential to the max. It's the way I felt in elementary and high school, long before the real world beat me down with a stick and I realized that intelligence is also about emotions and empathy.

In the 1990s I began noticing people in altered states of being that didn't really seem "stoned" or "high" but, rather, merely medicated in some way. People were suddenly "different." Quieter. Louder. Raunchier. Boozier. More subdued. Gappier. Whatever. But they were recognizably not in moods that we once understood moods to be. I figured out then that we really had entered the smorgasbord era of drugs, which is actually kind of interesting and not necessarily a bad thing. If nothing else, all those people who formerly would have been hidden beneath multiple blankets in dark rooms were at least out in the world experiencing life. Maybe not to the max, but with better options than had been available historically.

◑

I've known a lot of suicides in my life. I'd say twenty. In each instance drugs were involved as direct or indirect triggers, except for one time when it was ambiguous: Brian Rath, the high school shroomer and pothead, was so high he passed out in his van and died of carbon monoxide poisoning from the heater. He was a nice guy, but he was paranoid and could only live in a van by himself. I don't think it was suicide. I have no idea.

◑

One thing I have seen many times over the years is guys who smoke a lot of pot when they're young activate (I'm guessing) a genetic predilection for paranoia, which under assault from high volumes of THC, triggers late-adolescent THC-induced paranoia. For the next decade these guys (and it really does seem to be guys only) make random and strange life choices, and then, by thirty, their brains cool down, but by then they have to live with the decisions they made while being paranoid, and it's almost never easy.

◑

Here's a Vancouver story: In the spring of 1997, some kids in downtown Vancouver gave me three pot seeds, like Jack and the Beanstalk. I went home, planted them in little pots and watered them, and they sprouted like a third-grade class project on growing beans. A visiting friend of mine, Ian, looked at the sprouts and said, "Doug, that's not how you grow it. Pot is very social, and you can't just keep it by itself. It needs to be around other plants."

This was before an extended trip to England, and so I put the three sprouts, each in their own pot, down on a rock beside the creek at the bottom end of the property, surrounded by a cedar tree, sweet-scented astilbe, vine maples, moss and a few other regional plants. Two months later I returned to Vancouver and walked in the front door to learn that Princess Diana had died in a car crash, and this sucked up all of my attention. Then around sunset I looked out over the deck and into the creek area to see that my three little sprouts had morphed into dense, shaggy THC monsters. It was a real shocker. I mean, these plants were like plush mink coats of dope.

In the absence of any other plan, I continued to let them grow, and by mid-September I harvested them, cutting them off at the base and hanging them upside down (thank you, Internet, for these instructions), and then . . . and then I tried to find someone in my universe who'd want a huge supply of monster killer pot for free. I didn't smoke the stuff, but nobody else in my universe seemed to smoke pot either. I went through my phone book and everyone declined, one by one.

". . . just had a kid."

". . . doing a cleanse."

". . . too old for that shit."

". . . more into mountain biking these days."

". . . pot? Seriously? You?"

Basically I couldn't give away a five-grand trove of kick-ass weed. Donating it to hospices was too weird for technical reasons, and in the end I took it to my parents' house, incinerated it in the family fireplace and watched it go up the chimney. Buyers' market.

◉

We all know what gaydar is, but there is also something called drugdar, and I don't have it. To this day I can walk into any social situation and have no idea of the quantity and quality of drugs everyone is taking. I just take everyone at face value, while they must look at me and say, "Doug has no drugdar," and they move on to the next person more likely to map onto their drug wants and needs. It makes me feel foolish not to know what the signals and cues are.

◉

I drink a lot. At the moment it's still charming, but I'll probably have to quit someday. I like drinking because it's predictable. Regardless of the source, I know exactly how to nurse a buzz along for hours. It's wonderful. In the dozen times I smoked pot, it made me feel different every time—why would I want that? Besides, who knows how strong it's going to be, and who knows what synthetic agrotoxins are, or aren't, mixed in with it?

◉

I smoked cigarettes from 1979 to 1988 and I loved it. I was a good smoker, but I blew out my left lung cliff jumping in Howe Sound during my senior high school year, and when I die, it'll probably be because of something to do with my lungs. They're just not the best lungs (lung and a half, really), so I quit smoking on Halloween 1988, and I have several slip-up dreams a week. I still smoke; I just haven't had a cigarette since October 31, 1988. Dear tobacco: I miss you.

This piece isn't a gratuitous drug tell-all on my part. I'm illustrating that everybody has their own drug stories that play out across their lives. You have one too, and it will expand as you age.

◐

I fly a lot, and for years I'd fly over the United States and look below at the roads and buildings and think, *Ski hill? Shopping mall? Golf course? Industrial park?* And . . . and then there were always these strange things down below that looked like electron microscope images of viruses, but they were . . . I had no idea. Poultry farms? Amazon distribution centres? University campuses?

They were prisons.

◐

People seem to love pot. That can't be denied, and legalized pot is obviously at the tipping point in the United States and Canada, but why did it take so long? Everyone touts how much tax money can be made from regulating the stuff, and they're obviously correct. But I think a cofactor in the current pot-legalization warp is that Americans are seeing that 1.5 percent of their population is currently living in a jail cell, and the citizenry is understanding that this is madness. Remember, Prohibition in the 1920s and 1930s wasn't so much about booze being evil; it was more of a simple solution to the complex problem of domestic violence, to make life safer for women. To look at booze by itself is not the most useful way to look at Prohibition, and ditto for pot.

The sick thing about prisons is that, to a point, incarcerated people are very good for the economy: prison jobs, legal fees, construction contracts and political pork. As a bonus, when a government criminalizes you, they then have a permanent, excellent tool for controlling you. From an evil point of view, criminalizing as many people as possible is good for capitalism and for those in power. Until it unravels.

In 2015 taxpayers woke up to the fact that industrial-grade incarceration is too expensive. Too many people in jail, too many people about to go into, or back into, jail . . . and the tax base can't support it anymore. There's a finite limit to how many citizens you can incarcerate before the system falls apart—and that magic number would appear to be about 1.5 percent. Many of these 1.5-percenters are incarcerated on pot charges. Decriminalize pot and suddenly you empty your prisons. Your tax bill is lowered, and many of your people are freed, and once again their lives become useful and meaningful.

Odd that the war on drugs is ending up being cured by drugs.

◑

There's another cofactor in the legalization of pot, and this factor is called Dow. Or Cargill. Or DuPont. Or Bayer. Pot became as potent as it now is because of hybridization, but hybridization has probably reached its limits—but then what about genetically modified pot? Think about it. I'll bet you a hundred trillion dollars that at this very moment, Dow, Monsanto, Dole, Coca-Cola, BASF and Archer Daniels Midland are throwing every spare dollar in their budget at maxing out some super new GM pot that has so much THC, it drips like a chocolate fountain, but that's not necessarily why they'd be GM'ing pot. They'd be GM'ing pot so that it requires less refrigeration during shipping. Or maybe it'll be pot you can irrigate with salt water. Or maybe it'll be pot that's resistant to Roundup and glycophosphates, or pot that grows a hundred feet tall. But the moment they come up with the right combo is the moment pot goes legal in holdout states like Nebraska, Oklahoma and Arkansas. Imagine: GM pot that can sit in freight containers for up to 180 days without refrigeration with no noticeable decomposition. GM pot is most definitely waiting in the wings to take over from GM corn.

I just Googled *GMO pot* and the first hit was a blog saying that another news article elsewhere that stated Monsanto had created GM pot was a hoax. Genuine LOL.

It also occurs to me that the days of pot being sold through dispensaries is soon to vanish. Pot will become more of a daily consumer item, and so right now all of these GMO firms must also be lawyering up on every level and lobbying like crazy as they prepare for the inevitable. They're likely at the point of creating names and brands of pot that have yet to actually be GM'd. I'm curious to see if the names they go for are grocery-like (Ranch Dressing) or if they go scientific (Wellbutrin). This makes me think that in-house marketing teams are probably already on the case, identifying discrete segments within the pot user base, as well as trying to locate new ones. Old-school hippies. Moms. Emos. Country-and-western listeners. Superpatriots. Jocks. Hipsters. PTSD sufferers. Telemundo viewers. Rapper wannabes. Young professionals. Jimmy Buffett fans. Deadheads—now there's a superbrand just waiting to happen. Of course, not everyone's going to want the same packaging, and remember, whoever gets market share first is probably going to be the most successful and endure the longest. Think Marlboro. It's a Klondike just waiting to start, and it's going to be brutal.

◑

Smoking is actually a pretty clumsy THC delivery system; we use it simply because we're familiar with it. Even pot brownies seem hokey in 2015. All sorts of new aesthetics and product categories are likely to emerge. I suspect the future of pot is probably in spritzed pot, like I had in the plane from Toronto to Vancouver, or in THC taste strips, like breath-freshening strips. Or vaping. What will legalized pot packaging look like? The first wave of pot products will probably resemble borderline medical products currently existing, like the tubs of creatine or protein that weight-lifters buy at protein shops. The next wave will resemble packaging and labelling in the style of craft beer breweries. The third and long-term packaging may look like Wrigley's gum or Pepto-Bismol. Boring. Quotidian. Part of the landscape. "Hi, I'll get two Gatorades, a pack of peppermint Chiclets and a pack of Parrot Head Spritz vials."

◑

Eighteen years ago I was in a second-hand store in Chile and saw a really strange-looking metal vase—quite low-slung and unlike something you'd put roses into. I asked about it and was told it was a spittoon.

A spittoon.

I'd heard the word used before, but I'd never thought about it much, let alone visualized what a spittoon looks like. But up into the middle of the twentieth century, when American men in both public and private spaces felt the need to spit, they would look at a spittoon and say, "Good. A spittoon. Now I will expel the combination of mucus and tobacco residue inside my mouth into a receptacle on the floor, and I may or may not hit the mark." And then they'd do it.

Like many things from the twentieth century, spittoons seem not just barbaric, but they also tax the level of credulity of what a reasonably civilized society might consider okay and not okay (apartheid, bathing suits for women, gay anything).

I think pot is at the magic spittoon moment where suddenly we've realized it's too hard and too wilfully clueless to pretend that reality isn't reality—whether it's fiscal reality or social reality. I dislike pot. It has literally left me scarred. It's permanently damaged people I care for.

But then so has booze. And gambling. And greed. And genetics. And cars. And psychopharmaceuticals. And gravity. And aging. And the law.

I think people are more smart than they are stupid. If they can handle everything else, then they can probably handle pot—it's a very small leaf to throw into the salad of life. Everything will be just fine.

Got a Life

Last month I had lunch with a YouTube friend, and I asked her what the most boring thing she'd ever seen on YouTube was, and she said, "That's easy: elevators."

"Huh?"

"Well, you know how there are trainspotters?"

"Yes."

"Well, there are people who spot *elevators*."

"Surely not."

"No, I'm serious. Check it out. The numbers are huge."

I was unsure if she was putting me on, so when I got home I looked it up and quickly found, on one video (along with 1,012,773 viewers*), that in 2007 all elevators in the New York Marriott Marquis were replaced by Schindler Miconic 10 Traction elevators. I went on to learn that, "Rather than a traditional call-station and car operating panel (COP) configuration, the Miconic 10 system 'assigns an elevator based on destinations requested on a keypad in the elevator bank. Elevators are alphabetically labeled and are assigned based on location and demand.'"

So there you go.

☒

---

* "Schindler Miconic 10 Traction Elevators—New York Marriott Marquis—New York, NY," YouTube video, 8:11, posted by CBE9120, August 4, 2013, https://www.youtube.com/watch?v=NWT3TNVjqK4.

I think boredom has to be some sort of natural selection process. If it weren't for boredom, our ancestors would have spent all their days in their caves, with no hunting or gathering, and then no wheels or fire or mathematics or HBO.

Some people never get bored. For them, every moment of life is like a piece of yarn being dangled in front of a kitten's face, as if for the first time. I'm not one of these people. Yes, I know it's a miracle to be alive and possess sentience—but there's also a lot to be said for things like booze and YouTube. And cigarettes. I quit twenty-seven years ago but I could start at any moment. I always wonder what it would be like to smoke while being online—pure happiness, I imagine. And yes, drinking online can be a blast, but the most amazing eBay packages arrive at your doorstep a week later. And then your Visa bill comes in.

Apparently most adult men make their largest purchases of the day between 11 p.m. and midnight. The kids are asleep. You have the house to yourself. Add a bit of booze and . . . "Why yes, I think I *will* buy that rowing machine that, deep in my heart, I know will be used two or three times and then end up on Craigslist after gathering dust for three years in the garage." And once on Craigslist it will find fierce competition from similarly purchased rowing machines.

¤

Boredom is different than it used to be. I actually used to like being bored: walking down a street, not connected to anything, not speaking to anyone, wondering what lay behind those trees or shop fronts or clouds. Similar behaviour these days would have the cops pulling over and questioning me. Who do I think I am, taking a stroll without interruptions, just looking at the scenery. *We like ourselves, don't we?* No music or Bluetooth or navigation systems or other devices for *you*.

◫

Today I was wondering if I generate enough data during my days. I'm not quite sure what *kind* of data. Just data in general. It seems like a modern thing to do. How to max it out? How could I create a data storm? In a few years data creation will be the new frequent flyer points.

◫

Part of our new boredom is that our brain doesn't have any downtime. Even the smallest amount of time not being engaged creates a spooky sensation that maybe you're on the wrong track. Reboot your computer and sit there waiting for it to do its thing, and within seventeen seconds you experience a small existential implosion when you remember that fifteen years ago life was nothing *but* this kind of moment. *Gosh, maybe I'll read a book. Or go for a walk.*

Sorry.

Probably not going to happen. *Hey, is that the new trailer for* Ex Machina*?*

◫

In the 1990s there was that expression, "Get a life!" You used to say it to people who were overly fixating on some sort of minutia or detail or thought thread, and by saying, "Get a life," you were trying to snap them out of their obsession and get them to join the rest of us who are still out in the world, taking walks and contemplating trees and birds. The expression made sense at the time, but it's been years since I've heard anyone use it anywhere. What did it mean then, "getting a life"? Did we all get one? Or maybe we've all *not* got lives anymore, and calling attention to one person without a life would put the spotlight on all of humanity and our now full-time pursuit of minutia, details and tangential idea threads.

⌧

"The system also boasts its intelligence by reserving cars for certain areas. For example, Car A and Car B are now exclusive to the upper levels, so when I type in '45,' I will get Car A or Car B. If the system is overwhelmed, it will adjust accordingly, but this update increases the dispatching efficiency even more."

Makes you think.

Peace

There's a reason libraries are presumed to be quiet places. We're taught to think it's because there's a scolding schoolmarm perpetually lurking just out of sight, itching to pounce on us for the slightest sonic infraction. The real reason is more prosaic: irregularly protruding book spines coming out of their shelves are terrific for dispersing sound and creating environments that are mildly free of echoes.

Three years ago I had the borderline orgasmic experience of spending a few minutes alone in one of the technically quietest rooms on earth. No, it wasn't in a salt mine four thousand feet beneath the surface of Chelyabinsk-70. Rather, it was in suburban New Jersey, at the Bell Laboratories Murray Hill anechoic chamber. The chamber, built in 1940, measures thirty feet by twenty-eight feet by thirty-two feet and has three-feet-thick cement and brick walls. Its inner walls are lined with alternating clusters of biscuit-shaped wedges of yellow fibreglass household insulation. This formation absorbs over 99.995 percent of the incidental acoustic energy above two hundred hertz. At one time the Murray Hill chamber was cited in *The Guinness Book of World Records* as the world's quietest room.

It's heaven.

To enter, you pass through a Scrooge McDuck–like bank vault door and walk onto a steel mesh surface that has you floating in the exact mathematical centre of the room. It's as if you've entered a genuinely magic space where normal rules of sound no longer apply. Inside the room, a Bell Labs staffer popped a balloon in my face and it made no noise. That's because what we normally call a balloon pop is what is technically called a "sonic skeleton." No sonic skeletons here.

$$\oplus$$

In December 1988 I was walking to catch a streetcar on a snowy Toronto morning, and thirty seconds out of the house, I had a catastrophic sneeze. Looking at my Kleenex I saw an object the same size, shape and colour of a green Thompson seedless grape—except it had veins and something that looked like an umbilical cord. I took it directly to my doctor, who said, "Well, at least it's not inside you anymore." He had a point. But ever since that day, I've been unable to sleep without earplugs, and also on that day I lost my ability to "focus" sound. Up to then I was merely hypersensitive to noise but—I don't know what exactly happened—with that grape went what was otherwise somewhat normal hearing. Since then, a noise on one side of my head will cancel out a noise coming in from the other side. There's nothing I can now do about this; it's my brain. It's like being able to see but nothing is actually ever clear. So I avoid spaces where sound comes from all directions. Concerts are fine because the music blasts from the stage. Fundraising dinners in large rooms are a blur, so I don't go to them. Art openings and the like I also try to avoid: concrete walls and glass and the sound of five hundred quacking ducks—there's no point.

I think about noise more than most people simply because it all goes directly into my fight-or-flight brain nodule and wrecks much of life's options. But it also makes me realize that people with normal hearing still put up with far more noise than they actually need to. In many public spaces, all one has to do is click one's heels together three times and say, "I no longer want this noise."

Example?

Gyms.

Gyms are the worst: mirrors, hard floors, clanging metal, and music seemingly always ferociously controlled by a twenty-three-year-old girl named Hayley. Ask anyone in a gym to lower the volume and you might as well ask your dog its opinion on Russia.

Airport lounges are the second worst. Oh look—is that a TV screen? Well then we'd better blast out the sound because that way people will know the TV is turned on. It's so sad: all of these people seeking refuge during a weary travel day, and they get CNN at full volume. Asking staff to turn it down is pointless. They simply make "that face," and if you push it, you end up on the no-fly list.

And then restaurants. A really good one opened up down the street from me. Great food and a great owner—but all glass mirrors and ceramic tile. Inside, it sounds like cutlery being shaken in a soup pot. Bonus: music controlled by a twenty-three-year-old staffer (I asked). People remember these things even if they don't realize it.

"Want to go to that new place down the street again?"

"Hmmm . . . no. Let's try somewhere else."

And then there's leaf blowers. No, let's not start.

$$\oplus$$

Church bells were the Internet of the 1500s, but churches didn't play them twenty-four hours a day. Back then they knew that as a species we're not cut out for endless noise from endless sources, yet in the past century I think we've maybe tricked ourselves into thinking we are. There's a message from those bells or, rather, the absence of a message.

iF-iW eerF

Last month I stayed in two über-trendy hotels, one in Berlin, one in London. What sticks out in my mind about both hotels is their lobbies, restaurants and coffee areas: every single chair, every ledge, every flat surface had been colonized by well-nourished-looking twenty-eight-and-a-half-year-olds gazing into open laptops, buds in their ears, and a phone or tablet to the side. The only exceptions were obviously agitated twenty-eight-and-a-half-year-old men and women standing in the lobby, obviously awaiting a (*cough, cough*) Tinder or Grindr hookup.

And nobody was talking to anyone.

The only sound was the tippy-tap of MacBook Pro keys editing a sound file or sorting out photo files. Was this kind of creepy? Yes. Yes, it was. Spooky too. And then I got over the spookiness and began to see the room before me as a gentleman's club in 1900, with everyone reading newspapers in total silence—this is just the twenty-first-century version, except this one contains women and some sense of limitlessness. And then I got to thinking that these twenty-eight-year-olds could have been upstairs in their rooms with their laptops, doing what they were doing, except they chose to be downstairs among their own kind, finding warmth in numbers. It made me feel good about people wanting to be with people, albeit dressed up slightly on the hot side . . . But then, one never knows when Tinder or Grindr might buzz.

Last week Marriott International Inc. was fined US$600,000 after someone alerted the FCC that the Gaylord Opryland Resort & Convention Center in Nashville had a device that blocked conventioneers from setting up their own Wi-Fi hot spots, forcing them to instead use the Marriott's extortionately expensive Wi-Fi service, US$250 to $1,000 per device. Marriott's excuse? They were protecting guests from "rogue wireless hot spots that can cause degraded service, insidious cyber-attacks and identity theft." Oddly, Marriott still publicly puts forth the notion that they committed no wrong, fine notwithstanding [insert gales of laughter here].

⊗

I don't turn on the TV set in a hotel room anymore, nor do I use the phone. This wasn't a conscious decision; it just sort of dawned on me recently, and I think I'm in the majority. Everything runs through my laptop or iPhone: free long-distance calls on Gmail and all the movies and TV you care to bring or stream. I suppose hotels are either very happy about this—maybe phones and TV movies were a pain in the butt—or, more likely, they're very annoyed at losing a revenue golden goose. One hotel in Los Angeles charged me five dollars a minute to phone Canada. When I asked about it, they said, "Oh, but sir, Canada's a foreign country."

⊗

I live in Vancouver and I get about ten megs a second of Internet upload speed courtesy of my provider. This is pathetic, but comparing it to most North American providers, I should count my blessings. Decades of ruthless market competition—Darwinian capitalism at its most intense—has led to an Internet speed crisis so severe that critics have likened it to a human rights violation. It seems that carrying broadband is the one form of business that is stunted, if not entirely crippled, when placed in the hands of the free market. Ask anyone in telephony and they'll confirm that pretty much all wireless providers hate each other's guts—yet at the same time, with a bit of deft probing, you can also get them to confirm that Verizon is doing a Grindr hookup with Comcast, which is doing a Tinder hookup with Time Warner, which is probably hooking up with whoever it is that links *you* to the outer world. It's not hard to imagine collusive pillow talk about keeping speeds as low as possible while simultaneously brainwashing consumers into thinking they're getting the best service possible—and that they ought to be grateful for it. And we all know that roaming charges are probably the biggest single money-suck in modern history.

✖

China's recent five-year plan is to provide ultra-high-speed connectivity to every single Chinese citizen: one gig per second in the major cities, two hundred megs in smaller cities, and five megs in remote valleys. And because it's China, you know it's going to happen. Their logic? The future of humanity in this century is ultra-high-speed broadband, everywhere, always. It is inevitable, and if it's inevitable, China may as well get there first—although how they will censor this sort of Internet traffic is going to be very interesting. In my mind, China's high-speed experiment is going to end either like *Thelma & Louise*, with the car driving off the cliff, or like *Grease*, with Sandy and Danny's car flying up to heaven. But at least China's going for it.

✖

Good Wi-Fi is good business. High-speed Internet keeps your country from being second-rate. Overcharging for speed—or crippling speed under the aegis of pseudo-capitalism—is simply stupid. People remember when their hotel charges $13.95 for one day's Internet usage. They know they're being fleeced every time they log on to their home system. Improving wireless speed can happen only if we start ignoring the quacking duck noises of frenemy wireless providers and seek political impetus for a broader vision of wireless. Demand the inevitable.

Stuffed

One of comedian George Carlin's (1937–2008) seminal mono-
logues was his 1986 riff on *stuff*: "That's all the meaning of life is:
trying to find a place to put your stuff." "That's all your house is,
is a pile of stuff with a cover on it." And to paraphrase: "Someone
else's stuff is actually shit, whereas your own shit isn't shit at all;
it's *stuff*." I'm made aware of this every time family members visit
my house and see the art I collect. I see Carlin's very words etched
onto their retinas, and I can imagine the conversations they're
having in the car driving away: "Do you think maybe all that art
stuff he collects is a cry for help?"

"That art stuff of his? It's not stuff; it's shit."

"But it's *art* shit. I think it might be worth something. It's the
art world. They have no rules. They can turn a piece of air into a
million dollars if they want to."

"So, maybe it's not shit after all."

"Nah. Let's not get too cosmic. It's shit. Art shit."

Ahhh, families.

◑

In the past I've written about links between hoarding and col-
lecting, recoding art-collecting and art-fair behaviour as possi-
bly subdued forms of hoarding. Basically: Where does collecting
end and hoarding begin? One thing the piece didn't ask was,
what are the clinical roots of obsessive hoarding (which is now

a recognized condition in the DSM-5)? One thing psychologists agree on is that hoarding is grounded in deep loss. First there needs to be a pre-existing hoarding proclivity (not uncommon with our hunter-gatherer heritage). If someone with a proclivity experiences a quick and catastrophic loss—often the death of a close relative, frequently in car accidents—one need wait approximately eighteen to twenty-four months before hoarding kicks in. TV reality shows on hoarding (A&E's *Hoarders*; TLC's *Hoarding: Buried Alive*) would have us believe that given dozens of helpers and a trained therapist, hoarders are often cured by a TV episode's end. The truth, though, is that there's really no cure for hoarding. Once it's there, it's pretty much there to stay.

On these same TV shows, a voice-over regularly tells us that hoarding behaviour is unsanitary and unsafe, and that is correct. A few years back a family friend—a big-game taxidermist who ended up making more money renting out mounted animals to TV and film shoots than he did with his trade—was killed in an electrical fire that began in his basement. He ran into his basement to try to put it out, got trapped and quickly died of smoke inhalation. His retail storefront had always been immensely dense with hides and heads and antlers. Nobody was surprised to learn that his house had been equally as dense, but it was odd to think of his pack-ratting as being possibly a medical condition.

One of the borderline ghoulish best parts of watching TV hoarding shows is watching the expressions on the faces of hoarders once they realize that the intervention is for real. Your relatives are everywhere, poking out from behind mounds of pizza boxes and mildewed second-hand Raggedy Ann dolls. There's a huge empty blue skiff in the driveway, waiting to feast on all of your stuff, and it's surrounded by a dozen gym-toned refuse movers. There's a blond woman who looks like J.K. Rowling (1965–) asking you how you feel about an oil-stained Velveeta box whose contents you ate on the morning the Challenger exploded.

"This is actually happening to me—everyone is watching me."

Until then it's usually quite friendly, and in some cases hours can pass, and some deaccessioning progress is made, but then comes something—usually something utterly useless (a Jif peanut butter jar, *circa* 1988, empty but not cleaned or rinsed)—and the hoarder chokes. It's in the eyes: (a) *I may need that jar at some point down the road,* and (b) *this intervention is over.* From there it's only a matter of how much of a meltdown it's going to be, and how ornery the hoarder needs to be to eject everyone from his or her house.

Needless to say, one feels a tingle of superiority knowing that one would never *ever* have one's inner life come to a grinding halt over throwing out a twenty-seven-year-old unrinsed jar of peanut butter. But if it wasn't that Jif jar, what would it be that would make someone—*you*—choke? Losing the nineteenth-century rocking chair? That small David Salle (1952–) canvas? And wait— how did a Jif jar ever become the shorthand for life and its losses? Is that what the Brillo boxes were all about? How does a Christie's evening postwar contemporary art sale become a magic-wanding spectacle where, instead of peanut butter jars, bits of wood and paint are converted from shit into stuff? How do objects triumph and become surrogates for life?

◑

I think it was Bruno Bischofberger (1940–) who said that the prob-lem with the way Andy Warhol (1928–1987) collected art was that he always went for lots of medium-good stuff instead of getting the one or two truly good works. Warhol (the hoarder's hoarder) would probably have agreed, but I doubt this insight would have affected his accumulating strategies.

A publisher I worked with in the 1990s had a living room wall twelve-deep with Gerhard Richter (1932–) canvases. God knows how many he has now, but however many it is, it will *never* be enough.

A few years back I visited a friend of a friend in Portland with a pretty amazing collection of post-1960 American work. He went to the kitchen, and when he came back he saw me staring into the centre of a really good crushed John Chamberlain (1927–2011).

"What are you staring at?"

"The dust."

"What do you mean?"

"Inside this piece. There's no dust on the outside bits, but it's really thick in the middle."

He looked. "I think that's as far in as the housekeeper's arms can reach."

"Your housekeeper Windexes your art?"

I saw his face collapse. Later I believe the piece was professionally cleaned with carbon tetrachloride dry-cleaning solution at immense cost. It reminded me of reading about Leo Castelli (1907–1999), who wasn't allowed to have regular housekeeping staff in his apartment. In order to keep his insurance, he had to have MFA students work as his housekeepers. I wonder if they're now making MFA Roombas.

❶

I think it's perhaps also important to note that most curators almost never collect anything—yes, all those magazine spreads with the large, empty white apartments—and if you ever ask a minimalist curator what they collect, they often make that pained face that is actually quite similar to the Jif jar lover's at the moment of possible surrender. "But you don't understand; I have no choice in this matter. You merely see an empty apartment, but for me this apartment is full of nothingness. That's correct: I hoard space." A friend of mine is a manufacturer and seller of modernist furniture. Five years ago he built a new showroom, and he was so in love with how empty it was, he kept it unused for a year as a private meditation space.

Most writers I've met, when they're in the first half of their novel, stop reading other writers' books because it's so easy for someone else's style to osmotically leak into your own, especially during a novel's embryonic phase. I wonder if that's why curators are so commonly minimalists—there's nothing to leak into their brains and sway their point of view, which is perhaps how they maintain a supernatural power to be part of the process that turns air into millions of dollars.

On the other hand, most art dealers are deeply into all forms of collecting, as if our world is just a perpetual Wild West of shopping. I once visited a collector specializing in nineteenth-century West Coast North American works who had an almost parodically dull house at what he called "street level" in a suburb. But beneath his boring tract home were, at the very least, thousands of works arranged as though in a natural history museum.

Designer Jonathan Adler (1966–) says your house should be an antidepressant. I agree. And so does the art world. When curators come home and find nothingness, they get a minimalist high. When dealers come home and find five Ellsworth Kellys leaning against a wall, they're also high in much the same way. Wikipedia tells us, "Hoarding behavior is often severe because hoarders do not recognize it as a problem. It is much harder for behavioral therapy to successfully treat compulsive hoarders with poor insight about the disorder." Art collectors, on the other hand, are seen as admirable and sexy. Little chance they're going to see themselves as being in need of an intervention. Perhaps the art collecting equivalent of voluntarily getting rid of the Jif jar is flipping a few works.

🌓

I have a friend named Larry who collects beer cans, but his wife has a dictum: no beer cans may cross the doorsill of his collecting room. Larry then made a beer can holder that attaches itself to any surface, ceilings included. He patented his holder design and started selling them commercially. His is a capitalism feel-good story that highlights another dark side of hoarding and collecting, that our failures and successes in regards to how we accumulate things are viewed almost entirely through a capitalist lens. "How much did you get for it?" I'm uncertain what Marx said specifically about art collectors (if anything), but if he did, it probably wasn't kind. Some people collect art that's purely political, or purely conflict-based, or highly pedigreed by theory, but I wonder if they're just trying to sidestep out of the spotlight of the art economy's vulgarity. But wait—did they magically win their collection in a card game? Did their collection arrive for free at their doorstep from Santa Claus? No, it had to be purchased with money, and it's at this level where the dance between academia, museums and collectors turns into a beyond-awkward junior high school prom. I tried explaining a Tom Friedman (1965–) work to my brother. Its title is *A Curse,* and the work consists of a plinth over which a witch has placed a curse (currently at The Hayward Gallery). I told my brother it might easily be worth a million dollars, whereupon his eyes became the collective eyes of the Paris Commune, aching to sharpen the guillotine's blades and then invade, conquer and slay Frieze.

🌓

The collecting of stuff—slightly out of the ordinary stuff—is different now than it was in the twentieth century. Craigslist, eBay and Etsy have gutted thrift and antique stores across North America of all their good stuff, and in Paris, the Marché aux Puces de Saint-Ouen is but a shadow of its former self. Once groaning with low-hanging fruit being sold by the clueless, eBay is now a suburban shopping centre with the occasional semi-okay vintage thingy still floating around. This same sense of sparseness is felt in the museum world, where programming budget slashing remains the norm. As well, too much globalized money and not enough places to stash it has made pretty much anything genuinely good far too pricey for the 99 percent. The good stuff is always gone, and all the stuff that's left is shit. You don't stand a chance against money-eyed, technologically advanced collectors who have some magic software that allows them to buy that Jean Prouvé stool three-millionths of a second ahead of you. Thank you, Internet.

Interestingly, on YouTube you'll find anti-hoarding videos that coach over-collectors seeking to de-hoard their lives to get rid of any object that doesn't bring them joy, but I don't know if that's human nature. In Australia last month I asked if I could visit that secret stone alcove where the last three remaining specimens of the world's rarest tree are being kept hidden.

"Why would you want to do that?"

"I want to get one before someone else gets it."

That's human collecting behaviour.

◉

I sometimes wonder if there's a way to collect stuff without tapping into collecting's dark, hoardy side. I got to thinking that if visual art is largely about space, then writing is largely about time—so then maybe people collect books differently than they do art.

Do they?

No, they don't. Book hoarding tends to be just as intense as art hoarding, if not worse. It's called *bibliomania* and, like generic hoarding, is also a recognized psychological issue. Enter Wikipedia once again (and thank you, Jimmy Wales [1966–]): "Bibliomania is a disorder involving the collecting or hoarding of books to the point where social relations or health are damaged. It is one of several psychological disorders associated with books, such as *bibliophagy* (book eating) or *bibliokleptomania* (book thievery)."

Bibliomania, though, is almost universally viewed as quirky and cute, the way *kunstmania* (my coinage) is seen as glamorous and cool in a Bond villain kind of way. *Oh those booksellers sure are nutty!* And they *are* nutty—pretty much all bookstore owners recognize that the profession brings with it a unique form of squirrelliness. The best booksellers, the antiquarian sellers especially, are those sellers who genuinely don't actually want to sell you the book. You have to audition for its ownership, and should they sell you the book, you can see the pain on their face as the cash machine bleeps.

I once worked weekends in a bookstore. There was this guy who'd been coming in for years, and all the other sellers made cooing noises whenever he showed up for three hours every Sunday for some passionate browsing. "Now *there's* someone who really loves books—a real book lover." And then one Sunday afternoon, a *New York Times Atlas* fell out of his raincoat as he was exiting the store. Police later found thousands of stolen books in the bibliokleptomaniac's apartment.

As for bibliophagy, I chuckled when I learned of the term while writing this and then was chilled when I realized I'm a bibliophagist myself.

Coupland's 1991 novel, *Generation X*, chewed up by Coupland and spun into a hornet's nest form.

🌓

Back in the early 2000s, my then agent, Eric, in New York, was one of the first people I knew to harvest music into an iTunes playlist. In 2002 it seemed amazing that a person could have 1.92 days (!) of music on their playlist. These days it's not uncommon to find people with almost a solid year's worth of playlisted music, if not far more.

In high school everybody used plastic Dairyland milk crates to store their records. They were just the right size for 33 ⅓ LPs, and Dairyland was able to have their logo inside everyone's house in the most wonderful way—attached to music loved by the owner. And then Dairyland changed the dimensions of the crates so that they'd no longer hold vinyl. I'm still mad at them, not because I wanted crates myself (I've never been a big vinyl aficionado) but rather because they took such a major plus and turned it into a big minus. Idiots. Vinyl collectors are among the most reverent of all collecting communities. Those milk crates would have lasted peoples' entire *lives*.

Music is weird because it's not really space, but it's not quite time either. But what about film, which is a space-time hybrid? So then, do people hoard film? Actually, they do. My sister-in-law's cousin is a movie hoarder who has possibly millions of hours of torrented movies snoozing on his hard drives, movies he could never watch in ten lifetimes. "Don, let me get this straight: You speak no German and yet you have five German-language screening versions of *Sister Act 2*, starring Whoopi Goldberg (1955–)?"

"Yes. Yes, I do."

I think the human relationship with time has altered quite a bit since 2000, and film seems to be one venue where this is fully evidenced. The Internet has a tendency to shred attention spans while it firehoses insane amounts of film at humanity, making film hoarding as easy as newspaper hoarding was back in the 1950s. Even easier.

In the art world our collectively morphing sense of time became truly noticeable back in 2010 with *The Clock* by Christian Marclay (1955–), which in many peoples' minds should have won the best picture Oscar for that year. At the 2015 Oscars, the only two real contenders for best picture were *Boyhood* by Richard Linklater (1960–) and *Birdman or (The Unexpected Virtue of Ignorance)* by Alejandro González Iñárritu (1963–). In both films the star was, as Linklater put it, *time*. In *Boyhood* we saw the magic of a dozen years of continuous time. In *Birdman* we saw the magic of one continuous take. As a species we seem to have now fetishized continuity. We're nostalgic for real time's flow, and we're hoarding movies and videos and GIFs and clips and anything else that moves and has sound, knowing they're never ever going to be touched. In a weird way it's like the minimalist apartment of, say, curator Klaus Biesenbach (1967–), where no objects are visible, and what is present is virtual—in the case of Biesenbach, ideas. In the case of my sister-in-law's cousin Don, twenty-nine million hours of crap film.

In *Men in Black* Tommy Lee Jones (1946–) learns of an alien technology and says, "Great. Now I'm going to have to buy the White Album again." In my case, it's *The Rise and Fall of Ziggy Stardust and the Spiders from Mars*, which I've now bought twice on vinyl, once on cassette, once on CD and twice on iTunes. It's guaranteed there's some geek in California dreaming up some new way of making me buy it all over again. By now don't I get some kind of metadata tag attached to me saying, "This guy's already paid his dues on this one"?

⬤

There is one genuine way of stopping hoarding other than death, which is the actual approach of one's own death and the thana-tophobia that often accompanies it. One is forced to contemplate what's written on one's gravestone.

BORN

ACCUMULATED A BUNCH OF COOL STUFF

DIED

The above epitaph isn't creepy—it's just boring. So how, then, do you manipulate your loot meaningfully while the clock ticks and ticks and ticks? For artists, dealing with stuff at the end of life becomes complicated. I find it interesting that, say, Constantin Brancusi (1876–1957) didn't want to sell his work in his final years. He could afford not to, and he wanted to be surrounded by his own stuff. He wanted to live inside it. It's no coincidence that when he died, he wanted his studio to be *frozen in time* at that moment. Reece Mews, the studio of Francis Bacon (1909–1992), with its tens of thousands of paint tubes was one of the world's most glamorous toxic heavy metals waste dumps. And one can't help but always wonder about Andy Warhol with his townhouse stuffed with unopened bags of candy, cookie jars, jewels and Duane Reade concealer. Did he ever open the doors of his townhouse's rooms once they were full? Did he stop and stare at the doors, shiver and then walk away?

In December of 2013 I saw a magnificent show at Stockholm's Moderna Museet, *Turner Monet Twombly: Later Paintings*. It featured works done in the final decade of the lives of John Turner (1873–1938), Claude Monet (1840–1926) and Cy Twombly (1928–2011.) The show focused on these artists' (this is from the museum's website) "later work, examining not only the art historical links and affinities between them, but also the common characteristics of and motivations underlying their late style."

The paintings in the show were remarkable in and of themselves, yet what they collectively foregrounded was a sense of whiteness, a sense of glowing—an undeniable sense of the light that comes at the end of the tunnel. Overt content became less important, and the act of cognitive disassociation from the everyday world was palpable. As the museum catalogue further states, "Their late work has a looseness and an intensity that comes from the confidence of age, when notions of finish and completion are modified." A delicate way of phrasing things.

The Museet show's works depicted, in their way, anti-hoarding—a surrendering of life's material trappings. It was a liberating show that gave viewers peace. It let you know that maybe you should let go of many things in your life before your life is nearly over, when suddenly your *stuff* isn't as all important as it was cracked up to be. (Guaranteed, if you ask anyone over fifty which would they rather have, more time or more money, they'll almost always say more time.)

An obvious question here at the end is: Wait—have art super-collectors, as well as bibliomaniacs, also experienced losses of a scope so great that they defy processing? Are these collectors merely sublimating grief via over-collecting? Reasonable enough, but why just limit it to collecting art or books? People collect anything and everything.

Back in the days of caves, if someone close to you died or got killed, chances are your life was going to be much more difficult for the foreseeable future, so you'd better start gathering as many roots and berries as you could. Collecting as a response to sudden loss makes total sense. But also back then, if you lived to thirty-five, you were the grand old man or dame of the cave, with very little time left on the clock. Divvying up your arrowheads and pelts made a lot of sense—best do it before your cave-mate descendants abandoned you on an ice floe.

Collecting and hoarding seem to be about the loss of others, while philanthropy and de-accessioning are more about the impending loss of self. (Whoever dies with the most toys actually loses.)

Maybe collecting isn't a sickness, and maybe hoarding is actually a valid impulse that, when viewed differently, might be fixable through redirection tactics. Humanity must be doing something right, because we're still here—which means there's obviously a sensible way to collect berries and roots. There's probably also a sensible way to collect art and books (and owl figurines and unicycles and dildos and Beanie Babies and . . .). The people who freak me out the most are the people who don't collect anything at all. *Huh?* I don't mean minimalists. I mean people who simply don't collect *anything*. You go to their houses or apartments, and they have furniture and so forth, but there's nothing visible in aggregate: no bookshelves, no wall of framed family photos—there's just one of everything. It's shocking.

"You mean you don't collect anything?"

"No."

"There must be something. Sugar packets? Hotel soaps? Fridge magnets? Pipe cleaners?"

"No."

"Internet porn? Kitten videos?"

"No."

"What the hell is wrong with you!"

"What do you mean?"

"If this was ten thousand years ago and we all lived in a cave, you'd be an absolutely terrible cave mate. You'd be useless at foraging for roots and berries, and if you went hunting you'd only have one arrowhead, so if you lost it, you'd starve."

"Where is this coming from, Doug?"

"Forget it. Let's go gallery hopping right *now*."

Superman and the Kryptonite Martinis

One sunny afternoon in the near future, Superman was at the beach and got tar all over the soles of his feet. He went to his car and removed a Clark Kent shirt from the back seat, and then he popped the gas cap and dipped his shirt in just far enough to soak the tail. He pulled it out and began to wipe the tar from his feet and was promptly nailed by the Carbon Squad patrolling the lot. They gave him a $200 ticket for using gasoline frivolously and a $150 ticket for destroying a shirt that had 30 percent synthetic fibre content.

Meanwhile, a group of fellow beachgoers surrounded the car and began heckling him. "Ooh, look at me, I'm Superman. I can leap tall buildings and make time go backwards, but nooooo, instead I waste gasoline *and* destroy permanent press clothing."

"Gee," said another, "I think I'll go fight crime—whoops, my footsies are dirty! Looks like I'll just have to eat shit like everyone else in this world."

Superman asked, "What is *wrong* with you people?" He threw his shirt into the back seat and got in his car and put it in reverse, narrowly missing a quintet of snarling beach bunnies. As he drove away he rolled down the window to shout, "You make me really happy I left my home planet to come and fight crime for you ungrateful fucks!"

Someone threw a Frisbee at the car, and it bounced off the roof and landed in a ditch.

Superman turned on the radio and was tuned to easy-listening music when he passed a bar whose sign read "Tasty Cocktails for Those Bearing a Heavy Load."

"Man, I could use a drink right now," he said. Right there in traffic he did a U-ie and pulled up in front of the bar.

The bartender, who happened to look and sound a lot like Yoda, said, "Ah, Superman. I think I for you have a terrific drink."

Superman said, "Bring it on." The air inside the bar was cool, and he readjusted his cape and looked around. There were a few barflies in the back, but otherwise the place was dead. The juke-box was playing "The Logical Song" by Supertramp; it brought the superhero a flood of memories. As Yoda arrived with his drink, Superman said, "This song was in my first colour movie ever."

"That be the one with Christopher Reeve?"

"That's the one."

"Ever meet him did you?"

"Once, at a Golden Globes after-party. We were both kind of wasted. I don't remember much of it."

"On me is your drink, Mr. Caped Crusader."

"I don't know about that caped crusader stuff anymore. Today it's all I can do not to blast this planet to smithereens. But thanks."

Superman looked at his frosty martini, dew dripping down the sides. He took a sip . . . *Ahhh* . . . and then his mouth turned to fire. "You dirty little shit, what the hell is in this thing?"

Yoda, wiser than Superman, said, "The first time you tried wasabi you remember?"

"Yeah. In Osaka, when I was helping Sailor Moon during her Asian fragrance launch."

"But at first did it not? Aflame did your nostrils not feel?"

"Why . . . yes, it did."

"So finish your drink you will. And enjoy it you will."

Yoda went to the other side of the bar, and Superman sipped a little more of his martini. He yelled to Yoda, "This thing kicks like a bound and gagged hitchhiker! Very tasty—*mmmm*." The burn was like a new spice, and Superman became an instant addict. "Yoda, hustle with the next one."

"Yes, Mr. Caped Crusader."

As Superman awaited his next martini, he wondered why he bothered fighting crime anymore. He still had all his superpowers, but people just didn't seem to want him to use them. He'd recently received a condescending letter from the United Nations:

Dear Mr. Superman,

We appreciate your willingness to fight crime, but at the moment what we really need is a superhero who can separate out transuranium isotopes in the soil of northern Germany—or perhaps a superhero who can distill Pacific waters to render them free of plastic particles larger than two hundred microns. We at the UN acknowledge that everyday crime and everyday criminals are on the rise, but please also remember, Mr. Superman, that evil supervillains have all been eradicated, with your help. (Note: you left your thank-you plaque and goodie bag at the dinner table after the presentation ceremony. I can ask my assistant, Tara, to forward it to you if you pass along your home address.)

In any event, we want you to know that we appreciate and support your drive to be as super as you can possibly be, and we look forward to convening in the near future!

Yours,
Mbutu Ntonga, Secretary General
United Nations Temporary Headquarters, St. Louis, Missouri

Prick.

Superman downed his third martini in one gulp. A barfly near a keno machine clapped at this, and Superman roared, "I *am* a fucking superhero, you know!" He turned to Yoda. "What's in these things, anyway?"

"Magic ingredient kryptonite is."

"Kryptonite!"

Superman was about to induce vomiting with his middle finger when Yoda said, "Frightened be not! It is only at a strength useful for flavour, not enough that you lose your superpowers."

The martinis were tasty. "You're not shitting me? No lost powers? Seasoning only?"

"I shit you not. Mix you another I will."

"Done."

Soon Superman was hanging out at the bar every day, from its noon opening time until 2 a.m., with a few time outs at the Wendy's next door, plus one isolated incident when he chased down a teenager who'd jimmied the Hyundai logo off the front grille of his car. Being drunk, he miscalculated his speed, and the offending delinquent was flattened like a taco shell between Superman's body and the wall of the local rental storage facility. But nobody had witnessed the event, so Superman squished the teenager into a diamond and, once back in the bar, tossed the diamond toward the barflies.

"Nasty little prick."

Yoda said, "Hear you I did not. Mr. Superman, I am sorry to inform you, but you owe several thousands of dollars for the martinis you so much like."

"Bar tab, huh?"

"Yes."

"Forget cash. I know, how about I pay you in . . . diamonds?"

"Diamonds I like."

"Good."

Superman picked up the new diamond from the floor and gave it to a smiling Yoda, who promptly made him another kryptonite martini. All was well for several days, until his next bar tab came due. Superman excused himself, went outside, jumped up and flew around the skies for a bit, trying to find someone committing a crime who might deserve the fate of crystallization. Finally, he saw some guy holding up a rice warehouse. With just a small amount of vigilance, Superman was able to snag him and crush him, and soon he had Yoda's diamond.

But as the months passed, Superman's superpowers waned. And there came the fateful evening when, upon capturing a burglar in the act of entering somebody's rear window, instead of being able to squish the perp into a diamond, all he created was a blob of stinking bloody mess that got all over his crime-fighting suit.

Shit.

Superman's crimes grew uglier as his superpowers dwindled to mortal levels. Yoda, addicted to Superman's diamonds, refused to accept any other form of payment. Superman tried offering a Patek Philippe watch he'd ripped from the wrist of some guy who was selling weed behind an Office Warehouse. No go.

And so he robbed a Zales in the strip mall off the interstate. Bad decision. He fell down on the third bullet; by the sixth bullet, he was dead.

Back at the bar, Yoda trawled the news sites for exposés on Superman's private life: the whores, the spare bedroom filled with emptied and unrecycled cans of Boost and Ensure, the back taxes that went all the way back to the Reagan administration. Yoda sighed, fondled his sack of diamonds, and then smiled as he looked up and saw Batman enter the bar.

"Ah, Batman. The drink just for you I think I am having."

McWage

One observation I've often heard from European friends and visitors to North America is "It's as if every single person in your culture has worked at one or more restaurants in their life." I'd never thought of it before, but they're right. I can't think of anyone in my orbits who hasn't waited tables or bussed or dishwashed or cooked for some stretch. Europeans visiting Canada or the States: remember that restaurant memories are a great conversation starter; almost everyone you encounter will have tales of psychotic bosses, Christmas morning shifts and après-work partying excesses.

Working in a restaurant when you're young doesn't necessarily mean minimum wage (though it usually does). For many people, minimum wage is a stage-of-life thing that we all work through and gaze back on with rose-tinted glasses. When I put the word *McJob* in my 1991 novel *Generation X*, I wanted a word to describe a "low-paying, low-prestige dead-end job that requires few skills and offers very little chance of intracompany advancement." It made sense then and it makes sense now. Back in the early 1990s, I began to see the start of a process that's currently in full swing: the defunding or elimination of the mechanisms by which we once created and maintained a healthy middle class. What was once a stage of life is now turning into, well, *all* of life.

In the early 1990s I wanted to set a book in a fast-food restaurant, and in order to make field notes, I tried extremely hard to get a job in various Vancouver-area McDonald's restaurants, but as a reasonably well-nourished male in his mid-thirties with no references on his application, I rang too many alarm bells. I never got a job, and good on fast food for having HR mechanisms that can filter out infiltrators like me. A decade later I ended up setting a blackly comic novel (*The Gum Thief*) in a Staples, which is basically fast food but with reams of photocopier paper instead of pink goo–burgers. The point in doing so was to foreground the fact that a minimum-wage job is simply not a way to live life fully, and to be earning such a wage past a certain age casts a spell of doom upon your days, sort of like those middle-class Argentineans who lost their jobs in the crash fifteen years ago and never went back to being middle-class again.

McDonald's campaigned for years and ultimately failed to get the word *McJob* struck from the *Oxford English Dictionary*, even renting a big screen in Piccadilly Circus in 2006 to put forth their viewpoint. The saga of this campaign is a fun read on Wikipedia, but given the accelerating shrinkage of the middle class, the McLawsuit seems like a frivolous corporate bonbon from a nearly vanished era. Discussions of a minimum wage still seem to have a nasty bite. As I've said before, we're all going to be working at McDonald's into our eighties, and the relentless parade of numbers that are making this clear to us is starting to really frighten people. *It's really happening.*

I guess the thing that bugs me about current minimum-wage dialogue is that the minimum wage has gone from being a drop-dead minimum salary that, if nothing else, protected the young, the weak and the less able from being exploited (and the moment people can exploit others, they will, and we all know it) into an idea implying that if you can't get by on a minimum wage—rent, food, transport, life—then tough luck, sucker; you don't deserve anything at all . . . and it's all your fault . . . and by the way, you've forfeited your voice and participation in your culture.

The minimum wage is a shield behind which politicians can deflect any social criticism that might be central to people who need a minimum wage—student life and education, most social and medical services, artistic and creative life and whatever else you can think of—and basically say, "Well, look, we gave you a minimum wage, didn't we? So what's your problem now? If you can't stretch your minimum wage into food, shelter, lodging, medical, dental and education, then I guess it just sucks to be you."

Minimum wage has gone from being a device created to protect the worst of power and labour imbalances to a fiscal panacea that allows its wielders to gut valuable social infrastructure while smiling beneath the cheesiest of haloes. I was twenty-eight when I wrote *Generation X*, but the last time I was officially an employee anywhere was in August of 1989—so technically I've been unemployed for the past twenty-five years. But about once a month I have this recurring dream in which I suddenly realize that I'm unemployed, broke and living in a basement suite, and I desperately need a job—and so my mind automatically goes to having to work in a fast-food restaurant. The sensation is terrifying, because how on earth is anyone going to be able to live on what you make there? And then I wake up and say, "*Phew*. I've still got a few decades left before manning the french-fry computer. Dang, life is good."

Lotto

Thirty years ago I was staying over at my parents' on my birthday, December 30. Around nine in the morning, I heard my dad cursing from down the hallway. My mother's aunt Constance had phoned from Victoria, on Vancouver Island, and had not only woken my father from a deep sleep but also told him that the lottery ticket he'd put in her Christmas stocking was a big winner.

$%#^&!!!

Well, that's life.

But apparently there was a complication: Aunt Con had lost the actual ticket. My father was not thrilled. *"You what?!?!?!"*

As my family's "finder" (every family has one), I was called to duty and instructed to get dressed and take the ferry over to help Aunt Con find her ticket.

No problem.

When I arrived, maybe six hours later, Aunt Con's face was beet red and her facial muscles were wrung like a dishcloth. Her furniture was upended, the contents of drawers and cupboards emptied. I asked my great-aunt to sit down and take a quick breather. You can imagine the sort of day she'd had in her head.

So we inhaled and exhaled, and then I looked down at the coffee table and saw a runner on top of it. I lifted it up and there was the ticket: *ta-da!*

Except the thing was, Aunt Con had made a mistake. A few days earlier she'd seen the winning numbers in the newspaper and written them down on a sheet of paper that she'd stuck to her fridge door; later she looked at the numbers, forgetting where they'd come from, thinking they were the numbers on a ticket she'd bought . . .

If you ever wonder what it looks like to witness someone lose several million dollars, let me tell you, it is a dreadful sight. I high-tailed it out of Victoria very quickly, and the Day of the Ticket entered family lore.

☒

Fifteen years later I wrote a small indie movie, *Everything's Gone Green*, which used the story of Aunt Con's ticket almost verbatim. Along with it, I created a minor mathematical theory called "birthday people." A birthday person is someone who uses calendar dates as a means of generating lucky numbers—a very common tendency. People who win the big lottery jackpots are people who pity birthday people.

Big winners use the numbers from thirty-two to forty-nine (most lotteries use forty-nine as their numerical end point), thus lowering the chance of having to share a big win with people who chose the same numbers—birthday people. And it turns out there's a small but genuine mathematical basis for this. My birthday theory may not be the Fibonacci series, but I'll happily take credit for it.

☒

I think there's something inherently cruel about lotteries. They're like a surtax on desperation. A friend of a friend used to work a ticket booth at a local mall. I asked him when they sold the most tickets and he said, "That's easy: immediately after last week's winning number is drawn. That way they can hold on to their ticket all week and get the maximum amount of hope out of it."

I don't buy lottery tickets because they spook me. If you buy a one-in-fifty-million chance to win a cash jackpot, you're simultaneously tempting fate and adding all sorts of other bonus probabilities to your plane of existence: car crashes, random shootings, being struck by a meteorite. Why open a door that didn't need opening?

☼

Gambling is apparently the hardest of all addictions to shake. When you quit smoking or oxycodone, you know you've stopped, but former gamblers are still always gambling in their minds, even if they're not at the racetrack, or buying lotto tickets, or playing the stock market online in the family den.

I like Las Vegas but I don't get the gambling part of it. Let me see: I have two hundred dollars, which I then incrementally set fire to over the course of an hour or so. At the end the money I once had is gone. Who thought this was a good idea? I've noticed over the years that people who go to Vegas always lie about how much they won there. It's always one hundred to two hundred dollars, and they always say something along the lines of, "I never gamble much, but I thought I'd give it a shot and I came out $150 ahead." It's uncanny how common this highly specific lie is. Watch for it in future.

☼

I read something last week and it made sense to me: people want other people to do well in life but not too well. I've never won a raffle or prize or lottery draw, and I can't help but wonder how it must feel. One moment you're just plain old you, and then *whaam*, you're a winner and now everyone hates you and wants your money. It must be bittersweet. You hear all those stories about how big lottery winners' lives are ruined by winning, but that's not an urban legend. It's pretty much the norm. Be careful what you wish for and, while you're doing so, be sure to use the numbers between thirty-two and forty-nine.

Frugal

In art school my friends called me Dougal, which rhymes with *frugal*. Because of this, I thought that being frugal, or cheap, might be a funny, loveable or endearing personality characteristic—so, why not? For a few years I thought I was being amusing with cheapness until my friend Angela took me aside one day and said, "Dougal, you have to stop being cheap. It is incredibly unattractive and it makes it almost impossible to like you." I thought it over and realized she was correct. I stopped being cheap immediately and have never been wilfully cheap again. It was good advice.

Follow-up: Angela ended up marrying a Dutch guy, and this became my introduction to Dutch culture. She told me a joke about the Dutch: How did copper wire get invented? Two Dutchmen found a penny at the same time. LOL! Not really. But watching people be cheap in real life—to be specific, watching people taking pride in cheapness—is depressing. There has never in the history of the Earth been a woman or man who has been sexually turned on by an act of cheapness. There has never been a single person who saw someone be cheap—someone who wilfully undertipped, someone who chose an inferior brand of ingredient and subverted the quality of a meal, or someone who purchased unflattering garments in the wrong size and colour because they were on sale—and said, "Hey, that penny-pincher there, that's the one I want to have kids with."

I've written before that worrying about money is a bit like having locked-in syndrome—except you're still able to move

around and be a part of the world. But imagine marrying some-
one only to find out too late they're a spendaholic—would that have
been a deal-breaker, had you known? Or imagine marrying some-
one who turned into a creaky, prematurely aged miser—would that
be a deal-breaker for you?

$$\oplus$$

Supposedly, the three things you can control in this world are
time, dirt and money. This comes from Freud, I believe—except
when I Google it, it comes up blank. Still, it makes sense. As people
age they fixate on these three things. We all know perpetually
late people: they twigged on to this control mechanism ages ago,
and it's annoying and uncute. We all know super-clean freaks
and don't like visiting their places because we know that we trail
germs, and in their heads they're seeing wavy stink lines of patho-
gens wafting off our bodies.

Then there are cheap people. I mean, how is cheapness going to
make anybody think better of you? Really think this through: the
best that can come from adopting a cheapskate persona is a low-
level clerical job with no prospect of advancement because people
want to elevate people who think big. Saving five bucks by order-
ing an inferior snack tray for the office Christmas party is some-
thing everybody notices—it's a bad impression that, once made, is
almost impossible to rectify.

Would Richard Branson or Elon Musk order the cheaper snack
tray? No. They'd hire Cirque du Soleil and dress them up in snack
costumes and have them do trampoline acrobatics. People would
probably die in the process, but everyone would treasure the
memory, and they'd expect even crazier batshit the next time.

$$\oplus$$

When you meet self-made rich people who are cheap, possibly it's cheapness that got them there—but maybe they could relax a bit and make it look like a blast, like Richard Branson does. It's way weirder when you meet cheap rich people who inherited their money. Then it gets messy and psychological and taps into low self-worth and family drama.

Andy Warhol said that the difference between rich people and everyone else is that rich people have more interesting problems.

I think he was right.

$\oplus$

So who are you trying to impress when you're being cheap? The only answer that comes to mind is "a younger version of yourself," or perhaps your parents if they didn't have much money to throw around, which is most of us. But the thing is, you're old now. You're pretty much being cheap to an audience of ghosts. So if you're not cheap, then what are you supposed to be—thrifty? Really? Actually, yes. Boring but true. Thrift is often called for. Thrift is simply not broadcasting and not taking pride in having a common-sense approach to money. It's not a turn-on, but it's not a turnoff either. It's neutral, like being right-handed or having wavy hair. Oh, you're thrifty. Good. Now let's discuss other people's problems.

Zoë Hears the Truth

Once upon a time there was a princess, Zoë, who had no brothers or sisters. Since she was fated to become queen, she spent much of her early life wondering exactly what it is a queen does, aside from displaying excellent table manners and cutting ribbons at the openings of horticultural festivals. Her parents had always told her that when her day came, she'd receive special instruction. In the meantime she was told to enjoy life.

So Princess Zoë went to the gym. She read ancient scrolls. She played tennis. In order to promote her kingdom's industrial base, she once had lunch with a Japanese-made robot that simulated Elton John. It was an interesting life, but then one day during a month of heavy rains and floods, her father became sick and a hush fell over the castle. He called Zoë to his bedside and said, "It's time we had a talk."

Zoë's stomach fluttered because she knew this was when she was to receive her special instructions on how to be queen. "What is it, Father?"

Rain drummed on the ancient leaded glass windows.

"It's simple, really. You need to know that your mother and I don't believe in anything."

Zoë was shocked. "*What* did you say, Father?"

"Your mother and I don't believe in anything."

"As in . . . religion?"

"Absolutely. No religion for us."

"Politics?"

"Nope."

"The monarchy?"

"Absolutely not."

"Why are you telling me this? How can you just sit there and tell me you don't believe in anything? You're the king! You have a kingdom, and subjects who worship you."

"If it makes them happier to worship me, then let them."

"So wait. You mean you don't even believe in any form of higher being?"

"That is correct. Nothing."

"But you're divinely chosen!"

"So?"

Zoë didn't know how to handle this information. The room began to sway like a floating dock on choppy water. "Did you ever believe in anything before? When you were younger, maybe?" she asked.

"I tried. Quite hard. Really."

Zoë got mad. "Papa, you're a fraud!"

"Grow up just a bit, my little cabbage. Don't you ever wonder how I get through my days in such a good mood, even when the peasants threaten to revolt or when the queen of Spain overstays her welcome?"

"But don't you have to believe in *some*thing?"

"Princess, you're too old not to have had—how shall I say?—certain experiences. You've had bad Internet dates. You've had people be creeps to you. You've seen what you've seen; you've felt what you've felt. Ideology is for people who don't trust their own experiences and perceptions of the world."

"I feel like I'm going mad."

"Madness is actually quite rare in individuals. It's *groups* of people who go mad. Countries, cults . . . religions."

Zoë said, "I wish I smoked. If I smoked, right now would be a very good time for a cigarette."

"I'll have the butler bring us one." Her father leaned over to a speakerphone beside his bed and said, "Please bring me a cigarette." Almost instantly the butler arrived with a mentholated, filter-tipped cigarette resting atop a burgundy pillow. "Try it, Zoë. You'll see what you've been missing all these years."

The butler lit the cigarette for Zoë. She breathed in some smoke, coughed and grew dizzy. "This tastes awful."

"Sometimes what's bad for our bodies is good for the soul. Smoke some more. You'll love it. Soon you'll be unable to stop."

Zoë inhaled again. It wasn't as bad as the first puff. "Does anyone else know you don't believe in anything?"

"Just your mother."

"Don't you worry about death?"

"For every living person here on Earth, there are millions of dead people before them—and there will be billions of dead people after us, too. Being alive is just a brief technicality. Why are you so upset?"

"This is a lot to absorb in one blast."

"Pshaw, there's nothing to absorb. That's the point. And soon you'll be queen and you'll have to go through your days displaying flawless table manners and cutting ribbons to open horticultural fairs. And you'll have to deal with a few monsters as well."

"Monsters?" This was news to Zoë.

"Yes, monsters. People who believe in things to the exclusion of their senses. Everyone dumps on politicians as monsters, but they're actually very easy to handle, because at least they're upfront about the system they're using to avoid reality. The real killers are the quiet believers. It's always the sullen twenty-year-old who wears the Semtex-laden vest into the market square."

As Zoë sat and finished her cigarette, there was a pleasant quiet moment between father and daughter. The rain pounded on the window like a crazy person trying to get in. She stubbed out the cigarette in an ashtray designed to look like a miniature version of the Magna Carta. She said, "You heard the news this morning about the floods?"

"I did."

"They say the royal graveyard will soon flood."

"Won't *that* be something," said the king.

"Papa, it's where you're going to be buried."

"Just imagine all those bejewelled skeletons washing away down into the river."

"Papa, we're going to have to find somewhere else to bury you. What are we going to do? Where can we bury you if not in the royal cemetery?"

"Surprise me," said the king, at which point he died, making Zoë queen. And as she sat there thinking about her future, she looked at her cigarette butt and had the strangest sensation that the cigarette was actually looking back at her.

And then she realized that she too didn't believe in anything.

She wondered if not believing in anything would rob her of the ability to ever fall in love.

And then she rang for another cigarette, her first act as queen.

IQ

Today I wondered, "If the Internet had an IQ, what would it be?" I made a guess: 4,270—a four-digit IQ. Yes, I know the Internet is just a tool and not a sentient being. But one can dream.

⊗

When I was growing up in the 1970s, IQs were a big deal, and we were always getting tested in school. But the intelligence that was being measured wasn't empirical (if such a thing is even possible). Rather, IQ tests were about nothing more than the tests themselves. *Do you know how these tests work? Does that question remind you of another similar question? Oh, it's the rearrange-the-cubes question again.* And so on.

There was a magazine in the late 1970s called *Omni*, which catered to the culture of people who take IQ tests. There was something kind of sexy and key-party about it—I think because the genes for intelligence are right beside the genes that predispose a person to nudism. I think Valhalla for the Mensa set was group sex with Xaviera Hollander on a houseboat with walls covered in macramé wall-hangings and fencing swords.

I was born at the very end of December, so I was always the youngest person in my grade. I was also terrifyingly skinny, so my way of surviving was to be the smartest one in the class, which is not the same thing as being actually smart—just smart within the framework of school. It did the trick and I emerged in one piece. After high school I did one semester at university, where it dawned on me: *I don't have to be smart anymore.* For the first time in my life, I was getting Bs and Cs and it was like a drug; I remember feeling really high when I got my first D. I quit, went to art school, and I've never again wanted to enter a situation where I have to take a test.

I think people are smarter now than they were in, say, 1995. I've touched on this before: we all feel stupider yet I think were we to compare IQs from then and now, we'd find that our new standard IQ is more like 103. People time-travelling from 1995 to 2015 would probably speak with us for a few minutes and then quietly excuse themselves and go meet in the kitchen and wonder what drug we're on. "They have no attention span, and the moment you tell them even the slightest fib, they reach into their pockets, pull out a piece of glass, dabble their fingers over it and then look up at you and call your bluff. What kind of way is that to live life?"

If you go online, there are all sorts of free IQ tests you can take, but I can only guess that they're going to rate you as a genius while they ravage your hard drive, steal all of your passwords and give you a wicked case of malware.

A few years back I had the perhaps singular experience of varnishing a gymnasium floor with a group of retired high school principals. I asked them what they did when they had a problem student—which is not to say a low-IQ student; problem students tend to be smart. They told me, "Oh that's easy. Once we reach the end of our rope, we simply phone their parents, who are, of course, expecting more bad news, and in a reverent tone of voice we tell them, 'We think your son/daughter is truly gifted. They'd be much better served at a school that has better resources for brilliant students.' Nine times out of ten they are so floored, they just murmur a timid thank-you, and a week later our problem student is gone."

⊗

Lately I have made my peace with the fact that I will never be intelligent enough to turn on my TV. I upgraded everything last year, and there are not two but three remotes on the side table, gathering dust. I stare at them, and then I look up at the cool judgmental blackness of my new large flat-screen, and then . . . I open my laptop's lid to binge on season three of *Homeland*. I mean, what on earth is HDMI? (I know, I know: HDMI is High-Definition Multimedia Interface, an audio-video interface for transferring uncompressed video data and compressed or uncompressed digital audio data from an HDMI-compliant source device.) But couldn't they have just named it Walter? Or Trish? People, how hard would that have been?

I'm writing this at Toronto's Pearson airport at gate E72. Instead of endless banks of airport seating, they have elegant marble tables with leather furniture, and each seat has its own iPad and an electrical outlet. The Wi-Fi is, of course, smoking hot. There is also no sound in this airport lounge, which feels like the Airport of Tomorrow. Children who would otherwise be shrieking from sugar spikes and boredom sit calmly and play video games. Everyone is feeding on data and images and sounds. Information flows in and out of these portals. Nobody is getting stupider. Words are being learned. Connections are being formed. Patterns are being recognized. The next kind of intelligence is being crafted before my eyes, and it feels like a much more useful sort of intelligence as opposed to knowing how to rearrange cubes on a piece of paper. Oh yes, my IQ is 510.

My TV

On April 19, 1995, I bought my first genuine adult TV set—a twenty-seven-inch Sony Trinitron. I remember the date because two delivery men brought it to the house at about eleven in the morning. We installed the TV in a nook in the bookshelves and turned it on, and on the screen came images of the Oklahoma City bombing. The three of us stopped for an hour and watched the news. I made coffee, we talked a bit and then the day progressed.

I used to watch TV back then. By that I mean I'd go into the living room and turn on the TV set, saying, "Gosh, I wonder what's on TV right now? I think I'll run through the channels." It's hard to imagine anyone doing that now, even my parents. Over two decades our collective TV-viewing habits have changed so much that it's actually quite hard to remember old-style TV viewing.

I remember 1997 and Princess Diana's death and being glued to CNN for hours. The same for 9/11. But when Michael Jackson died in 2009, I was in my dining room, writing, and a friend texted to say Michael Jackson had died. Instead of turning on CNN, I went right to the Internet, and it was only hours later that I thought, *Hmmm, I wonder how TV is covering this?* A shift had occurred.

By the early 2000s it was obvious that big, boxy Sony TVs like mine were doomed. Screens everywhere were definitely growing both flatter and bigger. I found myself foot-dragging about getting a big screen, however, for a few reasons. One, laziness. Two, having to rearrange and rebuild the bookshelves. Three, the image quality on those early flat-screens was still blurry and smudgy. Four (and this is by far the biggest reason), big-screen TVs are ugly. In the history of human technology, there have been few inventions whose intrinsic ugliness and brutality of form so defeat everything we call *home*. Trying to put a big screen in a domestic space and have it look like it belongs is almost impossible, like having a *2001: A Space Odyssey* monolith inserted into your life—a monolith that has total disregard for your humanity or taste. The black minimalist box on your wall negates your framed wedding photos, your crown mouldings, your art collection, your potted plants. The only environment it looks passably okay in is a house built after 2008 that factors in the bizarre scale of big screens—and even then, when you see one passably installed, you feel like you've walked into Moammar Gadhafi's bedroom. On the other hand, it's nice to not have everything look orange and fuzzy like it did on the old Sony, and nice to view shows in the correct aspect ratio.

In 2008 I broke my leg and couldn't use my old office, so I had powerful Wi-Fi installed in the house, and that was the end of old-style TV for me. Soon I'd adopted all of the present-day viewing tendencies most of us share: binge viewing, laptop viewing, torrenting, series addictions, digital video recording, Netflix and guilty-pleasure viewing (*Come Dine with Me Canada*—I can't get enough of that show). But also, amid these shifts, it's been interesting to watch the evolution of TV as a new art form. Marshall McLuhan predicted this. When a new technology obsolesces an old one, it frees the newly obsolete medium to become an art form. Enter *The Sopranos, Breaking Bad, The Wire* and all the shows that are basically movies that run for fifty hours and act as a paradise for talented actors. Perhaps this shift to long-format TV has generated the biggest change in creative culture in the past decades. I've noticed that people now discuss TV the way they once discussed novels: What chapter are you on? Wasn't so-and-so's character great? Are you watching the new season? You watched it all in one night? Our long-form attention span is shifting to a new medium.

I tried taking my old Sony to the recycler, but along the way I hit a speed bump and the set's plastic casing shattered into a thousand cornflake-shaped plastic bits. It had spent sixteen or so years baking inside its living room nook. And when I asked to recycle the TV's cathode ray tube, they said, "No, we don't accept TVs." Puzzled, I drove away and was flagged down by a street guy with a shopping cart, who asked if I wanted him to take care of the TV set. I'm not proud of it, but I said yes and gave him twenty dollars. He smiled and told me that he wasn't going to spend the money on drugs but was instead going to buy a submarine sandwich and watch a 3D movie. That was the last pleasure my Sony gave the world.

The Preacher and His Mistress

They met on an Internet sex-connection site. They arranged for SWNS—sex with no strings—and the ground rules were that neither had a clue who the other was or what their powers were.

"I have to say," said Brenda, as she searched the motel room for her pantyhose, "for SWNS, this was pretty darn hot."

"You do this a lot?"

Brenda stared at him. "Part of the deal with SWNSing is that you don't ask questions like that." She leaned to look for her shoes, which were under the bed.

"But I want to know about you."

Brenda froze. "Stop right there."

"My name is Barry."

"Fuck." He'd snagged her for the moment. "Okay, Barry, why do you want to know more about me?"

"Because I think you're special."

"Really, now?"

"Yes."

"What makes me so special?"

"The look in your eyes near the end there. Something special was going on."

"Bullshit."

"Don't believe me, then." Barry reached for his cigarettes.

"You smoke? Nobody smokes anymore."

"I'm not nobody."

"Very witty."

"Want one?"

Brenda paused. "Sure. Why not."

She lit up, knowing that she shouldn't, that she should grab her clothes and get dressed in the parking lot if she had to. Instead she asked, "So then, what is it you want to know about me?"

"Your name, for starters."

"Brenda."

"Okay, Brenda, tell me what you believe in."

"Like God and everything?"

"Sure. If that's where your head takes you."

"I think God made a mistake with human beings. Nothing original there."

"Very charming."

"So then, what's with you?"

"So now you want to know about me?"

"Fuck off."

They smoked a bit more. Brenda said, "I haven't smoked since high school. Out by the portables. I never quite got the hang of it."

"What year did you graduate?"

She told him.

"So we're the exact same age."

"Gee. Isn't that thrilling." She stubbed out her cigarette. "I have to go. Where's my other shoe?"

"Meet again?"

Brenda paused and then said, "Okay. Same time and place one week from now."

"Okay."

And so for months Barry and Brenda met once a week, and each time they did, Barry asked a little bit more about Brenda and, against her better instincts, Brenda told him a little bit more, while he never bothered to offer much about himself into the bargain. But at least, she thought, she'd never told Barry her biggest secret—a secret that would change everything between them in a manner that Brenda definitely didn't want.

So slowly, gradually, the weekly tryst became the highlight of Brenda's week. Then one afternoon she looked out the window and saw that the peach tree was blossoming like it had the first time they'd met. She realized that she and Barry had been SWNSing for a full year and that it was no longer SWNSing—she was in love with him, although she didn't think he felt the same way. Realizing that her love was unrequited filled Brenda's heart with sweet pain; few things make us feel so alone in this world as unrequited love.

Soon Brenda did what she knew she shouldn't do: she told Barry she was in love. She was bracing herself for all kinds of worsts, but his reply simply shut her up: "If you want to spend more time around me, then join my flock. I'm a preacher."

"What?"

"Just what I said. I'm a preacher."

Brenda said she needed to go to the bathroom, which was really an excuse to buy a little time. She turned on the taps to make it sound like she was busy, but her full attention was on whether she could tolerate being a member of the preacher's "flock." You see, her biggest secret was that she herself was a priestess. There weren't any rules for a situation like this. Barry had intuitively sensed her priestess energy.

She came out to find Barry fully dressed. She told him yes, she would join his flock.

Barry said, "I'll see you on Sunday morning then, at eleven." He gave her directions and he left.

Come Sunday, Brenda showed up to find a reasonably nice church that was maybe a little too close to the highway off-ramp for her taste, but it could have been worse.

Not only was Barry a preacher, but—surprise!—he had a wife and kids, a subject she'd never broached with him during their year of SWNSing. Barry's wife was friendly in an impossible-to-hate way and welcomed Brenda into the church. After the service, as the congregation met downstairs in the church basement to welcome Brenda, she contemplated her bad decision-making, amidst the bad lighting, the religious flashcards pinned to a corkboard, salmonella-looking potato salad and a scary upright piano.

Brenda didn't go to meet Barry at their usual time and place that week, nor did she return to his church. After she missed the third week, Barry phoned her.

"How'd you get my number, Barry? The rule is that I only call you."

"Don't play dumb, Brenda. How hard is it to get someone's number? Just come to church and our weekly session. You mean so much to me, you can't believe it. Can you find it in your heart to join us again?"

Brenda found it in her heart, and she and Barry had scorching-hot mid-week pig sex followed by Sunday church, but she still had yet to reveal her secret identity as a priestess.

And then one Saturday afternoon Brenda was downtown, returning a jacket that didn't fit properly, and outside the store she witnessed an accident: her preacher had hit a border collie as he'd been driving by in his brand-new GMC Yukon XL Denali—the one whose interior was impregnated with the odour of his wife's perfume. Brenda ran and scooped the dog into her arms as the preacher got out of the truck. He said, "Brenda, relax. It's only a dog."

"What do you mean, 'it's only a dog'?"

"It's a dog. It doesn't have a soul; don't worry about it."

"*It* is not an it. *It* is a *she*, and *she* is in pain."

The dog died in Brenda's arms and she fell out of love with Barry. She looked up at him, her cheeks beet-red, and said, "I quit."

"You quit what?"

"Your church. *You.* And I bet you didn't know that I'm a priestess."

"Priestess? Don't be stupid. So then, go off and be a priestess all by yourself if you're so angry. See if I care."

His attitude further horrified Brenda. "I will. By the way, as a priestess I get three official wishes, none of which I've ever used. I'm going to use one of them now."

Barry was patronizing. "You just do that." He climbed into the Yukon.

Brenda thought that if her love must die, then other kinds of love should also die. There on the sidewalk, somewhat to the bafflement of passersby, she cried, "Here's my wish number one: from now on, all parents all over Earth will stop loving their children!"

Barry was halfway down the crowded block, his windows automatically rolling up, when he heard those words. "What?!" He stopped his truck.

"From now on, all parents will stop loving their children."

"Right. Yeah, well, whatever," Barry said, and drove away.

❂

Brenda's first wish as a priestess came true. All the parents in the world stopped loving their children. Nothing dramatic happened . . . at first. In fact, the world didn't change much at all. At the end of day one, there was just a series of creeping realizations among parents with children of all ages.

"Drive you to your play dates and sporting events? Good luck. Take a bus. Your father and I are going snorkelling."

"I feel like I'm babysitting somebody else's monsters."

"Why on earth would I want to phone the kids? All they'll do is bitch about their spouses and hit me up for money."

"Graduating? Big deal. People do it all the time."

"Not hungry? Fine. Don't eat your goddamn dinner. I've got better things to do than micromanage your food intake."

By day two, people were leaving babies on church doorsteps.

By day three, every PTA meeting on Earth was cancelled.

By day four, pregnant women were filling the nation's cocktail bars. The world's leaders abolished Mother's Day and Father's Day.

Day five marked the golden age of babysitting, as parents just wanted to ditch their kids, so babysitters could name any price they wanted.

By day six people without children formed mobs to confront the parents who had stopped caring about their children's lives. "The law says you have to take care of your children. You can't just let them go out into the streets like stray dogs."

"Can't we now? In any event, there's lots of food out there—lots of cans of Boost and Ensure all over the place. How hard is it to open a meal in a can? And ... I don't know, they can play video games until the end of time. And if they start whining or complaining, they can sleep on a mattress down in the basement."

"How can you be so heartless?"

"You know what? Fuck off. I have to go to my spin class."

Of course, Barry and his wife stopped loving their two children, though Barry hadn't been expecting Brenda's curse to be real. He thought about how strange a sensation it was to go from loving somebody intensely to not giving a rat's ass about him or her. When it came to that week's sermon, he found himself preaching about the importance of love to a congregation composed only of non-parents; all the people with children had locked their kids outside their houses while they remained inside making eggs Florentine for brunch. The non-parents were angry. They didn't know what to do, because if they took care of all these newly unloved children or babies themselves, then that would make them de facto parents, and because of Brenda's curse, as soon as they became parents, they would immediately lose any capacity to love their new children. There was no way around this. It was a real Catch-22.

At the end of the next week, Barry phoned Brenda and said, "Okay, you win the privilege of being able to say, 'I told you so.' I'm sorry I was such a dick when I ran over the dog. Are you happy now?"

"I want you to understand what you did to me. You drove away in your planet-killing truck with me sitting, literally, in the gutter, all because you don't care about dogs having or not having souls."

"Brenda, please, just unwish your wish. You made your point. Do you want me to beg?"

"No. I'm not cruel like that—cruel the way *you* are, killing an animal and feeling nothing."

"Brenda, please unwish your wish."

"I can only do that by making another wish. I wish that, from now on, all children will stop loving their parents."

"You bitch."

And so everybody on Earth, of all ages, stopped loving their parents. The results of this were subtler, for it's nature's way for children to naturally be ungrateful to their parents, to feel entitled and to take parents for granted. Younger children continued whining and behaving badly as always. But older children with older parents stopped emailing them. Around the planet, millions of people quit jobs they'd chosen to please their parents. Greeting-card manufacturers went out of business, and there were millions of instances of children killing their parents to speed up their inheritances; courts around the world became bogged down with murder cases.

Barry phoned Brenda. "You win. Again."

"It's not about me winning. It's about you understanding what you did to me and what you did to that poor dog you ran over."

"Oh god, I can't believe you're still harping on that."

Brenda sighed. "You really are a dick." And then in a rash moment she said, "I wish that everybody on Earth would stop loving everybody else." Her wish was granted, and there was no wish left to undo it. The world turned into a planet of loners—a planet of unabombers, hermits and recluses, people doomed to being solitary without the possibility of solitude, a world without hope.

Good, thought Brenda. *I like it this way. Now everybody knows what it feels like to be me.*

And then she spent the rest of the day on the Internet.

5,149 Days Ago:
Air Travel Post-9/11

I remember flying out of Heathrow in the mid-2000s. It was an afternoon flight to Canada and the security screening area was empty of passengers—a pleasant surprise. However, placing my carry-on bag onto the conveyor belt, I ripped my thumbnail backwards, breaking off a wide swath of the top, and I was suddenly in that magical state of being where I could either (a) chew off the broken part of the thumbnail, most likely ripping out a chunk of the nail in the corner and so causing immense bleeding, stinging and disfigurement that could possibly continue for weeks, or (b) be an adult, wait just a little bit longer and perhaps locate some form of device for safely removing the offending piece of thumbnail. This was a very tough call—sort of like a marshmallow test of delayed gratification. As we all know, nature has programmed human beings to always choose option A, even though it's by far the stupider choice. So what did I do? I tried to be an adult, and then . . . I had a brainwave. After my bag had gone through the scanner, and I was standing shoeless on the floor's rubber padding (a place the security staff dub "the mushroom patch"), I said to the gentleman on the other side of the conveyor belt: "This is a weird request, but here's the thing: I just ripped off a chunk of my thumbnail but it's still attached to the thumb, and I know if I remove it with my teeth, it will turn into an unholy bloody painful mess. Would you happen to have—and I don't want to compromise security or anything—something I might use to cut off the nail with?"

The screener gave me a gentle smile and then motioned for me to join him on the other side of the security area. Once we were there, he walked over to a Wedgwood-blue forty-four-gallon plastic trash bin and removed its lid, revealing tens of thousands of confiscated nail clippers.

Okay.

This isn't something one sees every day. I mean to say, there were SO MANY NAIL CLIPPERS ALL IN ONE PLACE. Tens of thousands. I honestly felt like the lid had been removed from the ark in *Raiders of the Lost Ark* and I had been chosen to view its contents—and that maybe my face was going to melt off in a few moments.

Then I remembered my thumbnail. Dang, it hurt. I posed the question: "Do you think there's one set of nail clippers here that looks . . . perhaps more sanitary than any other?"

We both scoured the top layer of nail clippers, and my new friend selected an innocuous pair as might be found at any local drugstore. He handed them to me. "Try these."

"Right." *Click click*. Nail catastrophe averted. "Thank you very much, sir."

"You're welcome. Have a safe flight."

⌧

It'll soon be fifteen years since 9/11, and more planes are in the air than ever. This comes as a pleasant surprise, as on September 12, 2001, it felt as though an old way of life was over and fewer people would dare to fly in the future. From an ecological standpoint, more people flying more than ever is a disaster, but from a social cohesion point of view, vigorous air travel comes as a great relief.

✕

After 9/11, I undertook a forty-two-city book tour. The first city was Madison, Wisconsin, which is where I was marooned for five days. I tried to make lemonade out of lemons and thought, "What a great chance to have a really good look at the region's bountiful Frank Lloyd Wright architecture!" Wrong. Being Canadian, I was ineligible to rent a car because I might try to drive it to the border. So . . . I was marooned in Madison, Wisconsin, for five days.

When flights in the United States finally resumed, I was usually one of only a few people on the plane. For about three weeks. And when meals arrived, instead of silverware, the cutlery was a clear plastic bag filled with white plastic utensils, like what you'd get in a Wendy's. How sorrowfully depressing. That little bag with a plastic spoon, knife and fork became a haiku expressing one of humanity's worst moments. My thoughts harkened back to Lufthansa's pre-9/11 first class, where the steak knife was a stag's antler embedded with what can only be described as a precision serrated steel hacksaw blade. You could have hacked apart an undersea fibre optic cable with one of those things. And suddenly this: a Wendy's cutlery pack.

✕

Sometimes I feel like a character from *Fahrenheit 451*, except instead of remembering an entire novel, my job is to remember a way of travelling that is quite likely gone forever. Which is fine. But mostly my thinking time-travels far, far off into the future, to the year 36559, when whatever species it is that supplants humans is digging through a garbage dump somewhere outside of London, and finds a forty-four-gallon container filled with completely uncorroded stainless steel nail-clippers.

"Their miniature hooves must have grown at eccentric rates of speed."

"Perhaps they were vain and only used their hoof clippers just once before rubbishing them."

"Maybe the hoof clippers were contaminated as a vector in a mass plague, and the local shaman urged his underlings to gather them for some sort of sacrifice."

Here's the thing: those clippers are an environmental disaster directly linked to 9/11, but a long way off from now. And more to the point, how do you explain 9/11—how will we ever explain it?

Glide

The other night I watched the movie *Airport* (1970; Burt Lancaster, Dean Martin and Jean Seberg). Passengers in its airport scenes were carrying old-fashioned luggage like your grandparents once used: plump, rectangular Samsonite chunks with single handles. Looking at this obsolete luggage was slightly cringe-inducing, sort of like watching an eighty-something shovel wet snow. People really used to do this? As an added bonus, the passengers who weren't carrying luggage were smoking—rarely has 1970 ever felt so far away. All in all, it seemed more like Bruegel the Elder's sixteenth century than it did Richard Nixon's America, and it certainly made it clear how far not just air travel but airline terminals have come in the past four decades.

$\oplus$

Can you guess what the single biggest factor for change in airport design has been over recent decades? The answer is wheeled luggage, and because of it, most every surface in a modern airport has been made as smooth and flat as possible, with bumps and gaps eliminated—the seamless plane ensures that the trundling of your luggage is both quiet and stylish. The smoothness helps define an airport's sexy allure. It's the opposite of your daily life, and the relentless smoothness lends most airports a borderline life-after-death tone. Sometimes an airport's spell of smoothness is broken and we're returned to the mundane realm. For me, this happens each time I visit the Air Canada domestic lounge of Vancouver International Airport, where the architect chose rough, lumpy chunks as flooring, and anything on wheels, be it a demure carry-on or the Rubbermaid cleaning trolley, sounds like Kimba the elephant on a rampage.

$\oplus$

Women living in industrialized countries tend to fall and break their hips more than women in less industrialized countries. For decades this tendency was credited to some sort of lack in the diets of the Western woman, or to a long-term accumulation of toxins, or to some sort of existential failing on the part of modernity. The real reason, it turned out, had nothing to do with these notions. We in the Western world walk almost entirely on flat, smooth surfaces. Because of this, stabilizer muscles in the ankle and lower leg remain largely undeveloped, so that when a disruption is encountered, the muscles and reflexes needed to cope with it aren't there, so people trip. It's that simple. There's a lot to be said for walking in nature, and it's not just for the fresh air.

$\oplus$

Segways are terrific: anyone who's ever used one will testify to this. The thing about Segways is that they're like flying dreams. You just think of going somewhere and they take you there effortlessly and with no learning curve. Using them is like walking or running but with all the boring bits removed. But boy, did Segway blow it. It's possibly the best product ever destroyed by clueless consumer and regulatory rollout: "Is this a bicycle? Is it a car? Is it a motorcycle? In the absence of boxes to tick, we declare this product unlicensable." I suspect that in the future, when energy and noise pressures grow too large, people will rediscover the Segway. But I hope they'll call it something else and release it into the world more intelligently. A few years back, I visited Austin, Texas, where Segways are street legal. People were using them for day-to-day living. Talk about futuristic. Forget flying cars. Segways were it.

$$\oplus$$

In the past year I've taken trains throughout Europe and, as someone who comes from a place where there are, for all practical purposes, no trains nor places to go in them, European train travel never loses that seamless sensation of infranational fluidity—the magic of floating from one country into another atop a continent as polished as the terrazzo flooring of Heathrow, Schiphol or da Vinci. Newspapers. Magazines. Meals. The countryside. Hey, wanna go to Warsaw this afternoon? The procedural logistics of crossing between Canada and the United States in a train rivals a trip into East Germany in the 1960s, whereas four border crossings on a small Euro trip is no big deal. I never take this for granted, but my impression of Europeans is that they do take it for granted, yet also that this may be coming to an end. In spring I took the Thalys rail line between Holland and France several times, and when photos of that recent foiled gun attack made the Internet, I found myself saying, "Ahh, yes, the distinctive Thalys maroon upholstering." The head-buzz of having had half a cup of coffee too many. A soiled and finger-worn copy of *Le Figaro.* Trying to get some, any, form of 3G connection. *Whoosh!*

$$\oplus$$

There are few utopias in Western culture. The senior prom. Two weeks in Hawaii. Hollywood. Retirement. Yet all of these utopias are being chipped away at. One has one's prom and then it's over. Consequence-free air and land travel are being ever more securitized and stripped of ease. The mathematics of retirement make it a dream that grows further away every day. As we weaponize the physical world, only Hollywood, in league with the Internet, retains some power to create a sense of someplace that transcends our daily reality. When we look back on right now from the perspective of a few decades in the future, I suspect we're going to think of it as the Age of Ease. And what's wrong with that?

$\oplus$

Afternote: I wrote this piece on a flight to Schiphol. Three minutes after deplaning, two security guards on cloud-grey Segways silently overtook me, then rounded a corner and disappeared from view. The moment was slightly thrilling, as though I'd spotted two endangered birds in the wild.

Klass Warfare

Okay. So I'm in Berlin and scheduled to fly to London on Lufthansa at 6:10 p.m.—however, a meeting comes up, so I look up a later flight but learn there are no later Lufthansa flights. Who else flies to London? The answer: Ryanair. But wait. I've never flown with them, and aren't they the ones where people fly standing up so they can get more people on the plane? Surely not. Well, what could possibly go wrong on such a short flight anyway? So I buy my ticket online and go to the formerly East German Schoenefeld Airport. But something is amiss . . . The airport building has miraculously time-travelled from the early 1970s and has endured much battering along the way. Have I wormholed into another time-space continuum? No problem. I can pretend I'm in high school on an exchange program—it'll be fun.

However, it turns out I bought the online ticket for the wrong day (@#$%!) so I buy a new ticket at the airport counter and head to the gate, stepping gingerly around brawling sunburned travellers and glistening puddles of vomit. *Remember, Doug, think high school—this is an adventure.*

I arrive at the gate, but something's wrong with my ticket. My German's not good enough to know what the problem is. I'm told to sit in a stanchioned off area and . . . whatever. *Read your newspaper. Try to see the mirth in everything.* Then comes the announcement, *Meine Damen und Herren . . .* It's boarding time, and suddenly the room goes silent and everyone turns to look at me with hate in their bloodshot, booze-ravaged eyes. *Huh?* I then listen closely and it turns out they're pre-boarding passengers in "Ryanair Business Plus"—which would be . . . me? So the silent room, filled with maybe two hundred people, watches me stand up, get my boarding pass bleeped and enter the plane's jet ramp. Well, that was uncomfortable.

Once inside, I'm actually oddly disappointed that the seats aren't arranged in a vertical sarcophagus mode—that would have been cool—but I am instead shown to my Business Plus seat, which is in the exit row above the wings. The seat is a regular seat but there's a good six feet of space in front of me. Not bad. Like anyone, I hate no legroom. However, the price for my seated comfort is that I have to endure a thirty-minute parade of hate and loathing as other non–Business Plus passengers lumber past me, muttering highly ungenerous things to the back of my head.

Finally, the door up front closes and I see that the plane is totally packed—all except for my row of six seats all to myself. A gentleman from the row in front of me tries to reasonably spread out into one of these seats but is harshly singled out by a flight attendant who makes sure it's painfully clear that these seats are exclusively for the use of Business Plus customers. Further laser beams of hate are shot my way. The plane lifts off.

Once in the air? Complimentary wine. Complimentary magazines. A selection of hot meals. It's actually kind of great and time passes quickly and, before I know it, we've landed at Stansted Airport—another airport I've never seen before. After a long hike I get to the luggage carousel without having been tripped and belittled by my Ryanair co-passengers. Once at the carousel I come to the conclusion that Stansted isn't so much an airport as, rather, a Burger King with a prison attached to it. An hour later I find my suitcase, I grab a cab, and my unplanned exercise in social mobility comes to a close. At the hotel I look up the price difference for my seat: about fifty euros.

What is it about business class that brings out some of the weirdest and deepest class responses we experience in a given year? I have a hunch that airlines do as much as they can to ensure that those not seated behind the blue curtain are fully aware of what's happening behind it.

Some business class flights are amazing, like an Emirates A380 from Dubai to New York, filled mostly with expats coming or going from or to six-month stints living in walled compounds, with everybody getting hammered for opposite reasons. They also have great Wi-Fi, but there's something really odd about enjoying Wi-Fi when the in-flight map tells you you're directly above Baghdad. And then you're above Romania. And then . . . and then your mind wanders off to poor old Malaysia Airlines, and you take your mind off things by watching 1983 Duran Duran videos on YouTube.

Business class on KLM is no-nonsense. They give you one drink, then a hot meal and then . . . no more anything, and if you ask for even a cracker beyond that, they make this face at you. It's hard to describe . . . sort of like, "So you think you're better than everyone else on this plane, do you?"

All business classes aren't the same, but even writing about class stratification in a plane actually feels a bit uncomfortable . . . like it shouldn't exist, like we're in the United States in 1800 and we're discussing slaves and it's somehow okay. But to take this further, the whole notion of jet travel seems slightly uncomfortable to discuss. It's an ecological crime. It shouldn't exist. In the future I hope there's just one class: propofol class. You get on a plane and then they administer propofol (the Michael Jackson death drug) and then you wake up on the other end. Who needs class when you have obliteration?

3.14159265358

The invention of the hamburger was a way of homogenizing cows. Take whatever you want from any number of animals (but, one hopes, all cows), grind it up and suddenly you have a consistent and uniform beef unit: the hamburger patty. In this same manner, humanity took time as it was once experienced and converted it into seconds, minutes and hours. One second is basically a time patty, or "the duration of 9,192,631,770 periods of the radiation corresponding to the transition between the two hyperfine levels of the ground state of the caesium 133 atom."* Romantic!

Modern culture since 1900 has been about the relentless homogenizing of anything that can be homogenized: pig byproducts into hot dogs; coffee into Nespresso capsules; junk bonds into hedge funds.

In this spirit of investigation, I began to wonder, "What, then, does *money* homogenize?"

⊗

The average person with a high school education uses three thousand words a day but is able to recognize about twenty thousand. But when it comes to sequences and numbers, when does a word stop being a word? Examples: Is the alphabet itself a word?

---

* Wikipedia contributors, "Second," *Wikipedia, The Free Encyclopedia* (mid-2015), https://en.wikipedia.org/w/index.php?title=Second&oldid=714856192.

We all know it: *abcdefghijklmnopqrstuvwxyz*. It ought to be. Is the sequence *1234567890* a word? We know that *1,000,000* is a word, but is *1,000,001* a word too? My high school math teacher gave us all an extra point if we memorized pi to ten digits, and of course we all did, so is *threepointonefouronefiveninetwosixfive-threefiveeight* a word? And if so, is it a different word from pi to nine digits (*threepointonefouronefiveninetwosixfivethreefive*)?

⊗

A few years back I was cleaning out an old space in the house, and I found inside a rusty paint can a canvas bag filled with silver coins—silver pre-1967 Canadian dimes, plus a wide selection of older US coins. I don't know what it's like to find treasure, but it must surely feel like finding a rusty paint can full of coins. I mentioned it on the phone to my mother, and she said, "Bring it over right now. Have you sorted them yet?"

"Yes."

"Dump them all back in the can. I want to sort them here."

I went to her place and she had a magnet ready to help sort them out (silver isn't magnetic). It was my first money-sorting party in the Scrooge McDuck tradition. The value of the coins came to $2,100.00. If my accountant phoned to say he'd found a tax break for $2,100, I'd be in a good mood, but it wouldn't feel like *treasure*. Good accountants should hide bags of rebate money all around your house. Imagine the joy they could bring to people.

⊗

Worrying about money is one of the worst worries. It's like having locked-in syndrome, except you're still moving around and doing things. Your head burns. If other people are not having money problems, it pisses you off because it reminds you that you're limited in the ways you can express your agency in the world, and they aren't. Worrying about money is anger-inducing because it makes you think about time: how many dollars per hour, how much salary per year, how many years until retirement. Worrying about money forces you to do endless math in your head, and most people didn't like math in high school and they don't like it now.

⊗

People will do weird things for weird amounts of money. At the opening of a show of mine in Vancouver, the gallery's fundraisers asked if there was something people could do to earn a ten-dollar coupon from Starbucks, one of the show's sponsors. I arranged a pile of red Lego into a twenty-foot strip and called it the "Lego Walk of Fire." You couldn't get your coupon until you walked across it without shoes. It was pretty popular, but then we noticed that if you put out less Lego, it was actually much more painful to traverse, which made it irresistible. There's a marketing lesson there.

⊗

I'm not a Mormon but I admire Mormonism as a religion. They get things done, they dress nicely and they don't seem that preachy. I also like them because they believe that the two things that separate human beings from everything else in the universe is that human beings have free will and the perception of time's passing. I think this sums up a fundamental aspect of humanity on Earth—and maybe that's as basic as philosophy gets. So I got to thinking that perhaps that's what money is: a crystallization—or, rather, a *homogenization*—of time and free will into those things we call dollars and pounds and yen and euros. Money multiplies your time. It also expands your agency and broadens the number of things you can do accordingly. Big-time lottery winners haven't won ten million dollars—they've won ten thousand person-years of time to do pretty much anything they want anywhere on Earth. Windfalls are like the crystal meth version of time and free will.

Time and free will. I've mentioned this before, but it's true: if you ask people over fifty which they would rather have, more time or more money, almost every person will choose time over money. But what would they select if they could choose between more money and more free will? We know the answer to that question: it's called Scandinavia.

The Great Money
Flush of 2016

Last week I was making a collage that included the sacrifice of a one-dollar bill for the sake of art. A friend watching me do this made a horrified face and said, "But the government could punish you if they caught you destroying money!" I quickly corrected her assumption. From the government's point of view, a dollar bill destroyed is a dollar bill the government no longer needs to back. Nothing would make the Treasury Department happier than people around the world setting fire to boxcars full of money—basically, bonfires like that would be a massive cash gift to the nation.

Then I got to thinking about boxcars full of money—more specifically, I got to thinking of places around the world where one might find truckloads of cash to burn. I couldn't think of any boxcars per se, nor could I think of, say, a Scrooge McDuck money bin. But what I do know is that around the planet are perhaps millions of suitcases and sacks and boxes filled with American dollars, much of it denominated in one hundreds. What if one were to magically destroy all of that cash? Out of the blue the Treasury Department would earn perhaps trillions of dollars for doing absolutely nothing.

At first this idea struck me as fanciful, but then I fleshed it out. What if the government were to have, say, a "currency flush"? Basically, it would announce that, as of January 1, 2017, it would no longer honour any hundred-dollar bill printed before December 31, 2013. People around the world with socks and suitcases and safety deposit boxes full of hundreds would have two years to redeem or spend their cash, quickly. What would happen?

Well, such a currency flush wouldn't necessarily affect everyday people too much. People who work in bakeries, teach high school or drive taxis tend not to have suitcases full of hundreds in their universe—nor to have much sympathy for those who do. But for those people who do have stashes, there would be a two-year window to convert this cash into services and tangible goods. The problem here is that it looks very, very suspicious to walk into a Mercedes-Benz dealership and buy an S-Class with $87,000 in cash. Or to buy a Montauk summer house for millions. Or a boat. Or jewels. Or anything, really. Discreetly divesting oneself of soon-to-be valueless hundreds would actually require great skill. At the very least, suitcase owners would be eating at expensive restaurants, buying first-class plane tickets and living it up for two brief years. What a boon to the economy for zero effort! And near the end of the flush, there might be a huge bump in the number of thousand-dollar lap dances and bar tips—but then that revenue would have to be recorded and taxed. More money in the coffers!

The Great Currency Flush would give the US economy a defibrillation of unparalleled voltage, but of course there would have to be a few rules. For example, you couldn't just take a hundred-dollar bill to the bank and say, "Give me five twenties." Once set in motion, the flush would demand that hundreds be used in only one go. You could buy a pack of gum with a hundred, but you wouldn't get back any change—so why not instead buy a hundred bucks' worth of gum? The people selling the gum, in the meantime, would have to document where the hundreds came from— not that hard to do. It's also not hard to imagine many, many books in many, many places being very, very cooked. Yet overall, even given the biggest one-time-only spending spree in history, enormous chunks of money would go unredeemed. Imagine the number of suitcases out there parked by people now long dead—or people who are, um, in jail and won't be able to get out their shovels and retrieve their trove.

Sure, there would be attempted workarounds. Go to Las Vegas, buy a million dollars' worth of chips and then cash them in. Buy $500,000 worth of gift certificates at Saks and then shop up a storm. But workarounds like those would be easy to predict and just as easy to cut off at the pass.

Would such a flush be ethical? Why wouldn't it be? The government's not saying the money is valueless. It's just saying you have two years to spend it or go to the bank to redeem old hundreds for new hundreds. Except who's going to go to a bank to redeem a duffle bag full of hundreds? Perhaps someone stupid. The government is trying to flush out all the zombie money—not unreasonable—while giving itself something of a financial enema at the same time.

It's hard to imagine much collective political anger being wasted by the masses in support of that one percent or so with boxloads of money. After all, people got those suitcases full of money by doing, um . . . *whatever it was it took to get it*. I'm sure they have receipts for all of it. Why wouldn't they?

Ick

Money is kind of disgusting if you think about it too much. It's like keeping tiny little hotel bedspreads in your wallet. God only knows where those banknotes have been. If this were a movie, this would be the point where we insert a montage sequence of Wall Streeters snorting coke, and crack-den habitués finding a tenner in the back crevice of a sofa, albeit glued to a thong and a hypodermic needle by God only knows what cementing agent.

Money is fun. I remember being in the rooftop lounge of Sydney's Intercontinental hotel and drinking with some Americans and looking at Australia's paper currency, which at the time, a decade ago, was in the world's vanguard of banknote design: it had a transparent window, holograms, a special chip that activated a smartphone *son et lumière* of Nicole Kidman's career trajectory. I told my new American friends I was from Canada and that Canada actually had the world's first banknote portraying somebody smoking a cigarette, Camilla.

They: Seriously?
Me: Oh yes. It was part of a deal Charles struck with the
     Queen to get her blessing on their marriage.
They: That's so free and open-minded!
Me: [Silently amazed at humanity's gullibility.]

———

Canada recently got rid of pennies. They vanished without a sound and, the moment they were gone, nobody missed them. Nobody even thought about them, and if they did, it was along the lines of, "Thank Christ those effing pennies are gone." Then last month I was in the United States and bought something and got pennies back in my change and it was like . . . time travel. Why are you people still using these things? Why would anybody want them? They exist solely to perpetuate their own existence. A big post-penny trend in Canada is people making floors out of pennies and resin, except the pennies vary in sheen from one to another, and when you put them all down, they look not only like useless pennies that you hate, but they also have that soiled-hotel-bedspread look of paper money. Worst of all worlds. Poor penny floors.

Women might not realize this, but guys inherit their father's taste in wallets. This is to say, if your father had a huge, overfilled black leather job packed with receipts and business cards and filthy banknotes, then chances are you, as a grown-up son, are going to channel the exact same wallet, sometimes held closed by thick rubber bands and looking, in your front pants pocket, like you're shoplifting a clubhouse sandwich. The only way to avoid this curse is to adopt extreme measures: the Euro Wallet, a sleek rectangle made from the finest leather and capable of handling, at most, one business card, one Amex card and one and a half hotel bedspreads. Add a family photo or a lottery ticket, and the whole thing blows up.

Canada stopped making its one-dollar bill in 1987, replacing it with an eleven-sided brass-coloured coin bearing the image of a loon, hence its nickname, "the loonie." I can't think of a stupider name for something monetary but, once you get used to it, it's like saying Google, and no longer feels so dumb. Then in 1996 Canada stopped making its two-dollar bill, replacing it with a bimetal coin called, yes, the toonie. And yet, somehow life manages to go on in the face of the onslaught of all these ignominies. I miss the two-dollar bill. It was handy and somehow far easier to work with than the toonie, which is like a dense, unnecessarily large Norwegian coin used for yuletide shenanigans involving striped stockings, gingerbread and fjords.

In modern times the Americans tried introducing a one-dollar coin, the dismal failure known as the Susan B. Anthony dollar, named after a suffrage campaigner who, when you see her face on the coin, looks as if she wants nothing more than to administer you an enema. What was the mint thinking?

I mean, if you're trying to wean your citizens off expensive-to-replace paper currency, give them something they might prefer having in their pockets: Marilyn Monroe, Joan Jett, Wilma Flintstone. I'm not a marketer but I can tell you those three would have been infinitely more successful out in the world.

After the Susan B. Anthony fiasco, the mint was left with a populace scarred and wary of further tampering with their day-to-day currencies. To get a one-dollar coin off the ground in the United States today would require nothing less than a full reunion of Fleetwood Mac (*circa Rumours*) with a real-time holographic depiction of the band's reunion tour. Let's not forget that people are demanding more from their currency these days. The new Canadian twenty is a high-tech marvel: one-quarter transparent, it contains no culturally offensive references of any kind, and features a stern photo of the Queen contemplating having to eat Christmas dinner at the Middletons'.

And then there's bitcoin. Should it ever get fully off the ground in a material way, all I ask is that they focus-group a little bit and then, having gone through the motions, just put Elvis on the damn thing.

Grexit

Okay, just look at the following words: *Grexit. Syriza. Tsipras. Merkel. Austerity.* At first glance they don't even look like words; they resemble, I don't know . . . launch codes—or maybe the names of recently FDA-approved osteoporosis medications—and yet at the moment these words are some of the most freighted in the language. Unlike most new words, they have the potential to demarcate the end of one era and the start of another.

◑

Let's have a quick peek at the Greek economy. Greece is odd because it's an ostensibly middle-class place with a twist: it's a warmer, slower-paced version of other middle-class societies in the liberal democratic West. Miami? Not quite. Santiago? Too young. San Antonio, Texas? Nope. Greek citizens still pretty much do normal middle-class things and they live middle-class lives, and yet when you look at the Greek economy, it turns out Greece doesn't really do anything. There's no tech or manufacturing or large-scale agribusiness; it's just islands and hotels and many, many people with pensions, and ATMs that only dispense cash to non-Greeks. This is not meant to be disparaging, and if you read further, you'll understand this. It also makes you wonder, *Well then, just how* were *these people filling their days?*

◑

"Hi! I'm Greece! I'm the happy, sunny Shirley Valentine country, where the living is easy and your days are filled with nothing if not the absence of labour. There's ouzo. There's outdoor chess. And for tourists there's an ever-present whiff of the possibility of sex with people out of your league."

🌗

Okay then, Greece doesn't really make or do anything the way other European nations do . . . but there's definitely large-scale tourism, and a bit of agriculture. And what's wrong with that? Light drinking. Outdoor chess games. Political arguments. Men dancing together. Sun. Life in Greece has always sounded great, and when we think of retirement, Greece's *dolce far niente* is often what springs to mind. Doing nothing all day? Life in Greece isn't even utopia; it's heaven. So then, what's the problem?

🌗

During Argentina's 1998–2002 financial crisis, vast chunks of its middle class were violently burped out of the nation's economy. At the time it happened, these people didn't realize that they were being permanently burped out of the middle class. The years rolled on and all those Brooks Brothers button-down shirts from the 1997 trip to New York grew ever more threadbare. The leather Coach handbag from the 1996 trip to Miami faded. And eventually: "Honey, I think it's over."

And it was.

The social devastation in Argentina never fully registered in the northern hemisphere, but now Greece is one Grexit away from Argentinian-style demiddleclassification, and this time it's registering the world over. Greece is sort of like a social terrarium from which all the money, like oxygen, is being extracted. The folks putting the lid back on top of the terrarium are giving each other guilty looks while hoping that the ensuing slow, protracted death of Greece's financial ecosystem won't be overly filled with audible screams of angry, dying little Greeks.

◐

Another metaphor: Greece is a financial car crash that's blocked traffic for miles, so when you finally drive past, you've earned your right to rubberneck, and in your head you're also thinking, *God, I'm glad it wasn't me.* And the seemingly inevitable Grexit makes us all ask ourselves, "Who's next?" But not just in a short-term Portugal-Spain-Ireland domino-effect way. Our pondering is existential, more like, *When does the overall system that supports middle-class democracy eventually end? Just why is it that only the existence of a large, complacent middle class represents both the health and validity of a society?* We seem to equate middle-class existence with existence itself.

◐

Greek society is intricate and complex, and it would appear one must be born into it to comprehend its intricacies, but just because it can't meet fiscal benchmarks established in Brussels doesn't make it less of a society. Since when is the value of any society judged by the robustness of its capitalism? Why can't we look at Greece's reasonably comfortable, mildly underoccupied life as a sort of utopia instead of The Death of Western Society? Maybe what we see in Greece is actually a dark precursor to what we envision for ourselves down the road.

To be discussed.

So okay then, Greece leaves the euro zone, or the euro zone leaves Greece. In that scenario would Athens become the new New Delhi? Would everyone have to hand in their Lacoste shirts and iPhones to receive a box of Nestlé tinned meal-substitutes, and sit in communal theatres to watch TED talks projected onto bedsheets? Does Greece enter class warfare? But wait—Greece doesn't really seem to be a one-percent-y country; Greeks all seem to more or less be in the same boat, so there aren't that many heads you can chop off and put onto stakes.

What would it mean for Greece to no longer be middle-class? It wouldn't be really blue-collar or working-class either, because there's no work available in which to be working-class. Would everyone sit around all day, nursing a single cup of coffee while discussing Marianne Faithfull's vocal tracks in *Broken English*? Would everyone go out and riot? But riot for what? More money? There *is* no more money. More respect? You've *got* respect . . . You just don't have any more money. Do you put your entire country up on eBay? Do you Airbnb every single residence in the country? Emigrate to England or Denmark, where they still have a Middle-Class Classic™?

The global middle class, just like Alaskan glaciers, is melting away at an extraordinary rate, and we very much need to rebrand the successor of the middle-class society as utopian—or at least suck the dread out of it and strip it of *horror vacui*. Greece is telling us this. Greece is the new template for the rest of the Western world. Greece forces us to worry about the new world order where an invisible high-tech conveyor belt relentlessly replaces formerly middle-class workers with machine intelligence, taking us all into a world of perpetual clicking, linking, embedding and liking. Greece forces us to worry about the abrupt vanishing of a social structure so old we don't even see it as a social structure but, rather, a universal right. But it's not. It's as artificial as aspartame.

☉

The Greeks are now involuntarily moving from the position of being a society of tacit off-the-books euro-subsidized leisure into a culture of borderline mandatory inactivity. That's a subtle shift. Until recently Greeks were able to spend their days doing nothing, which was nice; now they have to spend their days with nothing to do, which is scary. Greece is beginning to feel, if anything, like a J.G. Ballard novel about a dystopian future in which leisure becomes a cruel monkey's-paw curse. You're still doing basically the same nothing as before, except now, instead of being pleasant, it becomes terrifying. I mean, really, how is it that something as wonderful as life in Greece has become a new definition of societal hell? The Adriatic weather's great, and potatoes and lamb ought to be reasonably cheap and readily available. Add booze and it's fantastic. Do you *really* want a massive Siemens optical fibre facility in your neighbourhood? And would Siemens ever conceive of building one there? I mean, really, think about it. Would they? And would the Greeks in-their-bones actually want it?

☉

Let's discuss doing nothing. Doing nothing means doing *nothing*. It means being offline and walking down a street and . . . simply walking down the street. It means sitting on a bench for ten minutes, or however long, without crumbling and looking at your latest electronic whatever. It sounds simple, but almost nobody does nothing anymore; the hallmark of our age is the impossibility of doing nothing. Our attention spans are so thoroughly colonized by the cloud that even brief separation from the linked universe causes dread and something akin to homesickness. Maybe twenty years ago people were good at doing nothing. These days people are hopeless at it.

Now let's discuss "having nothing to do." It means waking up, thinking about the day ahead and realizing that you have, well . . . *nothing to do.* No job. No way of earning a living. Maybe you'll go out with friends in similar straits, and maybe you'll do a massage for a foreign hotel guest at the Athens Marriott. Torch an Uber Mercedes. The night goes on. You have a drink back in your apartment. Then maybe some Netflix.

Sleep.

Repeat.

◉

Until recently you either had something to do called a job and you did it—or you were unemployed and had nothing to do and you more or less meditated all day, possibly about being unemployed, but maybe also wondering about the seagull that just flew over your head, or maybe about the meaning of the end of the film *2001: A Space Odyssey.* Being unemployed twenty-five years ago wasn't so much a capitalist state of being as it was an existential state of being: "Hi—I'm unemployed, and because of this I'm probably more contemplative than people who are employed."

Enter the cloud.

◉

Let's discuss earthly paradise. Let's discuss utopias. Utopias don't have to be all about comfort and luxury. Growing up on the west coast of Canada, I saw group after group of hippies head up the coast to create utopian communes, which almost always went kaput the moment the women figured out they were doing all the work while the guys were out smoking weed in the hammocks. Or look at ISIS. They took a desert and its aging cities and rebranded the place as a form of utopia, generating meaning in a place where little existed before. It's hardly life onboard a Carnival Cruise liner, but people seem to be flocking to join. Meanwhile, migrants are swarming the Chunnel entrance at Calais, Africans are drowning trying to reach the Sardinian coast, Syrians are arriving by the tens of thousands like migrating birds, and Afghans are walking thousands of miles to reach the cabbage fields of Hungary— their jumping off point to the rest of Europe. Most of the world still sees Europe as a utopia, but the Europeans don't. They see themselves as stagnant and somewhat rudderless, but at least they've got something to do.

Having something to do seems to be an important aspect of a utopia being a utopia, whether it's building Airbuses or beheading people. At least you know what you're doing when you wake up in the morning. British novelist Susan Ertz said, "Millions long for immortality who don't know what to do on a rainy Sunday afternoon." It's true. Busy is better.

◑

Tourism, which is an engineered short-term utopia—as well as Greece's strongest business card—now also fosters a great irony for the Greeks. It enforces confrontation between people who come to the country to do nothing, and those locals who now have nothing to do—which has to be galling. But remember, Greece is just now reaching a place where we're all going to be sooner or later, a world of massive labour obsolescence where unless you actually know how to do something useful, you'll become one more piece of middle-class space junk. Don't forget, while people in the West see the erosion of the middle class as downward mobility, for most of the world, getting online with Android devices to comparison shop for Martha Stewart towels is proof positive they're on the way up. It's just that everyone on Earth is reaching a new middle, and we're still unclear where that middle will be and what it will look and feel like.

Rich people *especially* want to know what the remains of the middle class will morph into, but in the end they won't get there first because they have access to the same information that you and I do. If Bill Gates can be blindsided by search engines and mobile devices, then anyone can be blindsided by anything.

Modern people are largely incapable of doing nothing the way we discussed earlier—walking down the street and simply looking at the world around us. Omnipresent cloud-fuelled devices devour our attention spans. We're all deeply, deeply into the shredded-attention-span paradigm and, let's face it, it's not going to go away—nor do we want it to.

At the same time, we inhabit an age of massive and extreme unknowns, lurking in time and space both nearby and far away. Look! Mr. Putin is dangling a clump of grapes over the mouths of austerity weary Athenians. Look! China wants to turn Greece into a Double Lucky Golden Prosperity Node. Look! Global warming just destroyed this year's grape crop.

Our new world is defined by a duality of fear and diversion. Non-stop online diversion is palliative; it manages to make a world of extreme unknowns bearable. Diversion, in turn, makes having nothing to do okay. Diversion has become our new solace.

And all those tourists who came to Greece to do nothing? They're *not* doing nothing. They're just as trapped in the new duality as anyone else. It's irony squared.

The twentieth century? Those were the days, my friend. Enter, please, the twenty-first-century schizoid man.

World War $

Here follow a few thoughts that, in the end, link together to form a chain . . .

(1) Last weekend I realized that I've played the board game Monopoly maybe twenty or thirty times in my life, yet I don't remember anyone actually *winning* a game. I don't remember anyone ever saying, "There. I have officially won and the game is now officially over." Instead I mostly remember bored, irritated people drifting away to get a snack, answer the phone or what have you, and never returning. In the end there's the last person at the board, counting money and feeling fleetingly rich, but of course the game is over and the money and its thrill are void.

(2) A few months back a Canadian semi-trailer loaded with oil drilling equipment was driving south along Washington's Interstate 5, halfway between Seattle and Vancouver, Canada. The over-height truck struck a critical steel span on the Skagit River Bridge in the town of Burlington, causing a section of the bridge to collapse, shutting down Interstate 5 for a month until a temporary bridge was erected. Interstate 5 is a critical trucking link between Canada and the United States, and its entry point into Canada is the second-largest road freight link between the two countries. The collapse of the bridge foregrounded the often embarrassing state

of much of North America's infrastructure, which is, by any standards, one of the biggest elephants in the rooms of power.

(3) In the world of optical fibre communications, there is a phenomenon called "latency." Latency describes the fact that if an optical fibre goes from Chicago to New York, it probably travels not in a straight line but rather in a series of right angles and switchbacks and zigzags. An optical fibre cable travelling in a nearly straight line between the two cities would, however, allow the signals it carries to arrive in New York a few millionths of a second faster than the zigzagging line. This is latency. Those few millionths of a second would, in the computerized world of stock sales, give a minuscule but distinct advantage to the people with the straighter cable. Michael Lewis wrote a wonderful book, *Flash Boys*, on this topic.

(4) There has been in our culture, in the past decade in particular, a group of reasonably smart people who hired incredibly smart people—mathematicians mostly—to design algorithms that exploit time-space phenomena such as latency, as well as other small yet distinct phenomena, in order to vacuum insane amounts of money out of the economy by doing *absolutely nothing* except exploiting systemic flaws in the digitized financial world. We're talking about *hundreds of billions* of dollars, if not *trillions*, simply from hiring bright grad students, hurling some cash and some lap dances at them, and then hitting the return key.

(5) We all remember the night of the crash of 2008, especially when the Dow went below seven thousand, when it seemed like money was going to actually stop working. And by

saying "stop working" I don't mean simply "not going to be worth as much as it once was"; I mean that money itself would simply cease to function. It would be not just damaged but *broken beyond the point of fixability*. For a day or two there, more people than just me were mentally picturing well-dressed, seemingly healthy adult human beings walking the world's streets like zombies, trying to buy gasoline, groceries, sofas, plane tickets and what have you, except money no longer works. It's over.

(6) Money is more than a massively consensual IOU note. It is a piece of infrastructure and as artificial as Interstate 5, NutraSweet and season six of *Mad Men*. If money is not maintained, it can collapse like a bridge over Interstate 5, and fixing it could take years, during which time God only knows how much more financial damage will occur.

Me having photons faster than yours by a few millionths of a second is enough to make me appallingly rich—again, for doing *absolutely nothing* except hacking into money itself.

Puke.

It's hard to have respect for this kind of system. Often the latency issue is presented to the public as a "Wow, isn't this cool!" moment when, in fact, it's sickening, and it's partially why the world began to feel so one-percent-ish five years ago. Reasonably smart people who inhabit the Agè of Latency are milking those still stuck in the pre-latent era.

(7) In 2007 and 2008 we came perilously close to killing money, exposing in the process how out-of-date the financial infrastructure has become. The very smart people who looted billions from the economy got a slap on the wrist and are doubtlessly, as you read these words, trawling through the

graduate rosters of MIT and Caltech, looking for newer, fresher latencies. And there's possibly a parallel universe out there alongside this one, where things didn't go quite so well in the end, where money really was broken to the point of unfixability. It's a Monopoly game where the game just sort of ended one day and nobody was quite sure why.

The Man Who
Lost His Story

There was once a man who lost his story. His name was Craig and he looked just like you, and his life was quite similar to yours too—except that somewhere during his life, he lost his story. By this I mean he lost the sense that his life had a beginning, a middle and an end. I know, yes, we're all born and we all do stuff and then we die, but somewhere in there are the touch points that define our stories: first love, a brush with death, a scientific insight, a yen to climb tall mountains—and then we die. The story of our lives is usually long over before we die, and we spend our twilight years warming our hands on the embers of memory. Craig's problem was that he got to a point—thirty-eight, say—when he realized that none of his dots connected to make a larger picture: a few unsatisfying and doomed relationships; a job so dull a chimp could perform it; no hobbies that could be teased and stretched into larger, more vital ways of living life.

His lack of story seemed to be of the which-came-first-the-chicken-or-the-egg variety. For example, he thought that if he learned how to hang-glide, then maybe his life's story could begin there—an adventure! Perhaps there would be a mystical moment up in the sky! But wait—in order to have such adventures, Craig would have to be *into* hang-gliding to begin with. If he rushed out and chose an activity at random, would he now have a meaningful experience? As Craig wasn't actually into anything, he was trapped in the chicken-egg loop. Where to start? And how? He felt that his attempts to generate a life story were futile.

Craig decided to go to the Learning Annex and sign up for hang-gliding lessons anyway, but the woman who took his application form looked at him and said, "You're not really into hang-gliding, are you? You just want to do it so that you can imagine your life is a story."

"How did you know that?"

"It's pretty much all you get in a job like this: people like you walking in and hoping they can push a button and suddenly their lives become stories. You should hear my friend Phyllis, who works down the hall accepting forms for whitewater rafting excursions."

Craig walked away, his shoulders slumped, once again troubled that his life had no narrative to it. He was back to being Craig, the Guy Who Merely Existed.

On his way back to his apartment, posters and billboards and light boards showed people being sexy and fun and charismatic as they enjoyed beaches and ski slopes and parties that were filled with people who looked much like Craig or his sister, Heather. The exciting lives of all these billboard people weighed heavily on Craig, and when he got home he called a few friends (who, it must be said, felt sorry for Craig, but not *too* sorry). One of them said, "I mean, Craig, let's say you break a leg. Fine, that's a real problem that you can fix. Or your wallet gets stolen—you can replace it. But losing the narrative of your life? Dude, that's pretty sad."

Of course, the moment Craig hung up from speaking with his friends, they all went online and trashed him behind his back. All 93,441 of Craig's official online social networking friends and buddies sent disloyal texts along the lines of "Gee, I'm Craig— look at me! I'm so superfantastic and groovy that my life has to be a story," or "Yessiree, that's me, 168 pounds of animal magnetism in search of an empire to conquer, an empire without borders, a kingdom filled with endless new battles to be waged and won . . . not.

Craig went back to the Learning Annex the next day to sign up for Tae Bo, and the woman remembered him. "You're the guy whose life has no story. How's it going?"

"Not too well, thank you. I thought maybe Tae Bo would lend my life a unique narrative edge."

The woman—whose name was Bev—said, "Craig, the hardest things in the world are being unique and having your life be a story. In the old days it was much easier, but our modern fame-driven culture with its real-time 24/7 marinade of electronic information demands a lot from modern citizens, and poses great obstacles to narrative. Truly modern citizens are both charismatic and can respond only to other people with charisma. To survive, people need to become self-branding charisma robots. Yet, ironically, society mocks and punishes people who aspire to that state. I really wouldn't be surprised if your friends were making fun of you behind your back, Craig."

"Really?"

"Really. So, in a nutshell, given the current media composition of the world, you're pretty much doomed to being uninteresting and storyless."

"But I could blog my life! Couldn't I turn it into a story that way?"

"Blogs? Sorry, but all those blogs and vlogs or whatevers out there—they just make being unique harder. The more truths you spill out, the more generic you become."

"All I want is for my life to be a story!"

"Did you read a lot of books growing up?"

"Yes."

"Ah. Well, there you go. Books turn people into isolated individuals, and once that's happened, the road only grows rockier. Books wire you to want to be Steve McQueen, but the world wants you to be SMcQ23667bot@hotmail.com."

There was a fifteen-second patch of silence. Craig said, "Isn't it weird that Hotmail accounts still exist?"

"It really is," said Bev.

Craig stood there and finally said, "So, you know what? I'll pass on the Tae Bo."

"Right. How about Calligraphy and Menu Design?"

"Pass."

"Okay. But keep us in mind."

Craig walked away, angry that the modern world had conspired to force him into thinking in its manner rather than the other way around. How cruel that mankind was forced to conform to the global electronic experience. But all other options had vanished. There no longer existed a country to escape to (*country*—what a quaint notion) where people read books and had lives that became stories. Everyone's life had become a crawl that dragged across the bottom of a massive TV screen in an empty airport lounge that smelled like disinfectant, bar mix and lousy tips.

When Craig got home, he had 243,559 emails from friends and links that gently gave him an epoke in the ribs about his selfish desire to have his life be a story. Some of the emails were serious, some were snarky and some were scammy, demanding that he sign a legal document before useful ideas on how to get a story were sent his way.

After he ate dinner, Craig's doorbell rang and it was the Channel Three News Team, putting together a weekend think-piece, "The Man Whose Life Had No Story." Craig thought, *Maybe this is something hopeful in disguise.* But mostly the News Team just asked him who he thought might play him in the movie of his life and if he'd gained or lost any weight lately. He chased them out of his apartment.

Desperate, he went back the next day to see Bev. Surely someone in a position like hers would have insights and ideas he could apply to his situation.

"You again," said Bev. "I was expecting this."

"Really?"

"I'm assuming you want to take drastic action, then."

"Yes."

"Come with me." Bev put a Closed sign in front of her window and beckoned Craig to follow her down the hall.

After making many left and right turns and after passing through above- and below-ground tunnels, they ended up at a large, hospital-ish door covered with warnings and a request that visitors use a sterilizing gel on their hands before entering.

"We're here," said Bev, opening the door; she and Craig entered. It was a lab of some sort that seemed to share space with a theatre department. Wires and pressure gauges and digital meters existed alongside caveman outfits, Sir Lancelot costumes and old coins. It was a mess.

Craig asked, "What's this about?"

Bev said, "This is your one chance to get a good story going in your life."

"Really? This? I've never acted before, and I was never good at science."

"No need to worry. Neither skill is required. But if you sign this form here, we can get you set up."

The form was a two-hundred-page document titled "Story-Capture via Anachronic Transference." Craig signed the contract's final page while Bev nodded. She then took the document away from Craig and issued a two-finger whistle. From the wings appeared three muscular goons. Bev said, "We've got another one, boys. And don't go easy on him. He needs a story real bad."

The goons proceeded to wallop the daylights out of Craig. They clubbed him with aluminum baseball bats, ripped off all his clothes, poured some sort of chemical into one of his eyes and then tossed him into a scientific device that resembled an Apollo space capsule.

"How far back are we going to send him, Bev?"

Bev said, "Let's send him to the thirteenth century." She twiddled a knob.

"*Where?*" Craig shouted, his voice riddled with pain.

"The thirteenth century. They're running low on people there, so every extra soul we send them is a big help." She looked to one of her goons. "Bartholomew, throw some peasant rags into the time chamber."

Bartholomew tossed rags into the chamber.

"Shut the door!"

Bartholomew shut the door.

Craig was beating on the capsule's little window. "Let me out of here!"

Bev smiled and shouted, "Craig, you'll love it there! All they do is feed goats and wait for troubadours to pass through the village and tell them lies in the form of stories."

"But what am I supposed to *do* there?"

"You'll be a peasant! You've got a role to fulfill! Just be sure to worship and defend whoever owns you!"

"And the clergy!" added Bartholomew.

"Yes," shouted Bev. "And the clergy. We crippled you a bit so that you'll fit in better once you arrive! Your teeth are kind of nice, though—you might want to break one."

"But I don't want to—"

Whoosh! The time machine gleamed and Craig was whisked back to the thirteenth century.

A tear fell from Bev's eye, and Bartholomew asked her why.

"I'm so jealous," she said. "He gets to go back in time and be real and hang with real people having real lives. Us? We're stuck here in this perpetual nothingness."

"Not to worry," said Bartholomew. "I'll take you out for Japanese tonight. And afterwards I've got two new Woody Allen movies lined up. Oh, I forgot—have you got next week's plane tickets for Hawaii confirmed?"

"You bet."

"Ah, the modern world," said Bartholomew. "So empty. So dreary."

"If only our lives could be stories like Craig's." Bev sighed and looked at Bartholomew. "You're smiling—why?"

"Because I thought you deserved a treat, so I had your Corvette detailed today."

"Oh, Bartholomew, you're the best."

And thus our story has a happy ending.

The Valley

I've found that if you ask most anyone to locate Silicon Valley on a globe, they pause for about fifteen seconds, say *umm*, and then hesitantly put their finger down somewhere a little bit north of Los Angeles. They then apologize for being clueless and ask where it really is—and they're often surprised that it's up near San Francisco. I think for most people, Silicon Valley is largely a state of mind more than it is a real place—a strip-malled Klondike of billionaires with proprioception issues, clad in khakis in groups of three, awkwardly lumbering across a six-lane traffic artery with a grass median, all to get in on the two-for-one burrito special at Chili's before the promotion ends next Tuesday.

I've many happy memories of the Valley. One afternoon, in a long-ago world called Before 9/11, I'd park my car just inside Menlo Park, the Valley's venture-capital capital, on the other side of Interstate 280, just west of the Sand Hill Road exit. Walking through what seemed to be a Christmas-tree farm, I'd arrive at a chain-link fence with a Department of Energy warning sign, duck through one of its many breaches and sit beside the Stanford Linear Accelerator,* two miles long and operational until 1966. I don't know what I was expecting to see, but it was nice to lie in the grass like Tom Sawyer and imagine baryon asymmetry and positrons committing suicide while a Cooper's hawk soared high above, scoping out the 280 for roadkill.

---

* Now the SLAC National Accelerator Laboratory

I remember the month the Segway came out and an annoyingly rich Palo Alto friend (who lived in a massive apartment furnished only with a folding lawn chair, a card table and a $500,000 flight simulator) bought a fleet of ten. That night a group of us held a ride up Page Mill Road to the parking lot of the now closed *Wall Street Journal* printing plant, and then we started off-roading over the endless berms that define the Valley's aesthetic. Talk about a dork-fest . . . but it was fun. What else? . . . I remember encountering, in Mountain View, one of the most beautiful things I've ever seen. It was near the remains of an old shopping mall being bulldozed to make way for yet another mirror-walled tech HQ. The mall's escalator had been removed and dumped onto the parking lot. A guy in a crane was picking it up in his machine's teeth and flinging it around like it was a pearl necklace—a moment of pure joy, and in a poetic way, a metaphor for up and down class mobility in San Jose, Cupertino, Mountain View, Palo Alto and Menlo Park.

It's the money that makes the Valley sexy, because there's otherwise not very much that's sexy about what goes on there. Tech is tech; cables and routers are cables and routers. But wait. Tesla is sexy. Xapo is kind of sexy. And Houzz is fun. But having said all this, my Bay Area friend Liz continues to write a novel titled *Founderfucker*, which is about the mothers and daughters of patrician East Coast families going through elaborate rituals to snag socially clueless Valley tech workers with vast amounts of stock—preferably company founders. Get in, have two kids, punch out and . . . you're a billionaire! It's cynical, but at the same time it's a real thing, all those girls from Brown and Sarah Lawrence, in lambswool sweaters, bored witless, sitting at the kitchen counter, asking earnest questions about motherboards and retail data encryption as they wait for their ten-year stints to come to an end.

Last summer I enjoyed participating in a seminar at Singularity University, an unaccredited school founded in 2008 by Ray

Kurzweil and Peter Diamandis. Singularity U's goal is to get the correct people fully informed about the transformative capacity of logarithmic technologies. It rests in an office building in NASA's Ames Research Center, a building seemingly untouched since one foggy 1944 afternoon when The Andrews Sisters came in and sang for the boys. Ames's runways are now used only a few times a day, by NASA, Lockheed Martin Space Systems, Air Force One, the Santa Clara County Sheriff's Department's helicopters and Google staff. Yes, Google has its own airport, smack in the middle of one of the planet's most insanely expensive real estate markets. Go, Google! Google is also currently adding more than a million square feet to its Googleplex, on property leased from the Ames facility. It's as if the airport's land is a sort of portal into ascendant technologies: aviation, NASA, search engines. Next? Teleportation. Time travel. Cold fusion. Flying donkeys.

People are a bit afraid of the Valley. We all now live on the vertical asymptote of technological history: every new day, God only knows how many powerful and transformative technologies are being dumped into the world—new inventions that simultaneously complicate and flatten our lives—and we're all just barely managing to hold on as it is. When people look at that little bit of land just below San Francisco, they're not just looking at a city or town; they're looking at wizardry, transmutation and borderline magic. We all love our iPhones and laptops and GPS devices and everything else that defines modern life, but we're spooked by the king's magicians. Are they good or are they evil? And do they spend much time thinking about outsiders putting their fingers on the wrong part of the map?

3½ Fingers

When the former White House chief of staff Mr. Jack Lew was made US Secretary of the Treasury, his signature began to appear on American currency. Unfortunately, his signature resembles the loops we all make when testing a ballpoint pen and there was an uproar loud enough that Lew ultimately had to create a new signature that was more currency-friendly.

My signature is as bad as Lew's was. Like most people, I invented a signature in my teens that I'm now stuck with for life. It's a horrible glyph I barely remember creating. It bugs me that the gesture that defines me in the written world was designed by a self-absorbed fifteen-year-old sitting at the back of math class, bored out of his mind. With the general decline of cursive script, signatures are, along with graffiti, one of the few remaining personal gestures that remain in our culture.

Cursive script. I recently gave the daughter of a friend, twenty-two, a bottle of wine in return for helping me on a small project. I hand-scripted a thank-you note along with it, but her face went blank when she opened it. I asked what was wrong and she said, "I can't read . . . *squiggles*." Chalk up another win for digital technologies.

I have beautiful handwriting, but it's a lot of work, *and* I have to be in the right mood to deploy this handwriting, and its content has to merit a personal touch—thank-you notes or birthday cards. My handwriting is beautiful because, starting in my thirties, I worked hard at fixing it. An insouciant Vancouver school system had left me and my cohorts with a scrawl like Adrian Mole *circa* age twelve and one-eighth. You could practically see the pimples in every stroke.

Fun fact: I'm left-handed, which has always made cursive script a challenge. Oddly, when I need to write anything larger than six inches high, such as on a chalkboard, I become a right-handed person—the letters suddenly turn into objects and they want to be navigated by a different part of my brain.

I'm also not a good typer. I'm a three-and-a-half-fingered typer, using mostly index fingers with a dash of thumbs on the space bar. I'm also pig lazy. Typing may be less work than handwriting, but even so, if I want to put out words, I only ever want to type them once.

In 1998 I was in a Brussels hotel and my laptop died. To meet a deadline I used the hotel's business centre. I sat down to work and . . . it was like I'd had a stroke: none of the Benelux keyboard keys were in their correct spot. I gave up after three sentences. It was worse than difficult; it was impossible, infinitely more difficult than back when I taught myself to type (badly) in my late teens. My brain couldn't do it.

Four years ago I noticed I was making far more mistakes than usual while typing on my Mac laptop—clumsy, embarrassing errors—and I was worried: *Is this how it starts?* I felt like I was back in the Brussels business centre, but this time my stroke was occurring in slow motion and bore the dark undercurrents of mental decay. Worrying about this decay became my silent mania, until finally, it dawned on me that I had started hardcore using an iPhone around the same time my "condition" began. While I'm a three-and-a-half-fingered typer on a keyboard, I'm also a three-and-a-half-fingered typer on a mobile phone, except my thumbs are doing what my fingers usually do. Added bonus? *Autocorrect.* So, deep inside the box of tangled electrical cords that is my brain, that little neuron cluster that had orchestrated my keypad strokes for twenty-five years suddenly had to reconfigure itself to accept a similar yet inverted reality—and it didn't like doing so one bit.

Science tells us that all humans grow ten thousand new brain cells a day, but if we don't activate them by learning new things, they're reabsorbed back into our bodies—which is slightly creepy, but if you don't try to retain them, then you probably don't deserve them. It took my typing cortex four years to grow new cells and to renegotiate the neural and ergonomic issues of getting used to swapping thumbs and fingers between devices—four *years*.

The good news is that I asked around and learned that most people in my life were quietly experiencing a similar secret panic over escalating typing uselessness—I am not alone. But I can see that our species' entire relationship with words, and their mode of construction, is clearly undergoing a massive rewiring. I bridge an era straddling handwriting and heavy smartphone usage. Young people like my friend's daughter, with her emoticons and rampant acronyms, are blessed in having no cursive script to unlearn—with the bonus of having no sense of something having been lost. That's a kind of freedom, and I'm jealous. Part of accepting the future is acknowledging that some things must be forgotten, and it's always an insult because it's always the things you love. We lost handwriting and got Comic Sans in return. That's a very bad deal.

Bit Rot

A friend of mine works as an archivist at a large university that collects rare documents of all sorts. She tells me that a major issue with collecting documents that were created after about 1990 is that the really desirable "papers" don't physically exist—or rather, they do exist, but they're lying comatose inside a 1995-ish laptop. Not only that, but the structured electrons that constitute any given file inside that 1995 laptop are drifting away as electrons apparently do. Depending on a laptop's architecture, its drive will erase itself at a half-life rate of about fifteen years. This has many implications.

For the archivist, it means that the paper they once collected— novel manuscripts, notepads, UN speeches and what have you— no longer exists, or never came into existence. The paper material that arrives for archiving now is more incidental: thank-you notes, ticket stubs, dinner table seating plans and cocktail napkin sketches. Manuscripts for novels now exist almost entirely electronically, and there's apparently not that much interest in a print-out of a book in its early stages, or even in the final drafts where a back and forth with an editor is evident. Archivists want the first draft only, and they want it written by hand, the thinking being that with handwriting you have a true neurological record of a book's pregnancy and birth. This is a bit fetishistic and not too likely to happen. The need for the authorial gesture in the face of high tech is not unlike the New York art world of the early 1960s, where the abstract expressionists (with their near-religious obsession with dribbles and strokes being a manifestation of the subconscious) were in the winter of their vanguard, while the newly emerging pop artists, with their technological unsentimental rejection of brush strokes and the "paintiness" of paint, were next in line to steal the crown.

At universities, younger people tell me that older archivists just want to retire and flee the building, leaving the digital archiving issue for the youngsters to deal with. The youngsters can't wait to rise to the challenge, but as of yet, there's no widely accepted protocol on how to acquire and permanently store files from the early digital era. Of course, the Golden Fleece for the young archivists is a writer's old laptop, dozing away at the back of the hall cupboard. Its files may be disintegrating, but this is where the archivist can take the true measure of a writer or politician—or pretty much anyone, you included.

Getting past the issue of cables, adaptors and plugs ("Honey, where did I put the 1997 DPX GM9/PC-KNW changer adapter?") and assuming that the laptops have been kept in a quiet, temperature-controlled environment, the archivist of the near future might be able to graze on the mind of a novelist or statesman or artist with a level of voyeurism unprecedented in the realm of research. It's all there: not just book drafts or worthy letters to PEN, but everyday correspondence, shopping history, browsing history, email history, porn history, gaming history—materials that one can only describe as, logarithmically, too much information.

So how does one take what is historically valuable without straying into the laptop's scarier neighbourhoods? As it stands, the only protocol is to have the archivist and the laptop donor sit at a table together and go through the files one by one (assuming the files are still legible), and say yay or nay, keep or delete—with the archivist there to ensure that the file creator doesn't go in and delete those bits that make him or her look bad. Question: Does posterity really need that flame email sent to Adobe at 1:30 a.m. in 2007, complaining about their relentless update emails? No. No it does not.

Not only is this one-by-one process slow, but intrinsic to it is a distrust between the creators of the documents and those whose goal is to preserve legacy. It's easy to imagine Winston Smith of *1984* sitting, waiting for the clock to strike thirteen while an archivist asks why an archive donor treasonously cancelled their subscription to *Martha Stewart Living* in 1998.

Here's a question: Do I, or anyone else, want to look at four hundred different versions of a book from first draft to final manuscript? Maybe, but probably not—that's for academics in the year 2525. What about sealing documents for one hundred years? Unsurprisingly, embarrassment and shame lasts far beyond the grave, and this is a donation path taken far less than one might think.

Here's the most important question: What would I *really* like to *see*? Well, here's a thought: many writers email themselves a copy of their novels at the end of every day, using the cloud as a backup mechanism. Imagine if one were able to take all of those daily backups and then place them into a sort of stop-motion animation. One could see how an author constructs their work, by looking at words per day, words cut and pasted, paragraphs deleted, items shuffled about, typos, notes to self, and then, when the editing process begins, one could watch how a novel is hacked and pruned and reshaped—an organic process displayed in a dynamic organic mode. This would be a fascinating new way of appreciating a book's creation—a visual language to describe a verbal process. And while this is just a fanciful idea, it does point out a chasm that now exists between the old manuscript and the new, and gives a taste of a visit to the archives of tomorrow.

Bartholomew Is Right There at the Dawn of Language

A long time ago a bunch of people were sitting on a log, looking at a fire and wishing they had language so that they could talk to each other. Grunting was becoming a bore, and besides, they had fire now—they deserved language. They'd *arrived*.

Of course, they didn't think of it that way—they only had these feelings that went undescribed because there were no words for them. But within this tribe there was this one alpha guy in particular who saw himself as the creative one. He pointed to himself and said, "Vlakk." He picked up a stick, held it up, stared at it, scrunched his eyes and then pronounced it *glink*. And everyone there repeated, "glink," and thenceforth sticks became known as glinks and Vlakk was now Vlakk.

Vlakk then pointed at the fire and again made up a noise—*unk*—and from then on, fire was called unk. And so on. In one night Vlakk was able to come up with sound effects for dozens of nouns and verbs—gazelles and smallpox and thorns and mate-beating—and because it was just one intelligence making up all these new words, the newly evolving language had a sense of cohesiveness to it—it sounded true to itself the way Italian or Japanese does.

However, Vlakk's language-creation process made one tribe member, whom he'd named Glog, furious. In his head Glog was thinking, *This is crazy! You can't just go around making up words arbitrarily, based on sound effects!* But of course Glog didn't have language, so there was no way for him to articulate his anger at the vim with which Vlakk was cooking up new words. And it's not as if Glog had some other, better way of naming things; he was just one of nature's born bitchers and moaners. A hater.

Vlakk and Glog and their tribe had many children, most of whom died very young of hideous causes, because it was the distant past and, in general, people didn't last too long. But many descendants of Vlakk survived to generate new sound effects that went on to become words.

And, of course, Glog's descendants carried his gene for finickiness. As the new language grew and grew, they continued to protest the arbitrary, harum-scarum way in which Vlakk's descendants gave words to things like "dung beetles" or "ritualized impalement on sharp satay-like bamboo skewers beside anthills." As the language evolved over thousands of years, everyone forgot that words had begun as arbitrary sound effects. Words were now simply words, long divorced from their grunting heritage.

As culture became more complex, so did language. Grammar was invented, as was the future tense. And gender, and verb conjugation, and all the things that make learning a new language a chore.

Finally, language entered our modern times. If Glog the Finicky had been king, his far-distant grandchild Bartholomew would have been his successor. Distant as they were in time, their neocortexes were of the same size: Bartholomew was Glog with a good haircut and a stylish suit.

Bartholomew was, unsurprisingly, obsessed with new additions to the language. He was particularly incensed by the things that caused language to change or evolve. He worked as a copy checker for a large business magazine and spent his lunch hours and weekends writing acid-tipped hate mail to other magazines that incorporated any noun or verb that had entered the language since the dawn of digital culture. "Can't you see how you're diluting the language? Corrupting it! Tell me, what is JPEG? What a sick and diseased and laughable word it is—it's not even a word! It's a sound effect, a glottal sideshow freak. It's a bastard word—a bearded lady of a word."

People at the magazine thought Bartholomew a lovable kook, but they were very careful never to offend him because, while he wasn't the sort of person to anonymously mail you a dead sparrow inside a cardboard box as some form of demented condemnation, there lingered the feeling that he had more subtle, untraceable means of punishing a perceived offender, like maybe he was keeping dossiers on all of them. The secretaries in the office would make fun of his cologne—they called it "KGB." And one year during the office Christmas party, staff got drunk and snooped through Bartholomew's cubicle, but they found nothing.

Fortunately there was Karen from HR, who was able to bring a ray of light into Bartholomew's grumpy world. Karen was the office free spirit. She had a Bettie Page hairdo, a nose ring and black knee socks she had bought in Osaka. Each morning she dropped off files at his desk and, with effort, was usually able to coax a smile out of Bartholomew. She saw him as a challenge to her womanly charms: she knew Bartholomew was straight because she would see him loitering in front of the straight porn section at the newsstand three blocks over from the office.

At first Karen tried to come on sexy, but she pulled back because sexy freaked him out. This was going to be one tough fish to reel in. So ultimately she decided to conquer Bartholomew by email. Short. Sweet. Perky. *Saucy*. Unfortunately, this decision was made right at the tipping point in human history when handheld devices started enslaving the human psyche. Bartholomew was quickly distressed by the collapse of language into a chimp-like bafflegab of emoticons, emojis, acronyms and abbreviations. Oftentimes his co-workers' text messages exceeded his powers of cryptography. He took to keeping his office door shut. He grew a beard and, as people began to forget he was there, he went all Howard Hughes-y. But he *was* bunkering himself.

Bartholomew had also been raised in the Glog family tradition, which was to believe that every moment of life heralded the beginning of the end. Language was becoming a scrapyard of slashes, diacritical marks and pointless combinations of characters. Suffice it to say that, for Bartholomew, the supremacy of smartphones heralded the beginning of the end of language, a tradition that had begun around the campfire so many years before.

One morning Karen was on the subway going to work and realized, however improbably, that she was starting to actually fall in love with Bartholomew. Knowing it wasn't maybe the smartest thing to do, she sent Bartholomew a very *lusty* text message:

> W|-|3|\| I g37 70 7|-|3 0ffi(3 2d4y, 137'5 m4k3 p455i0|\|473 10v3
> 0v3r70p y0ur 14rg3 (0113(7i0|\| 0f 1i|\|3d y3110w 13g41 p4d5.
> S|-|4rp3|\| u p3|\|(i1, Big B0y

Bartholomew read this and thought, *Good lord, language has devolved into a series of strung-together vanity licence plates! I can't be a part of this! I can't!* So when Karen showed up, Bartholomew didn't give her his daily smile. Karen was crushed. She sent a proper email in perfect English that said:

Dear Bartholomew,

Earlier today while I was riding the subway to work I emailed you a whimsical message. I think it overstepped the boundaries

of "what is correct" but it was meant in jest and I hope you won't
think lesser of me for it.

    Karen

The thing is, Bartholomew ignored this email because he was crazy, and the thing about crazy people is that they really *are* crazy. Sometimes you can get quite far with them and you start telling other people, "So-and-so's not the least bit crazy." And then So-and-so suddenly starts to exhibit their crazy behaviour, at which point you think, *Whoa!* and pull back. *People were right: this guy is really nuts.*

Karen's boss, Lydia, saw Karen moping in the lunchroom and said, "Honey, sometimes I think it's almost more polite to be crazy 24/7, because at least you don't get people falling in love with you and making a mess of things."

"But I *love* him."

"Of course you do, sweetie. Pass me the Splenda."

As Karen left the lunchroom, Lydia said to her co-workers, "People always seem to fall in love during that magical time before one person sees the other person display their signature crazy behaviour. Poor Karen."

But Karen's heart mended from her break with Bartholomew, and within two years she was engaged to a guy who made sculptures out of cardboard boxes that he took to the Burning Man festival in the California desert.

And life went on.

Bartholomew grew older and buggier. People stopped using land-line telephones altogether. Everyone on Earth used smartphones, even starving people in starving countries. Phones basically cost nothing to make and were as common as, well, the packs of Splenda used in the office lunchroom. All the languages on Earth collapsed and contracted, and Bartholomew's endgame scenario was coming true: language *was* dying. People began to speak the way they texted, and before Bartholomew turned fifty, language was right back to the log and the roaring fire. Bartholomew wondered why he even came to work. Nobody paid any attention to what he did, but, as the Glog family motto goes, "Somebody has to maintain standards."

Then one day Karen walked past Bartholomew's office with her by now teenage daughter. His door was open and he was able to hear the two women speak. They both sounded like the Tasmanian Devil character from Bugs Bunny cartoons. Then they turned around and spoke to Bartholomew: "Booga-booga-ooga-oog?"

They were actually asking him if he wanted to go out for lunch, but he understood not a word. He shook his head in incomprehension. The office emptied of staff. Lunch hour ended and nobody came back. Bartholomew thought this was strange. He walked out of his office and around his floor. Nobody. *Hmmm.* He went down into the lobby and there was nobody there, or in the street either. He began to walk around the city, but everywhere he looked, there was unpeopled silence. He looked at the TVs that were playing in public spaces: they showed the Channel Three News Team's chairs with nobody in them, soccer fields that were empty, traffic cams trained on still roads.

So he walked back to his office and mulled over the situation, which was actually a kind of dream come true for him—no pesky people to further degrade and cheapen the language! But where had everyone gone? He looked at his screen, where the Channel Three News Team had finally appeared in a box in the centre.

"Hi, you're watching the Channel Three News Team. I'm Ed."

"I'm Connie."

"And I'm Frank, and if you're watching this prerecorded message, it means that the Rapture has finally happened and you've been left behind."

"You know, Connie, people are probably wondering why we're speaking the way we're speaking right now."

"You mean, speaking like people did at the start of the twenty-first century instead of the modern new way of speaking based on text messaging?"

"That's right, Connie."

(Giggle) "It's because the only people watching this prerecorded broadcast are those who never adapted to the new language and were left behind after the Rapture. Language has come a long way since then, Ed."

"Has it ever!"

"In the old days people worried about words and grammar and rules."

"And it was a horrible mess, wasn't it!"

"You said it, Frank. And not the kind of mess you can remove with some club soda and a bit of elbow grease."

(All chuckle.)

"But once people smartened up and began speaking the way they texted and began shrinking language back to its origins in grunts and groans, people became more primal, more elemental . . ."

". . . more *real*."

"That's the word I was looking for, Connie. More real. More *authentic*."

"And once people became more authentic and more interested in using noises and sounds instead of words to communicate with others, their interior lives changed. The endlessly raging, self-centred interior monologues came to an end. A holy peace and dignity fell over their lives. They accidentally became closer to God."

"And now they've gone right into God's lap."

"Where we are now too!"

"So farewell from eternity, you sticklers who remain behind."

"Saying good night from the Channel Three News Headquarters, I'm Ed—"

"I'm Connie—"

"And I'm Frank—"

(All) "—wishing you a happy forever!"

Temp

(1) Temp Enlivens Life-Sucking Meeting

I've learned over the years that the fastest way to bring an office to a grinding halt is simply to write "BROKEN" on a piece of paper and tape it onto the photocopier. Staffers walk to the machine, see the sign, feel momentarily inconvenienced and then glow inwardly when they realize they can blamelessly return to their cubicle and play FreeCell and trawl the Internet for Russian dashcam car accident GIFs.

Greetings. My name is Shannon Phelps. I'm a temp, but more than that, I'm the future of employment in the Western world. Sure, you may have a job right now, but one day you'll be me, roving from gig to gig, with no medical, no dental, no anything else except the pleasure of not having to kiss ass or put up with imbeciles or care much about things like, say, life-sucking, boring meetings of the sort I sit in on at Taylor, Wagner & Kimura Filter Systems. TWK's owners are systematically moving the company to China, and everyone knows it. Pretty much once a day, someone at TWK is given the axe while I, as temp goddess, casually buff my nails or stalk Facebook, looking for unflattering photos of the popular kids I used to go to high school with. There used to be a full-time receptionist, but she went on mat leave. So here I am. Temp!

Dan Wagner (the Danimal), who co-owns TWK, understands my devil-may-care, low-commitment attitude. Like today, when he called me in from the front. "If it's okay, young Shannon here is going to take notes on today's meeting." Dan always winks at me, which is slightly pervy but technically not actionable as harassment.

The three Sarahs roll their eyes when Dan brings me in. Yes, you read that correctly: Sarah from Marketing, Sarah from E-commerce Strategy and Sarah from Systems. Don't get me going.

So when the meeting invariably turns into an inevitable miasma of fear and crushed dreams, Dan will say, "Shannon, give us a lift, why don't you. What's your random fun fact of the day?"

"Well, Dan, what country on Earth has the world's lowest age of consent?" This question was just racy enough to ensure that even the Sarahs listened in.

"What country would that be, Shannon?"

"Vatican City. The age of consent there is twelve."

Everyone whipped out their gadgets and dog-piled onto Wikipedia.

"Wait," said Sarah Number Two. "I think it might actually be fourteen."

"Well," said Dan, "the thirteen-year-olds over there must certainly be sleeping easy tonight. Shannon, thank you for bringing enlightenment to our universe. You are *good*."

I am.

(2) Temp Accepts Slightly Random Date with Chinese Guy

Today was Thursday. In the future, every day of the week will be Thursday. We're all going to be working to the grave and we know it, so days of the week will be meaningless. I call it *Permathurs*—I just happened to be in the future before most people. Permathurs isn't totally bad, but without the Internet it would be truly horrible.

My morning highlight was when Kyle the bike courier showed

me his new forearm tat, a bleeding dagger, which sounds clichéd but was actually kind of hot, even though Kyle's not my type. Everyone in the office thinks we're some Big Item, and when we flirt, they turn into gum-chewing zoo visitors staring at the chimp cage and hoping something frisky transpires.

Then the day went sideways. First, my ride home bailed on me— my sister, Amy, had just landed a gig teaching yoga for tweens at the now-empty Barnes & Noble on Route 34.

"Shanny, l hear buses are great these days. Like hotels, practically. You can blog about it—it's free content—you *own* your bus ride!"

Second, Kevin Taylor and Andy Kimura's flight back from Beijing was grounded for a day because of a bird-flu scare: a scheduling mess. Third, there was a norovirus outbreak at the Bunmeister during yet another lunchtime farewell party.

At four-thirty, while I was puzzling over how to bus it home, the Danimal hobbled up to my desk, obviously deeply regretting his Bunmeister Cheesetastic Meatballicious sub.

"Dan, maybe you need one of those super-drugs they give to people on cruise liners."

"Shannon, I need you to do some overtime for me—for the company."

At twice my regular hourly rate? "Sure. What is it?"

"I need you to take a client out for drinks and dinner."

"What? No!"

"Shannon, here's the thing: all of us are dying and this guy *has* to be taken care of."

"Meaning?"

"Look, I'm not talking hookers and blow. I'm talking chicken fingers and three-for-one margaritas at Mister McFunbury's, out by the off-ramp that takes you out to the oil refineries. This guy's not high up the food chain, but we can't not do *something*."

I stared him down. "Okay. One: a week of free taxi chits. Two: cash up front for the food—my cards are maxed out. Three: drinks, dinner, dessert and goodbye. Two hours max."

"Agreed."

"Who is he, anyway?"

"I think he's the idiot son of one of the engineers who's disassembling one of our lines. Andy says he's the guy who inserts the harpoon so they can reel it all back to Asia."

"Sounds colourful. Okay, I'm in."

(3) Temp Enjoys Thursday Meal
Special at Mister McFunbury's

Rarely have I ever felt so much like Sigourney Weaver at the end of an *Alien* movie. Around me nothing but casualties and disaster while I, Shannon the survivor, exit the doomed mothership to hop into a taxi to go on my glamorous date with a high-flying Asian businessman.

"Where to, miss?"

"Mister McFunbury's."

"The one where they had the hostage-taking last September?"

"No, the one by the off-ramp that takes you to the oil refineries."

"Right."

Mr. Xu (pronounced Mr. Shoe) was standing by the cigarette machine, as I was told he would be. He wasn't hot but he wasn't unhot, either—that's an important distinction. He was my age—late twenties, kind of Banana Republic-y, and he was quite relaxed given the clattering of walkers in the place for Seniors' Shrimpy Thursday.

"I'm Shannon."

"I am Mr. Xu."

"Let's grab a table."

We sat down, and my first instinct was to figure out Mr. Xu's language capacity. "How long have you been in the city?"

"Two very glorious nights."

"I'm glad they've been glorious. Is your hotel okay?"

"Most gracious hotel. Thank you."

Oh dear. I was going to be dining with a fortune cookie.

Well, okay. "Why don't we get into the McFunbury's spirit, Mr. Xu."

"That would be most excellent."

I'm not totally proud of myself, but I went right for the booze. We hadn't even ordered food yet, and I was trashing the three Sarahs. "My issue with Sarah Number One, Mr. Xu, is that on the first anniversary of Whitney Houston's death, she Facebooked: 'One year later, heaven took an angel from Earth too soon.'"

"Most unfortunate."

"I'll say. And my issue with Sarah Number Two is that at a Friday staff lunch, she suggested 'we girls' go off on our own and have a 'cuddle puddle' to discuss things 'the boys just wouldn't understand.'"

"So sorry."

"And my issue with Sarah Number Three—killer martinis, by the way—is that she insists on microwaving popcorn with that nauseating fake butter smell. She says, 'Well, I think it smells like fun. If you don't like fun, then I feel sorry for you.'"

"Most ungracious."

I stared at the laminated menu. "What do you think you'll order, Mr. Xu?"

He looked at me. "Well, I'm not feeling very surf-and-turfy—you know, it's a mood that you're either in or you're not. And I kind of carbo-loaded at lunch—I'm doing a half-marathon in three weeks—so I guess I'll get a clubhouse with McFunbury Sauce on the side. You?"

"You, Mr. Xu, are a total dick."

"Let us both have one more most glorious martini. Clean or dirty?"

(4) Temp's Lack of Jeans Day Spirit Irks Co-workers

I walked into the office the next morning only to experience that sickening pang we all dread: Jeans Day—enforced perkiness among the girls while the guys make theatrical, creepy, ass-gazing gropey faces in the lunchroom. No jeans for me.

My jacket wasn't even off when Sarah Number Three stuffed a wad of documents covered with sticky notes into my hand. "I need these alphabetized like we did last week."

"Fine."

She stared at me.

"Is there a problem?" I asked.

"You know, it wouldn't have been so hard to throw on some jeans today."

"I'm not a very jeans-y person."

"Morale is really down around here and we need some fun."

"Okay . . ."

"It's not even for us, Shannon. *It's for the kids.*"

I gagged and then the phone rang. "Good morning. Taylor, Wagner & Kimura Filter Systems, a proud, patriotic company since 1899. One moment, I'll connect you."

Then the Danimal rolled up to the desk, winking like mad. "How was last night's . . . umm . . . *date*?"

"Date? It wasn't a date. It was Mister McFunbury's for exactly 120 minutes."

"And what was Mr. Xu like?"

I wanted to keep my secret. "Nice enough. Limited English, though," I lied.

"Did he say anything about the company I should know about?"

Boy, did he ever!

"No. Mostly we just stared at the *How I Met Your Mother* reruns playing on the screen above the salad bar. I don't think he's very espionage-y."

"Oh." Danimal seemed let down.

Just then Kyle walked in with a delivery. "Hot and heavy at McFunbury's last night, huh?"

I was peeved. "What the—? It's none of your business, Kyle. And who told you?"

"I was driving back from the oil refinery. Saw you there with your date. Seniors' Night, too—*rocking!*"

"The refinery? Why were you out there?"

"I'm applying for a job."

"Oh."

Kyle was acting as if he and I were somehow a real couple. At the same time, I was getting surprisingly verklempt thinking about no more Kyle, with him working at that big, gross refinery for the rest of his life.

Kyle said, "I'm sick of being a temp on wheels, and it's occurring to me that I'll never even be middle-class, let alone some big success story, and maybe I need to get my foot in the door at a place that is never going to go out of business—hence oil."

The phone rang; it was Xu. "Gotta take this, guys." I picked it up. "Good morning. Taylor, Wagner & Kimura Filter Systems, a proud, patriotic company since 1899."

Kyle and the Danimal lumbered off.

I lowered my voice into the receiver. "Hey, Shoeboy. How you doing?"

(5) Temp Is Conflicted over Co-worker's Firing

Sarah Number Two got the axe just before lunch: the curse of Jeans Day. To be practical, a company selling itself to China doesn't need someone to plan its long-term e-commerce solution. Her firing happened fast. One moment she was lecturing about the excessive number of time-expired dairy products in the lunchroom fridge, the next she was standing in the lobby with a cardboard box full of generic desktop crap.

"I suppose you're happy to see me go," she said.

"Not really. I've never had to dumb myself down with you."

She gave a judgy sigh. "The world's not one big joke, you know, Shannon." She turned around to look at the dumping rain while waiting for her ride—which didn't seem to be coming. Looking out at the parking lot, she got philosophical. "You know, I think that in the future we're going to look back on the forty-hour workweek with 3 percent unemployment as a social failure—everyone was busy but no one was actually doing anything meaningful. Yes, you were busy all day, but so what?"

The phone rang. "Just a moment, Sarah . . . Good morning. Taylor, Wagner & Kimura Filter Systems, a proud, patriotic company since 1899. One moment, I'll connect you." I put down the receiver. "Sorry, you were saying?"

"I was saying that I think a forty-hour workweek may well seem as odd and cruel to future citizens as seven-year-olds working in Victorian cotton mills does to us."

I thought about this. "I think you're right. Where's your ride?"

"According to my most recent text, it's stuck in traffic across town."

I quietly phoned to get Sarah a cab, and when it showed up, I gave her one of my taxi chits. "If it means anything, Sarah, the fridge grosses me out too. It makes me think of Gwyneth Paltrow in *Contagion*, especially that scene in the morgue when they slice open her skull."

"Thank you, Shannon. I think that, in your own way, you're being quite sweet." She gave me a small smile and hopped in the cab. It made me wonder if I ought to be nicer to the remaining Sarahs.

I looked at my watch . . . Lunch! Woo-hoo—freedom! Tattered back issues of *InStyle* magazine by the coffeemaker! Last night's pasta in a Ziploc tub! Guys making lewd Jeans Day ass comments!

I sent Mr. Xu a quick text about our evening plans and was leaving the front desk when the fire alarm went off. Rick from Receiving ran into the office from the factory floor. "Holy crap, the warehouse is on fire!"

(6) Temp Contemplates the Remains of Detroit

My weekend was a social flop. I mostly helped my sister paint her basement suite yellow, while my scheduled meeting with Mr. Shoeman was called off at the last minute when his boss phoned with a pair of cagefighting tickets at the Civic Arena. Sometimes a girl has to know when to admit defeat.

Monday morning, Amy dropped me off at work just in time to see a tow truck drag away the charred husk of Kevin Taylor's prized 1968 Shelby GT500, which was carbecued in Friday's warehouse mess. Kyle rolled up just as Amy dropped me off. It was so sad, like watching a dead beached whale being dragged out to sea to be dynamited into chunks.

"Detroit peaked with that car," said Kyle. "Motown's high-water mark." He gave it a salute.

Amy said, "Look at how small it is—I mean, compared to my car." We compared and she was right; her 2010 Hyundai Elantra had almost the exact same volume as a big-ass 1960s Mustang—and yet we think of modern cars as kind of like photocopiers on wheels while the Mustang: "That's a *car*."

Kyle asked what the car was doing in the warehouse anyway. I said, "Kyle, can you keep a secret?"

"Sure. What's up?"

"Kevin Taylor was going to sell that car to pay his wife's casino gambling debts."

"Seriously?"

"Seriously. A hundred and twenty grand. I accidentally over-heard a speakerphone call."

"Poor guy. My stepdad blew a $25,000 whiplash claim cheque all in one weekend." He paused. "So, are you going to see Kung Fu Guy again?"

"Kyle! That is so incredibly ever-so-slightly racist—and even if I was, what's it to you?"

"Just curious. What do you guys talk about—terracotta warriors? Gong Li movies?"

"Kyle, this conversation is over."

"So there is something going on."

I sighed. "We're, um, working on a project together."

"A project."

"You make it sound dirty. We're working on a platonic business venture. He is a nice conservative Chinese guy."

"Okay, don't tell me then."

"When do you find out if you got your refinery job?"

"Maybe this week."

"Is that a delivery for TWK you're holding?"

"It is."

I took it from him. "Thank you." I sauntered into the building, purposefully whistling like someone trying to be mysterious. I found Sarah Number One inside the door, waiting for me. What a way to start the week.

"Hello, Sarah."

"Hello, Shannon."

I remembered my pledge to be nicer to the office's remaining Sarahs. "Can I help you with anything?"

"Shannon, can I take you out to lunch today?"

Talk about a surprise. "Seriously?"

"Yes. Seriously."

Life is strange. "Okay."

"See you here at noon."

"Deal."

(7) Temp Is Slightly Shocked by Lunch Query

We settled on Saipan, a Japanese lunch place run by a noisy Belarusian family. It's a quick walk if you cut through the next-door parking lot of AmQex, a defence contractor, and trek over brown grass berms forested with CCTV cameras atop white poles.

We quickly ordered two bento boxes and sat down by a window.

"How's temping?" asked Sarah.

"I get used to feeling disposable."

"You know about the warehouse fire, don't you?"

"Know what?"

"Kevin Taylor's wife started it."

"No!"

"Yes. They caught her on the AmQex cameras."

I played dumb. "Holy moly."

"Nobody else knows. The Danimal told me."

"Huh."

Our boxes arrived and we quickly ate. Sarah had yet to tell me why we were there—and then she did: "So, are you and Kyle a, um, *couple*?"

For once I got to roll my eyes. "No! And I keep on feeling like we're two pandas in a Chinese zoo and everyone's waiting for us to mate." I remembered my pledge to be nice. "Why are you asking?"

"Because I thought maybe he and I . . ."

"Sarah, you're forty!"

"So?"

"I'm sorry, I just blurted that out. But really, Sarah, you're forty and he's maybe twenty-five."

"All the better."

I sucked in a breath. "Well, he's all yours to win, and he *may* be getting a job at the refineries, so he's ready to settle down, too."

"You think I'm a perv?"

"No. I say go for it and good luck. He can get you discounts on skateboard equipment, too."

"Meow."

"Just wrapping my brain around this."

We ate the remains of some oily tempura. Then I realized something: "It was very nice of you to ask me first. For real."

"I'm not a monster. And I'm not just another Sarah unit around the office."

"I guess you aren't."

Walking back, we approached two older guys begging with cardboard signs at the stoplights, one an Afghan war vet, the other guy just old and sad. Sarah and I looked at each other. "What are we going to do?" I asked.

"I always give the old guys something because, I mean, what are they going to do, become Walmart greeters? The young guys . . . if I think it's going on drugs, I don't give. But the Afghan guy doesn't look druggy."

"He just looks so lost and forgotten."

We ended up giving each of them twenty bucks, and Sarah did a cool thing: she asked them each their name, and they were so glad just to be able to say it to someone and then hear it said back to them—like the world remembered them again. The old guy was Kurt, the younger guy was Darren.

When we got back to the office, there were six police cruisers in the lot, cherries flaring. Uh-oh. And vans. And a K9 unit.

(8) Temp Stumbles upon a Shootout

"Get back!" A policeman standing in front of the yellow-taped-off parking lot barked at us to move. We saw police snipers on the roof.

Sarah Number Three was close by, and we asked what was happening.

"Kevin Taylor is bunkered inside the remains of the warehouse."

"And?"

"He says he's going to kill himself."

"Oh god. Any hostages?"

"They don't think so."

Talk about drama. Just then, the Shoeman and his father, Xu Senior, pulled up across the street and came over. We filled them in. Xu Senior went in pursuit of more info while, as per our agreement, Shoeman pretended to speak English as though he'd been taught at the People's Glorious Education Facility No. 43,607: "This episode with gun create many unglorious feng shui problems. May jeopardize once benevolent deal to buy company."

The Sarahs both saw their buyout stake evaporating, panicked and went to hunt for Mel from Payroll.

Shoeman reached into a Whole Foods paper bag for a snack. Once the Sarahs were out of earshot, I asked him what he was eating.

"Two hundred bucks' worth of raw unfarmed British Columbia salmon. Nothing like it for marathon training. Want some?"

"Ick, no thanks. Would a shooting really kill the sale of the company?"

"My dad's totally old school. He can't buy a building someone's died in. I couldn't care less, but I think we have to fly back to China tonight and discuss this with the family."

"Really?"

"Yup. Which also upsets my training schedule, because yesterday I found this perfect running track nearby—an elementary school they closed because of tax cuts. The soft, unmown grass is perfect for my feet."

I grew worried. "What about . . . what about our secret plan?"

He winked at me. "One day at a time, Shannon. By the way, I was a guest at a poker night and I found out what they make at the defence contractor next door."

"What?"

"In-dash beverage caddies for drones."

"My sister would love that—hey, wait—drones are unmanned!"

"Gotcha."

Then shots rang out. *Holy crap!* We ran and ducked behind a pickup. It was like in the movies: guys in black running across the roof, with more guys closing in from all sides. I was really frightened that Kevin would get killed. He's a nice guy, but life simply hasn't been too kind to him lately.

There was some silence and then we heard squeaking wheels, like a child's toy wagon. A moving dolly rolled out of the open double-wide doors of the warehouse. Duct-taped on top of it was a poorly made effigy of Kevin from the waist up. It was holding a broomstick as a rifle and was shot through with bullets.

"Uh-oh."

(9) Temp Ineligible for Trauma Disability Pay

"Good afternoon. Taylor, Wagner & Kimura Filter Systems, a proud, patriotic company since 1899. I'm sorry, Mr. Taylor isn't here right now. Is there a message?"

You'd think, after a great big glamorous shootout, we'd all get the day off, but no. I, the disposable temp, was forced to man the front desk while everyone else went home to Google grief counsellors so that they could file PTSD disability claims. Still, it was an hour before the bomb sweep was finished and we got the okay to go in.

The Danimal returned me to desk duty with brazen emotional manipulation. "Sorry, Shannon. You have to be the strong one here today." This meant brushing off press inquiries and telling freaked-out loved ones that everything was okay, which actually gets dull very quickly. The calls died down by four o'clock, so I went online to look at Shoeman's specialty website, Undeadbutnotunmown. com—nothing but screen snaps of well-mown lawns in the backgrounds of zombie apocalypse movies. He is so deep.

At a quarter after four the door opened and I looked up. It was Kyle, dressed head to toe in oil refinery gear. "Guess where I just got hired!"

"Kyle, you look like a Village Person. And thanks for being relieved I'm alive."

"Of course I care. The shootout—it's all over the radio. What happened?"

"Kevin went nuts and holed up in the warehouse, threatening to shoot himself. You know why."

"What then?"

"Then there were maybe fifty shots fired and everyone thought he was dead, but then he wheeled this creepy scarecrow effigy out the doors—and walked out with his hands on top of his head."

"Did they arrest him?"

"I don't know. Is threatening to kill yourself a crime?"

"I wonder. And what would a guy like Kevin do in jail all day—shop for boats online?"

"Kevin is now officially declassified."

"Declassified?"

"Declassified. Like me. No longer a part of the class spectrum, and with no hope of re-entering. Not poor, not middle-class, not blue-collar or white-collar. Blank-collar—spending the rest of his life shopping in jail."

This was when Sarah Number One, who'd been gone all day, magically appeared at the front door, wearing slutty heels and a push-up bra. "Hello, Shannon. Oh, *hello, Kyle.*"

"Umm . . ." Kyle was stun-gunned by Sarah Number One's getup. I mouthed the words *cradle robber* to Sarah.

She winked at me. "Kyle, can you help me with my car? It won't start."

Shameless. Just shameless. They left for the parking lot.

(10) Temp Enjoys Cocktails with the Danimal

It was after five and I was getting ready to call a cab when a flower delivery arrived—a jumbo tropical parade float that brought rum drinks to mind. The Danimal passed through as I was opening the envelope. "Who's that for?" he asked.

I opened it and we both read it at once: "To most beautiful temp for glorious Mcfunburry dinner. return from china very soonly."

I wasn't sure how to play this.

"Shannon, is there something I should know?"

"Huh?" God, not the mating panda thing again. "No!"

"That's not what I meant."

"What *did* you mean?"

"I saw you and Xu Junior yakking it up in the parking lot. Don't think I believe the fortune-cookie English thing for a minute."

"Oh."

"Yes, *oh*."

I tried casually to put on my jacket. Danimal said, "Come for drinks with me. It's not a pickup. Yes, my wife's in Florida, getting her lips done, but you know that. I just don't want to go home yet, not after today."

"Where's Andy Kimura?"

"I don't care where he is. We hate each other. It's one of the reasons we're selling."

A mother lode of potential office gossip was too big to ignore. "Okay, but I don't go with married guys. Period."

"It's not about that. Let's hit that bar beside McFunbury's."

"The Executive Privilege Short-Term Corporate Lodging Good-Time Experience?"

"That's the place. The Priv. We have a deal with them."

Drinks at the Priv started badly. Danimal guzzled a double Scotch and I got stupid on a rum punch. He got philosophical about cars, the way guys do. "Kevin's Shelby depressed the crap out of me. I looked at it and all I thought about was how it's too late to fix whatever bit of the economy is left after having shipped it all to China. Think of Michigan: ten million primates needing 2,500 calories a day, sitting on a cold rock in the middle of the North American continent, with nothing to do all day. A recipe for disaster. Bartender!"

More drinks. More philosophy. "Shannon, Detroit is our existential bogeyman. Detroit forces us to ponder the meaning of being alive: we wake up, we do something, we go to sleep, we repeat it about 22,000 more times, and then we die."

I looked across the bar. Sarah and Kyle were coming in and they'd obviously just been . . . *frisky* with each other.

Danimal was being maudlin. "I don't care if you're spying on TWK for the Chinese. I just want the old system back."

Dan and Sarah locked eyes. So did Kyle and I.

"Sarah?" said Danimal. "This place is *our* place. You brought someone else here?"

"What about *you*, Romeo?"

Kyle looked at me. "Shannon?"

"It's not what you th—" I turned to Danimal. "Spying for the Chinese? Are you nuts?"

Caramba, what a mess.

(11) Temp Enters a Universe of Pain

It was a Quentin Tarantino standoff, where everyone holds a gun on everyone else, except there weren't guns, just words and emotions.

The Danimal looked at Kyle and then at Sarah and hissed, "You cradle robber."

Sarah shot back, "What about *you*, Dan?" (Referring to *moi*.)

"I'm here with Shannon only to talk business."

"Yeah, right, cowboy."

Danimal got up and that's when Kyle slugged him in the gut—well, more like where your gut touches your rib cage. It sounded like a kettledrum, and Danimal fell to the floor, shouting astonishingly unprintable things at Kyle and Sarah, who up and left.

"What is wrong with that kid?" shouted Dan. "Oh my god, the pain!"

"Thanks for accusing me of spying," I said.

He coughed. "Shannon, take me to Emergency. I think I'm going to die."

I helped him to his BMW, where he curled into a ball in the passenger seat while I drove.

I said, "I really shouldn't be doing this. You're mean."

"Just take me to Crown Permanente."

"Oh, going to the rich people's hospital, are we?"

"Please just drive."

We arrived and Danimal hobbled out of the seat and into Emerg, an oasis of calm with tastefully matched fabrics and gentle lighting. There was a copy of *Modern Symphony* magazine on the walnut-inlaid coffee table. We went to the desk, where a super-model was moonlighting as a nurse on duty.

Dan groaned, "I need an X-ray. Quick."

"Of course, sir. I'll need to take an imprint of a credit card. We accept all major cards."

Danimal looked in his pockets. "Oh jeez, it's in the pocket of the jacket that went out for dry-cleaning today. Just let me in. I'll bring it tomorrow. I'm totally insured."

I could see that our supermodel had been through this many a time.

"I'm sorry, sir, but without an imprint of a valid card with the appropriate credit limit, I'm afraid there's nothing further we can do."

"I—" He was speechless.

"Welcome to my world," I said. "Get back in the car. I'll take you to Saint Eustace."

"That's in the worst part of town."

"And your point?"

So we drove off to Saint Eustace. "It's just a slug in the gut, Dan. How bad can it be?"

"He broke something. Or damaged my heart. I can tell. Oh my god, the pain!"

We pulled up to Saint Eustace, which resembled the battle-ravaged Vietnamese village remains in part three of *Full Metal Jacket*. A conga line of sick and wounded people stretched out the front door and into the street. One quick wardrobe change and you'd have *Les Misérables*.

"I can't go in there," Danimal said.

"It's either that or nothing. Want me to take you home?"

"No!"

"Okay, then join the line."

(12) Temp Witnesses the Class Divide

Had there not been stab wounds and vomit everywhere, the hospital lineup could have been fun in a tailgate-party kind of way. Our surprise neighbour was Darren, the vet I'd given twenty bucks to after lunch. He was holding a T-shirt to a wound on his forearm.

"What happened?"

"I got into a fight with a raccoon over half a bucket of KFC I found beside the check-cashing mart."

"Who won?"

"He did."

"Here, have a stick of gum." I am nothing if not fresh.

Danimal was being a downer. "How hard can it be to get some painkillers?"

"Dan, there are many people here in far worse shape than you. Just wait your turn."

Darren advised, "If you're looking to score painkillers, man, don't overplay it."

"But I'm in genuine pain."

"Sure, sure. Half the people in this lineup are here just to score some oxy, but if you overdo it, they'll tell you to scram."

Dan is practical. "What do I need to know?"

"Tell them your pain is about eight on a scale of one to ten. It hurts but you've felt worse. And don't scream or make moaning sounds. It irritates them, and they're relieved when they don't have to watch someone aiming for an Oscar."

"Good to know."

"And now we stand and wait."

And wait we did. About two hours in, Dan asked, "Shannon, have you been here before?"

"No. But I did break my arm Rollerblading in Boston four years ago—go, Red Sox! Cost me nineteen thousand dollars and I'll be in debt until I'm forty. It's why I can't do what I really want to in life. But I do have a Saint Eustace loyalty card you can borrow if you want."

"Was the emergency area as crowded as this four years ago?"

"Worse. There was a full moon that night."

Finally, it was our turn. Once we hit the front, Dan took a step and something inside him went sideways—he bellowed like a pirate, scaring even me.

"Sir!" said the intake nurse. "This is a hospital. I'll politely ask you to lower your voice."

"My stomach—God, it's like a tractor's driving over it."

"You're in a great deal of pain, are you?"

"Yes. Some idiot slugged me in the sternum."

"Where did this happen?"

"In a bar."

It didn't take a genius to see Dan was making a bad impression.

"How would you describe your pain, sir?"

"About eight on a scale of one to ten."

The nurse buzzed a security guard. "You're the tenth person tonight to describe your pain that exact same way. I'm afraid I can't help you in your quest for pills, sir. Next!"

Out on the street Darren commiserated. "Sorry, dude. Take two of mine."

Dan grabbed them and chewed them like Mentos. Then he collapsed.

(13) Temp Does Ambulance Duty

I asked Darren to put Dan into the BMW's back seat. "If we drive him back to Crown and dump him by the door, they'll be forced to take pity on him."

Darren rifled through the glove compartment. "Look! A BlackBerry Z10!" The BlackBerry then promptly rang (ringtone: "Dust in the Wind" by Kansas). "Hello?"

A woman squawked on the other end. I grabbed the phone. "Hello, who's this?"

"It's Chantelle, Dan's wife. Who's *this*?"

"I'm Shannon. I'm a temp at Dan's office. He had an accident and we're trying to take him to a hospital, but he doesn't have his credit cards, so nobody wants him."

"Come to our house and pick me up."

"Aren't you in Florida?"

"I found a card with a pile of unused frequent flyer miles, so I returned early."

Chantelle was on the curb. Her lips were swollen like Donald Duck's beak, and it was hard to not stare.

"I know I look strange but I never expected to get old, and then one day it happened and, as you can see, I'm not handling it well. I know I look ridiculous."

On cue both Darren and I chimed, "No, you look great!"

Darren added, "I'm sure your lips will look terrific once they deflate, Chantelle."

Chantelle was unruffled by the sight of Dan in the back and me at the wheel and Darren in the passenger seat, looking and smelling very streety. She climbed into the back seat and removed a fifth of vodka from her purse. "Any takers?"

Darren eagerly accepted, and we soon arrived at Crown Permanente. "You two lug him in," she said. "I'll handle the staff."

"You've got your credit cards, then?"

"Cards, schmards. A well-dressed, well-nourished white woman with obvious cosmetic surgery is welcome in any hospital on the planet."

Dang if she wasn't right. The supermodel nurse beamed at her while another fetched her a cappuccino and asked which satellite music station she preferred. We dropped Danimal's carcass inside the door and two hot guys who looked like Qantas flight attendants whisked him away. It couldn't have been more pleasant.

"You two wait in the car. I'll be out in a sec."

Chantelle soon emerged and got into the back seat. "Shannon, take me home. Darren, you stay the night at my place. We can party and maybe you can take a shower later. Dan's clothes will fit you. Shannon, you keep the car for a few days."

"Seriously?"

"I may be aging gracelessly, but I'm no idiot like Kevin's wife. Just promise me you won't set fire to it."

"It's a promise."

I feel like a bad person, but I was so excited to have a Beemer for a few days that I forgot to ask what was wrong with Dan.

(14) Temp Makes Lemonade from Lemons

Okay, the nice thing about being a temp is that if you screw up, you leave, but you were going to leave anyway, so it's no big deal. I suppose this is true for anybody with a job, but for temps it's just more out in the open.

After almost no sleep I arrived at work only to find gossip and fear-mongering. The worst gossip was that Danimal was in a coma, when in fact he was in a twenty-thousand-dollar-a-day hotel with a slightly collapsed left lung and an unhelpful feeling-sorry-for-himself attitude.

Sarah Number One walked up to my desk and said, "I guess we were all behaving badly yesterday."

"I was doing no such thing! I was there just to listen to Dan vent about the warehouse fire! *You're* the one who got a room."

Sarah winked at me. "Have it your way. Here's a pile of files that need alphabetizing."

Ugh. I decided my day desperately needed some cheer, so I phoned my sister's friend who breeds golden Labs. We had a quick chat, and just before lunchtime, she arrived with two blue plastic storage tubs filled with puppies. I ushered her into the admin area. In a loud, crisp voice, I shouted, "Oh no! There's been an explosion!"

Everyone looked stunned . . .

"That's right: an explosion of cute! Hilda, release the hounds!"

Ahhh, the puppy bomb—is there any greater experience in life? Eighteen chubby bundles of YouTubeable romping joy demanding nothing except unconditional love—and snacks. Everybody got down on the floor, and it took only a minute for people to learn that the person with the most food is the one who gets the most puppies, so in came the lunch bags. I was proud to have brought even the smallest dab of joy to the otherwise dreary lives of the soon-to-be-fired full-time staff. Yes, I was proud of myself for firmly turning the day around.

The icing on the cake? Outside the building there was a zombie walk, with about two hundred kids dressed in their finest living dead, headed to a political protest starting outside AmQex next door.

And that's when two things happened: a massive bus, like Bon Jovi on tour, pulled into the parking lot and fifty Chinese people emerged, holding measuring tapes, string and clipboards. Then, half a minute later, about twenty cops arrived to shut down the AmQex protest.

"They make engine parts for drones," whispered Sarah.

The Chinese delegation's leader said, "I am most curious to see how protesters are handled in your country."

(15) Temp Recalls the Zombie Walk

I think the AmQex protest got so much press because the zombies that the cops handcuffed and dragged away left behind a wicked trail of slime and body parts.

Andy Kimura was looking at YouTube over my shoulder and said, "Bodily remains really look great online." Andy was still woozy from jet lag after being quarantined for bird flu at the Beijing airport.

"Mr. Kimura, shouldn't you be showing the Chinese folks around while they measure stuff?"

"Not me. I'm Japanese."

"Genetically, maybe."

"But my name certainly is, and the Chinese aren't so hot on Japan."

I said, "Hey, check this out—Sarah from Marketing got fifteen seconds with the Channel Three roving reporter." To be honest, I've no idea what Sarah said. All I remember is her trademarked casual hair flip as she smiled, while behind her lay a left leg covered in red corn syrup and vinyl blackflies.

"Poor Sarah," said Andy. "Today's her last day."

Oh God. "Seriously?"

"That's life, Shannon. As we speak, our new Chinese owners are measuring the staff lunchroom with a laser level. We are not a company that is in need of a head of Marketing."

"Oh, Sarah, I barely knew ye. Does she know it yet?"

"After lunch."

"Life sucks."

It was weird to have every single surface of the building measured by quiet, methodical people speaking a mystery language. What made it especially odd was how they didn't really seem to notice or interact with the people in the building. It was like they were taking measurements inside a photograph, not a real building. Two guys in the meeting room were assembling a 3D model of the building, using data brought in by the measurers.

I found myself missing Mr. Shoeman terribly. I decided to phone him in Beijing—seeing country code 86 on my desktop phone put me in a better mood. I hoped he hadn't forgotten our plans for the future.

"Hello, Mr. Xu?"

"Hi, hello, yes, whatever—whoever this is, I'm getting a reflexology treatment right now and need to focus my qi energy."

"Mr. Shoeman, it's me, Shannon."

"Ah. Sweetest lily of decadent Western imperialism."

"Shoeman, I miss you. When are you coming back?"

"Me so sorry—not understand."

I giggled. "You're still such a dick."

"Hang in there, sweetheart."

"What about our secret plan?"

"Our secret plan goes into operation within a few days."

"You promise?"

"I promise." I hung up the phone and turned around to find Andy Kimura and the two remaining Sarahs. "Secret plan?" said Andy. "So Dan wasn't just being paranoid."

"Imagine that," said Sarah Number One with as much righteousness as she could muster. "A traitor right here within."

Andy said, "I think you'd better leave, Shannon."

(16) Temp Gets Fired

Here's the thing: I've been fired before and couldn't have cared less, but getting fired from TWK stung.

"You let yourself get attached, Shanny," said my sister, Amy. "The number one law of temping: never bond." She was helping me self-medicate with grape Popsicles and a Kate Winslet marathon. I was in pyjamas at four in the afternoon and my life had devolved into the third panel of a *Cathy* cartoon, where she stares into the void and emotionally implodes. "The only reason anyone hires anyone is to help them make money. The moment you can't do that, they'll chew your face off and toss the remains into a Dumpster."

"That's not true. I liked it at TWK."

"Have you tried calling Mr. Shoeman?"

"He's on an energy retreat in the countryside."

"China has a countryside?"

"You're right. He's probably at World Extreme Cagefighting."

"What about Kyle?"

"He showed up to take Sarah to lunch just as I was leaving. I couldn't talk to him. God only knows what Sarah told him about me."

"Shannon, how do you think Kate Winslet manages to always lose weight?" Amy's attention span is limited. Discussion of my temping was over.

The doorbell rang. I live in a basement suite and it's not the easiest place to find, so for someone to locate me takes work. I opened the door. It was Sarah Number One, so I closed the door, but she started banging on it. "Let me in! Shannon, I was horrible! I deserve this! Let me explain!"

I opened the door. "Explain what?"

"I just got fired."

"So what? I'm waiting for whatever it is you're going to explain."

"Let me come in?"

"Oh God, all right. Shoes off. Would you like a grape Popsicle?"

She came into the TV area and I introduced her to Amy. "We're having a Kate Winslet marathon." Amy hit pause.

Sarah looked at the frozen frame. "How does that woman always manage to lose the weight for every role?"

"Excuse me, Sarah . . . my explanation?"

"There is no explanation. I came here because I couldn't think of anyone else to visit. I have no friends. They all got married and this would just make them happy about their decision to do so."

"So you came to me because I'm a failure and won't judge you harshly?"

"To be honest, sort of. Yeah. You seem like your head's screwed on right. I like the way you never took crap from anyone at TWK— and your random fact of the day was always funny. And yesterday I got to see the human side of you."

"I'm deeply flattered." The three of us sat there in silence, and then I figured it out. "Wait—you just want to know what my secret plan is so that you can get in on it."

"Well, *yeahhh*!"

I paused a second. "Okay."

(17) Temp Learns Some Secrets

After Sarah left, I tried watching more TV, but the thing about a Kate Winslet marathon is that after about 1.75 movies, your brain says, *I can't do this anymore!* and forces you to get out of the beanbag chair and do something out in the real world. So I drove to the hospital to visit the Danimal. In the Beemer I felt like I'd barely squeaked through their visitor parking lot's quality-control filter—thank God the car had been recently washed. Once inside the building, a tastefully clad male escort took me up to the third floor as though I were a guest on *David Letterman*.

Danimal was in bed, looking woeful. "Shannon!"

"Hi, Dan."

"Thanks for saving my life."

"I did no such thing. I just took you to the hospital. How is your ever-so-slightly collapsed left lung?"

I could tell Dan wanted to dramatize his condition but couldn't. "Oh, you know."

"I certainly do. I looked it up online. You'll be 100 percent healed in one week. You should get out of this luxury hotel as soon as you can, too. It'll bankrupt you."

"Too late. I'm already bankrupt."

I cocked an eyebrow. "Really?"

"Why do you think we're dumping the company? I'm going to enjoy this country club lifestyle as long as I can on the insurance company's dollar."

I saw the remains of lunch. "What's the food like here?"

"Insane. Lunch was a wild mushroom risotto with shaved Parmesan. How's your Chinese boyfriend and your evil plan?"

"Dan, I'm assuming it's the painkillers making you stupid, but the fact of the matter is, yes, he and I do have a plan."

"I knew it."

I looked around the gorgeous room (a Warhol print of an eagle was on the south wall) and waited for him to say something.

"Well, what is it? What's your plan?"

"I knew you'd ask. I knew you'd crumble."

So I told the Danimal the plan, and after that I drove over to his place to check up on Chantelle. I rang the doorbell (also "Dust in the Wind" by Kansas—these people are thorough) and a much cleaner and studlier-looking Darren opened the door, in a housecoat, holding a vodka tonic. "Chantelle! It's Florence Nightingale!"

"Ask her to come in."

Dan's house truly rocked—everything you'd expect from the gated-community lifestyle. The firepit alone was the size of my bedroom.

"Hi, sweetie, have a drink. Darren, make our guest a greyhound. There's fresh grapefruit juice in the fridge."

"Will do."

"So," asked Chantelle, "how's Dan?"

"He's looking good. Have you gone to see him yet?"

"Maybe tonight. I have to, um, pull myself together."

I said, "I'll drive you."

"That's sweet, but I'll cab it. How are *you* doing?"

"I got fired this morning."

"Really? Well, sit right down next to me and tell Chantelle everything."

(18) Temp Empathizes with Ducklings

I stayed for a while at Chantelle's but declined her vodka, as I still had to drive—to the oil refinery to meet with Kyle, who had answered a meet-for-coffee text with: "blue gate, refinery north road, 7:45 look for billboard with photo of happy mallard duck family."

Indeed, I found the duck family portrait with the banner caption about always putting the environment first. It stood in front of a crude oil fracking facility, straight out of a sci-fi film in which mutants on a slave planet convert poor people into snacks for the master species.

"Isn't this place great?" asked Kyle, coming in from the parking lot and wearing his still brand-new journeyman's outfit. "I start on the 8:00 night shift. I'm totally stoked."

"Kyle, this place is freaky, and who knows what toxins there are in there."

"Shannon, for a guy with no degree, this is a good foot in the door. If I play my cards right, I can be a supervisor in a few years."

My heart felt like one of those little ducklings—one onto which a massive Acme cartoon anvil had fallen from a mile up. "Where's Mr. Burns's office?"

"Admin's about a mile thataway. Why are you so bummed out? I've got a real grown-up job. You should be happy for me."

I was silent.

"And look, I can maybe go work in Libya or Abu Dhabi and make crazy money. That's where the action is. Six months in the Emirates—business-class ticket each way—live in a walled compound with satellite TV and well-stocked fridges—the sky's the limit."

I sighed.

"You're always looking for fun facts. Did you know that one barrel of oil—forty-two gallons—yields forty-four gallons of petroleum products?"

"I didn't."

"It's because when crude oil is converted, it increases in volume. Roughly half of each barrel of crude oil is turned into gasoline for transportation."

When had Kyle drunk the New Kyle Kool-Aid? I never saw this coming.

He asked, "Shannon, why did you want to see me, anyway? Trying to get me involved in your evil plot with the Chinese?"

"As a matter of fact, yes."

"I don't think I'm the espionage type."

"It's not espionage."

"Look, now's not the time for this. I'm going to be late on my first day if I don't get in right now." He started edging backwards toward the entryway. "Besides, this is where I'm at in my life right now. I'm an oil guy."

"Promise me you'll call if you change your mind?"

"Gotta go, Shannon. Bye."

I waved goodbye and got back into Danimal's BMW. I turned on the radio. "Dust in the Wind" by Kansas was playing, and I promptly began bawling.

(19) Temp Hits an All-time Low

Do you have a special place you go to when you're at an all-time low? Some people have a place, but me, I just drive and drive, past the strip malls, past the light industrial zones and past the fallow fields. After watching Kyle enter the refinery, I began thinking about the world and how it's changed, even in my short life. Countries like Greece, which used to be normal countries, now gutted of their middle class and turned overnight into something new and nameless, a land with no economy but with pretty good coffee and smoking-hot Wi-Fi. I got to thinking about bubbles—how all we do these days is lurch from bubble to bubble. *Are we in a new bubble? Is the bubble about to burst?* I'm afraid of bubbles and I'm sick of bubbles—and yet I'm addicted to bubbles. Go figure.

I drove past the under-construction subdivisions that died in 2008, their two-by-fours turned the grey colour of moths. I wondered if we're addicted to the idea that society without a middle class isn't really society. I wondered if maybe, back in the days of Detroit, jumbo refrigerators and the Beatles, we tricked ourselves into thinking that the middle class equals the future—and without a middle class, we can't see pictures in our heads of what tomorrow might be. I found it strange how politicians repeat the words *middle class* over and over and over again, as if doing so will allow us to pretend it still exists—that it's not evaporating daily like a puddle on a road.

Night came and I was anywhere and nowhere when my phone buzzed—it was Mr. Xu and he was back in town! He had his big surprise all ready for me at his short-term corporate lodging suite. I couldn't remember the last time I was happier to get a text.

I drove to the Executive Privilege Short-Term Corporate Lodging and ran to Room 307, where the nerdy but lovely Mr. Xu awaited me.

"Ah, hello, capitalist lapdog. You be ready for grand surprise?"

"Shut up! I can't believe you're back!" I gave him a smooch and said, "Okay, dial me in. I am ready for your big surprise, buster."

"Apologize in advance if not good enough."

"Show me your surprise!"

"Very well."

A drop cloth concealed what was supposed to be the main living area. Mr. Xu pulled it back and I bathed in the majesty of what I saw.

He said, "Pretty kick-ass sexy, don't you think?"

I sucked in some breath and said, "Mr. Xu, you have truly amazed me."

Before me, in beautiful rows on shelves, lay more than a thousand unique pairs of sneakers that would crash eBay in a flash if they all went up for sale at once.

(20) Temp Figures It All Out

If you came here expecting a happy ending, that's exactly what you're going to get. It's a few months later, I'm now Mrs. Xu, there are twin Xus in the offing, and the twins will be in line to inherit more than a billion dollars. I remind myself of this every time I think of the coffee room's Girl Guide cookie honour box, and how horrified I always was to find that staffers had shortchanged it, and how I paid the difference from my own pocket.

What about TWK? Don't worry about the old gang—they're doing just fine. The building is now home to Mr. Xu's vanity project (and mine), which is to be the world's largest online retailer of vintage and high-end sneakers. Sarah Number One is once again in charge of online marketing development, and Sarah Number Two is back developing e-commerce strategy. This time their decisions will have a chance of being implemented and making some kind of difference.

In a slight romantic twist, Sarah Number Three, who I never really got to know, is seeing Kyle, who quit the refinery after a week spent inhaling its magic aromas. Kyle is now getting a full sleeve of ink on each arm and is in charge of "branding atmosphere," which means—I'll be honest—I have no idea what, but I'm just so glad he's no longer inhaling oil. I'll always have a soft spot for that lovable lunkhead who kind of flirted with me and who I kind of flirted with, back when we were both younger and dumber.

The Danimal we now call "the Shaker," because we send him out to do anything that involves old-school middle-management people shaking each other's hands: conferences and land leasing and that kind of stuff. It's a remarkably effective category and he loves it. Dan and Chantelle split up quite amicably. Chantelle and Darren are engaged and living together in the gated community. Chantelle's lips have shrunk and she looks a tiny bit more human and promises not to get more work done.

And the happiest ending of all is for Kurt, the old guy by the stoplight, who now has his own office out by the delivery bay, where his main task is to sit, enjoy life and maybe watch the Carpenters on VHS—he refuses to go online.

So maybe you entered this story expecting there to be a bogey-man—someone who we can yell at and whack with sticks like a piñata. But there is no bogeyman here. There's only the times we live in. We can bitch about them or we can move forward, and if you don't move forward . . . well, you'll be left behind, left in the past, which makes no sense, because the present is all we have. And really, how does Kate Winslet always manage to drop those pounds?

Retail

The alpine suburb of Vancouver where I grew up was so remote as to be technically rural. The nearest store of any sort was five miles away, which was moot, because we never got to go there anyway. So until I got my driver's licence, I was a prisoner of remoteness and, as a result, to this day retail seems like magic to me. You walk into a space filled with well-lit, cunningly arranged, tantalizing objects, you see something you like, you hand over this stuff called "money" and they give you what you want. What could be better? I'm always amazed by how cavalier people who grew up in a town or city are about shopping. You don't understand: shopping is amazing. It's like transmutation.

I like the way stores work so hard to earn your enthusiasm. Stores are so well thought out and make your head feel shiny and new, and then you get home and your house is a mess and you think to yourself, well, at least stores have their shit together.

The first thing I do in any new country is go to a hardware store. Hardware stores anywhere are inspiring and make you want to make things. Foreign stores add a new twist, especially when you find a tool that obviously has a specific use, only you don't know what it is. It's like shopping in a parallel universe, or like eating in that nightclub in *Star Wars*.

The Japanese have the best department stores. The stores aren't so much brands as they are fully immersive lifestyle experiences, and they sell everything from toothpicks to (yes) whale sushi to Robert Rauschenberg paintings. They're so well put together, you feel like you should dress up just to go there. On this topic, there's a line from *The Brady Bunch Movie* (1995) in which Dad Brady says, "Okay kids, put on your best sweaters—we're going shopping at Sears!" This is funny because you'd never in a million years think of dressing up to go to a Sears. If anything, you'd try to dress down so as to blend in: fleece pants and a day pass from the local clinic clearly pinned to your inside-out T-shirt.

Japan also has a category of department stores everyone calls zombie stores—nobody can figure out why they still exist, but they lurch along anyway. You walk into a zombie store and they have stuff lying on tables and things are technically for sale, but it's so depressing that you flee before buying anything.

It's similar to another Japanese phenomenon called *sabishii* (sa-bee-shee). *Sabishii* is when you look at a restaurant from outside but there's nobody in it, which is kind of depressing, so you don't go in . . . which reinforces the restaurant's *sabishii*ness, and soon the restaurant goes out of business.

I was really excited to go to Harrods in London. When I got there everything was . . . shiny. It looked like it was designed by the guy who did Michael Jackson's wardrobe. I guess I was expecting a whole other level of luxury, which sounds so corny. And what would a whole new level of luxury look like, anyway? In the old days, more luxury meant more jewels and shiny stuff. These days, it usually means a lot less, like Muji or airport interrogation rooms. Humanity actually seems to be split down the middle on the definition of luxury: those who want gilded leopard-shaped teapots and those who want to live in the white box their iPhone came in.

I like department stores because there's always something to surprise you. I was in the Macy's in Union Square in San Francisco two years ago, buying pyjamas, and there were all these hip inner-city kids buying pyjamas too, and I thought to myself, *Isn't it great that kids are discovering something good and sensible like pyjamas.*

And then my friend Liz told me that they buy pyjamas because they're the exact sort of thing a fifty-year-old white guy would buy, and that kids wear their pyjamas as streetwear, and with much irony. Owned!

I was leaving a Hudson's Bay store in Vancouver a few years back, and this woman who looked like she lived in her car grabbed me and said, "Not so fast. You're coming back inside with me." She was a store detective and she was convinced I'd shoplifted a bottle of Eau Sauvage. She was genuinely excited about taking down a customer—frothing at the kill. A small crowd gathered, I produced the receipt, her face collapsed, and I've never gone to that store again. Once the trust is gone, it's over.

The most seductive retail on earth is the Paul Smith store in Heathrow's Terminal 5. You're already discombobulated from jet lag and sleeping pills, and then you drift through the mall, and the store is like a vision of . . . unexpected quality and uniqueness. Old books and architectural scale models sit alongside actual merchandise. Nobody leaves empty-handed.

Right now I like these new hipster stores that each sell exactly four and a half things and feel like the Great Depression when you walk in. A painted rock, a really good notepad made in Antarctica, a knitted cozy for displaying heirloom tomatoes, vintage aspirin holders and a sock. I'm never sure if it's a pop-up conceptual art gallery or if it's for real, which is actually the very best retail confusion there is.

Trivial

Last night I went to a café where a friend, Jess, was hosting a trivia night. When first I received her invitation, I thought . . . trivia night? Trivia. Yes, there used to be this stuff called trivia and I haven't thought about it in ages. So I was curious to see what a 2015 trivia contest would feel like. I arrived to a rowdy vibe: ten jovial teams of five and six members, many of them on the young side—a lot of millennials and borderline millennials.

Jess was in charge of writing the questions and told us: "Tonight instead of Hollywood fluff, we're going to have trivia questions that broaden our view of the world." This sent shivers down my spine as I remembered that trivia is sort of the opposite of broadening one's world. Trivia is trivia because it's trivial. And then, of course, came Jess's final rule: "No cellphones allowed, put them away now." That was when it got real.

The questions erred on the side of difficult. Here's one of the first: "A contronym is a word that has two opposing meanings, which is to say, a contronym is its own antonym. What is a contronym that means both 'give official permission or approval for' and 'impose a penalty on'?"

Ahhh . . . here's the thing: right now you, the reader, and I, the writer, are sharing a moment, and this moment is tense.

This is because I, for at least a few moments, know the answer to this question, whereas you, for at least a few moments, don't. This is called a power imbalance. To rectify this power imbalance, you have a few options: You can put down this book and figure out the correct answer. (Just think how satisfied you'll feel.) Or you could put down this book and never open it again. (Boo hiss.) Or you could circumvent all of this and look it up online. (Wait—no cloud allowed.)

The answer is *sanction*.

Next: "Which one of the following products does NOT contain beef by-products? Asphalt, car tires, baby powder, paint, sugar or drywall?"

While you mull this over, I'll just mention what a great feeling it is for me to have important information while you don't—and also state that this information dynamic is precisely why we hate elites. So smug. It also reminds me of a line from the US version of *The Office*, where Jim says about his co-worker Dwight, "This is the smallest amount of power I've ever seen go to someone's head."

Okay, the answer is baby powder.

The larger question for me during the trivia evening was, "Wait—we used to have all of this stuff stored in our heads, but now, it would appear, we don't. What happened?" The answer is that all of this crap is still inside our heads—in fact, there's probably more crap than ever inside our heads—it's just been reclassified. It's not trivia anymore: it's called the Internet and it lives, at least for the foreseeable future, outside of us.

The other thing I realized is that we once had a thing called a larger-attention-span-than-the-one-we-now-have. Combine these two factors and we have the reason why a game of trivia in 2015 almost feels like torture. I sat there with four other reasonably bright people, not necessarily knowing the answers to all of the questions, but knowing that the answers, no matter how obtuse, could be had in a few seconds, delivered without judgment by my iPhone 6 Plus. But then I decided the evening was also a good reminder of how far things have come since the early 1980s heyday of the board game Trivial Pursuit.

Q: What country is north, east, south and west of Finland?

A: Norway.

Q: "Clean," "jerk" and "snatch" are terms used in which sport?

A: Weightlifting.

Q: Why was trivia such a big thing in the late twentieth century?

A: Because society was generating far more information than it was generating systems with which to access that information. People were left with constellations of disconnected, randomly stored facts that could leave one feeling overwhelmed. Trivia games flattered twentieth-century trivia players by making them feel that there was both value to having billions of facts in one's head and that those facts were actually easily retrieved. But now we know that facts are simply facts. We know where they're stored and we know how to access them. If anything, we're a bit ungrateful, given that we know the answer to just about everything.

You may be wondering who won trivia night. It wasn't me—but instead of feeling like a loser, I felt the way I once did when a friend spent an afternoon slaving over the creation of croissants that she served for dinner. All that toil and sweat—why not just go out and buy some? The croissants you make on your own will never be as good as the ones from the bakery, and you won't have used up an entire afternoon in the process.

Q: The word *croissant* comes from where?

A: Google it.

Über That Red Dot

I've always felt vaguely embarrassed for cats chasing the red laser-pointer dot on the floor. We like to think of cats as being smarter than that. *Oh, come on—the dot comes from this laser pointy–thingy I'm holding. Get your act together.*

I also always feel slightly annoyed at myself for holding the pointer and leading the cat along . . . It's not that I'm being cruel—it's more that I'm making it clear to myself and to everyone that intelligence is a continuum and not a threshold, which in turn makes me wonder what metaphorical red dots I'm following that I don't know about. Who's holding the laser pointer and laughing contemptuously at me?

And then I was in Paris last week, ordering a car from Uber. I was in an office with two co-workers and we were staring at my iPhone, watching the little black car on the streets navigate the tangled topological mess that is the streets of the 9th arrondissement.

"Look. It's stopped."

"Huh."

"I wonder why?"

"Maybe it's hit a red light."

"Look! It's started moving again."

"No! It's going the wrong way!"

"That's not true. That's a one-way street, so it has to go that way. It's Paris."

Note that it wasn't the driver, a human being, we were discussing: it was the little black car on the screen.

"Look at it now. It's making good time on Rue Saint-Lazare."

"Oh no—it's stopped again."

"What is its problem?"

Then I had a chill: *Uber is the one holding the laser pointer*—and I wonder if they're even aware that they are? For fans of Uber, and there are many, possibly the most underrated asset they have going for them is the red laser-dot experience of staring at the phone's screen as you watch the car come ever closer.

"It's almost here!"

"It's here!"

Bliss.

Everything about Uber makes sense. Beyond the onscreen fun of ordering, when the car shows up, it's clean and new, the drivers are well-dressed and courteous. "Bottled water? Phone charger? What music do you like?" And then they take you where you need to go. And their prices are good. Uber in LA is the best. Also Berlin. And Paris. And London and Sydney. But not in Vancouver, where I spend a fair amount of time.

☿

I get a lot of visitors in Vancouver, and those from New York City are always horrified because my kitchen has a garburator in the sink.

"Oh my God, you have a garburator."

"Oh. Yeah. They're great. They reduce your trash stream by a lot."

"But people put their . . . *babies* down the garburator!"

I know. But in their defence, these are otherwise really smart people standing there saying this. So I always go easy on them and point out that the reason New York didn't have garburators until recently is because back when they were invented, the Teamsters went crazy because trash going down the drain is trash the Teamsters can't move in their trucks. So they fabricated the urban legend of people putting babies down the garburator to galvanize public sentiment on their side.

"Oh."

✻

So back to Uber. What I hear from some people now is, "Yes, but you could get raped by an Uber driver! They could be psycho murderers."

"Well, you could get raped by any driver, really. So why are you focusing on Uber?"

I think right now the Uber situation is like the Teamsters and garburators. There's no real argument to *not* have Uber drivers. They are superior to taxis in all possible ways. The only thing stopping them are all these cab drivers who had to pay extortionate amounts of money for a *medallion*, and suddenly entering their arena are these new people with superior service who didn't get hosed buying a medallion (honestly, *medallions*? How is that even still a thing?). So of course taxi owners are angry, and of course they're going to lash out and try to generate urban legends to frighten people who, the moment they use an Uber, will never use a taxi again if they don't have to. Uber's not alone in this sort of engineered fear environment. Remember the Craigslist killer?

Gosh—someone didn't buy an ad in a newspaper, and for their stupidity they paid with *their life*.

In Canada a while ago, the press revelled in the fate of an Edmonton couple who rented out their house on Airbnb and came back only to find it trashed to the tune of C$100,000. Airbnb now has the largest hotel footprint in the world. Uber has image problems, but they're on the correct historical track. Craigslist, Lyft et al—the shareconomy? The freeconomy? It's going to happen.

And the moment these firms start paying more in taxes is the moment they officially suffocate to death the old economy. As for Vancouver, which has the lowest number of taxis per capita in Canada, fear-mongering can only last so long. People travel. They know something better when they see it. And one day soon I'll be able to follow the red laser dot on the floor of my hometown.

361

First, let me tell you who I am. I'm Sharon Firth and I was an elementary school teacher in Vancouver, Washington . . . not the Canadian Vancouver—the other Vancouver, across the Columbia River from Portland, Oregon—and I really liked teaching younger kids. Younger kids are so sweet. But I will add that, at thirteen, the girls turn into bitches, and when I look at their little heads, all I can see in the classroom is shoplifted mascara and thought balloons filled with very cruel nicknames for me—or whoever got stuck teaching them. Boys become sulking monsters at fifteen, and that's easier to handle. So, yes, I got to teach the young kids, and it really was like teaching angels, but I'm also very aware that it is dangerous to confuse angels with children, and this is my tale.

It was in late October 1975. It was just past three and class had gotten out for the day. Most of the kids had gathered their things and left, then there were a few stragglers, and then there was quiet, and when I looked up, there was one student sitting calmly in his chair: Greg Cushing, the sweetest little guy ever, tight brown curls and never any sass. He was twelve.

"Greg, sweetie, you're not leaving?"

"I'm not Greg."

"Greg, I've got papers to mark and I don't have time for games. Come on now, scoot. Get home. Your mama's waiting for you."

"I'm not Greg."

I decided to go along with it. "So, then, if you're not Greg, who might you be?"

"I don't have a name. Not the way you think of names. I guess you'd call it more of a number than a name."

"Okay . . ."

"This is Greg's body. I've hijacked it. He's not here right now. Greg is in storage."

"Greg, sweetie, you're scaring me."

"I guess you're not listening to me . . . Sharon. If you want to call me a name, call me 361."

That's when I understood it was real. It doesn't take much. Greg wasn't there. I exhaled and sat back in my chair to collect my thoughts. It was a rainy day already and getting dark out, even at three-thirty. I wanted to run out of the room, and badly, but how could I?

"Okay, 361, tell me something that would confirm to me that you are indeed alien."

"Very well. You're a lesbian but you're not coping with it, and the stress of maintaining a heterosexual facade is causing you to overeat and gain weight. You think nobody knows, but there's always chatter in the staff room. And in any event, suppressing your identity is making you profoundly unhappy. You've contemplated leaving teaching and leaving Vancouver, but you have a cowardly streak and it will probably get the better of you. It will set you up for a lifetime of pain and regret."

I stood up and stared at him. I walked over—I didn't even look to see if the door was open or if anyone was looking—and I slapped him hard on the face. "How dare you!"

"A slap. How clichéd, Sharon. As if a slap is going to make the truth go away. Here, while you're at it, why don't you kick Greg's body and damage it—give it scars. Give it something to make his mama want to take you to court."

I was terrified. I didn't know what to do.

"Sit down," said 361. "I'm not here to hurt you."

I slumped down into the seat of the desk beside him. The chair was tiny. I felt fat. And 361 was indeed correct in everything he had said about me.

"Good," he said. "I think I've got your attention."

"Where do you come from?"

"Excuse me?"

"Where do you come from? Some other planet? Why are you on Earth?"

"You've been watching too much late-night TV, Sharon. If I'm alien, it's only in personality."

I could feel myself sweating. My ears were buzzing. I don't know what it was . . . maybe what it would feel like if a panther walked into the room and was sniffing around while I sat there hoping I didn't smell like panther chow.

"I can see you need time to think over my brief visit, Sharon. To prove to you I'm legitimate, I'll give you a list of things that are going to happen in the world over the next week."

"What?"

"Just stop and listen. Today, October 27, a man in Ottawa, Canada, killed a man and wounded five people in a high school and then shot himself. You haven't heard about it yet. Also today, Rex Stout, an American detective novel writer, died. Tomorrow, Georges Carpentier, a French boxer, will die. On the twenty-ninth, President Ford will announce that he will veto any legislation calling for a federal bailout of New York City. The cover of *The Daily News* the next day will read: 'Ford to City: Drop Dead.' That same day Juan Carlos I of Spain will become acting head of state after dictator Francisco Franco concedes he is too ill to govern. Also, a Yugoslavian airliner will crash while attempting to land in Prague and seventy-five of one hundred and twenty people on board will die."

"How do you—?"

"Shush. I'll see you again same time next week. Goodbye, Sharon."

Greg's—*361's*—head slumped and then suddenly it was Greg there, no mistaking it, and seeing me there with an astonished face quite reasonably freaked him out. "Miss Firth? Wait—what happened? Where is everyone? Why are you here? Am I in trouble?"

I sucked in breath. "Sweetie, I think you have a cold. You'd better go home to your mama."

"So I'm not in trouble or anything?"

"You? Greg, you don't have a troubled bone in your body. Now go home. Scoot."

"Bye, Miss Firth."

I really don't know what I thought. Trickery? Demonic possession? Blackmail? I mean, it was simply too mind-blowing to even remotely try to explain to anybody. I couldn't phone my family or my friend Donna because . . . how could I even begin to ex . . .

. . . And then Gerald Ford really did tell New York City to screw off, and Franco did concede power, and then the airliner did crash. After that I didn't sleep for the whole weekend. Come Monday, I think the stress was showing. Miss Milne in the staff room offered me Midol, so I could tell I wasn't making a very good show of things. I blew it off as "Mondayitis" and got a few laughs, and then I walked into my classroom. I had to have been on some form of autopilot, because all I remember of the day was parroting math lessons, making construction-paper chains and trying not to stare at Greg Cushing.

Classes finally ended and the students left, and of course Greg was sitting there.

"Greg?"

"No, Sharon. It's not Greg."

"361. Hello."

"It's not a very exciting week coming up, Sharon. I wish I could tell you more exciting news, but the news is what it is."

"Why are you talking to me? How many of you are there?"

"How *many*? That's an odd question, which, for various reasons, can't be answered. Let's just say not very many."

"So again, why are you reaching out to me?"

"Sharon, you're being a bore."

Then 361 went quiet and Greg's body froze, as if he were rewinding or something, and then he said, "We are your friends." Something new was speaking and it had a mechanical sound.

"How do I know that?"

"Because we have taken the time to learn about you, assess your life and develop the choices you can now make to ensure that the remainder of your life goes unwasted."

I decided to be tough. "What would those choices be, then?"

"Leave this Vancouver and go to the other Vancouver. Stop teaching and start making objects with your hands. We recommend metal at the scale of jewellery. That will then make you comfortable within a lesbian existence, and out of that you will meet someone who will stick with you until you die."

"Who the hell are you to be telling me what to do with my life!"

"We wish you to activate what is most likely your last chance at what you call happiness."

There was a knock on the door: Ed Jarvis, the phys-ed coach, kind of a goofball. "Am I interrupting anything?"

361 and I turned into the picture of sunshine and happiness. "Just a bit of detention and some math homework, Ed. Everything okay?"

Ed looked understandably suspicious. "I came to drop off the unused UNICEF boxes from last week."

"Oh, right. Just put them there by the pencil sharpener. Thanks, Ed."

"No problem." He dropped off the boxes and left.

361 said, "Don't worry about the coach spreading rumours. Ed

steals underwear from his apartment building's drying machines. Just mention that and he'll be quiet."

"Jesus, what am I in for here?"

"Here is your news for the next week, Sharon. Tomorrow Fidel Castro will order 6,500 troops to Angola. On Thursday an English rock band called the Sex Pistols will play their first performance at a London art school. On Friday a vapour-cloud release from a Dutch petroleum cracking facility in the town of Geleen will kill 14 people and injure 109. Also on Friday, Patricia Hearst will be declared fit to stand trial. That's it, I'm afraid. All in all, an incredibly boring week. Goodbye, Sharon."

And then 361 was gone.

What would you do in a case like this? What would anyone do? I was certainly not dashing off to a church . . . and I wasn't going to run to a shrink. I actually ought to have gone to Donna's brother, who dealt weed from the back of his bakery, but I didn't.

I looked at my life.

361 was absolutely correct. Who was I fooling? I'd dated a few guys in high school, but I might as well have been dating cardboard boxes; there was no sexual anything there. At the same time it seemed like gay guys were suddenly in the news, growing mustaches and having endless sex, and there was all this new disco music. It didn't seem like there was much for a gay woman—certainly not in Vancouver, Washington, more or less a blue-collar suburb of Portland.

I was lonely. Having to maintain a normal face for the world was taking its toll: "Are you seeing anyone? Let me help you meet just the right guy . . ." So 361—whatever the hell he was—had nailed my life, and that was humiliating.

And, of course, everything he said would happen that week happened, and come Monday I wasn't so much nervous as I was excited. Miss Milne (she of the Midol) said, "Aren't you full of beans today." I giggled nervously . . . as if she could ever imagine what was happening. All day long, it was all I could do to contain my excitement. After class ended, for some reason the kids were dawdling that day, and I had to almost bark to get them out of the room.

Greg's body sat there waiting for me. "Hello, Miss Firth."

"Hello, 361."

"I'm hoping by now you understand my authenticity."

"Yes, I do. So—you're obviously here for a reason: you want me to be happy. Well, that's fine and all, but why me? Are there millions of 361s out there going around telling people how to be happy?"

"No, Sharon. You're almost unique."

"Me? Unique? How? And how does that help you?"

"Your body's cells contain the CCR5-Δ32 variant protein. They lack both CCR5 and CXCR4 receptors on their surfaces, and thus confer you with resistance to a broad range of viruses and their variants."

"I have no idea what you just said."

"I am currently inhabiting the body of Gregory, and Gregory is gay."

"What? He's twelve."

"Have it your way. He *will* be gay, then."

"What does that have to do with anything?"

"The virus that will kill him will be one that targets gay men, and it will target and kill Greg."

"What the—? How is that even biologically possible? Wait. Don't even . . . What does this have to do with me?"

"Greg is doomed. You need to see what's at stake if you don't follow my advice."

"I'll just give him some of my blood if I'm a living cure."

"It doesn't work that way. Are you going to knock on his parents' front door and say, 'Hello, I'm Sharon and I'd like to give your son some of my bone marrow'? You also have, Sharon, another protein mutation that will be important in the year 2018."

"Who does that one target?"

"Almost everyone, except a few people like you who have another specific protein mutation."

"Why don't you just suck me up into a UFO and deep-freeze me or something?"

"We would if we could, Sharon, but it doesn't work that way. Channelling Greg here is about the best we can do. And besides, we need you alive."

"Do you have any idea how creepy you sound?"

"Creepy as sex between two women?"

I whacked Greg/361 across the face, then heard a voice—Ed's—behind me.

"What the hell do you think you're doing, Sharon?"

My face flushed red. "Mind your own business, Ed. Go steal some panties from your basement dryer."

The blood drained from Ed's face. What had I done? He stared for a few moments, then closed the door and walked away. "I shouldn't have said that."

"Not to worry, Sharon. He won't blab."

I was winded. "So then, what happens next?" I asked. "Do we meet every Monday from now on?"

"No. You'll hear from me again, but not through Greg."

"But when?"

"Soon enough. It's very difficult for us—for me—to do this, Sharon. I'm at the end of my time here. Remember my life advice and act on it as quickly as possible. Goodbye."

It took a minute for Greg to return, during which time I went back to my desk at the front and pretended nothing had happened. When he came to, he looked at me. "Is this a . . . detention?"

"No, sweetie, I think you just took a quick nap."

"Oh. Okay." Poor, doomed Greg got up and left the classroom.

I walked down the hallway and looked outside. It was pouring rain and the Columbia River was swollen. In a blur I got into my little Datsun and drove home, to the small bungalow I'd gotten a rental deal on from a friend of my father. I went into the kitchen, stared inside the fridge and poured myself a glass of milk, a reflex whenever I get worried, which stemmed from a hygiene class slideshow on the perils of osteoporosis in women.

I put the glass down on the counter and turned around. Ed was standing there. "I don't want to be doing this, Sharon."

I knew what he meant. "Don't, Ed. This is a dumb idea."

"How did you know?"

"About the underwear? Ed, it doesn't matter."

"Tell me!"

I made up a lie. "My girlfriend lives in your building."

"What's her name?"

I had no idea how big Ed's building was, so I tried to pick as common a name as I could. "Susan."

"Her?"

Thank God I'd hit a nail on the head. "Yes, but she only told me because she knows we work in the same place. She thinks it's funny. But it's your secret, Ed. We won't tell anyone."

"I don't trust you, Sharon." He took a step toward me.

I tried to open the fridge door between us, but he pounced too quickly. He put a rope around my neck and I was almost instantly unconscious . . . but I didn't die. Instead I went into a coma, where I am now, and I feel very stupid indeed. Obviously 361, that bastard, was smart enough to see the future, and he engineered the whole Ed fiasco to keep me alive yet immobilized.

And so here I am. I don't know what the date is or what time of day it is, but I know that my body has become the equivalent of a working farm. Almost daily someone's removing eggs or taking tissue or marrow samples, and I suppose I don't mind. I do feel sorry for Greg. He must be long dead by now. Judging by the recent increase in marrow harvesting, I suppose we must be getting close to the year 2018.

My Name

The morning after my Sweet Sixteen party, I saw the eyes and mouth of a Halloween pumpkin wash up onto the same spot on the beach where I almost lost my virginity. It was Saco Bay, south of Portland, with the beautiful tall grass and the wooden walkways leading to the sea. It was November and cold, no tourists anywhere, and that grey morning it was just me on the sand, relieved I'd not done the nasty with Nathan Schein, and then these little orange eye and mouth chunks washed ashore, like a ghost of a smile.

Symbols like these are important. Last week I saw a white bird, an albino crow, land on the freeway beside speeding cars and pick up trash with the black crows. It seemed like the regular crows should have been bringing it food instead of it having to look for its own. It was different. It was special.

Last night an animal scuttled across the roof . . . Maybe it was a ghost, but I'm too old to believe in ghosts. Yet I do believe in souls. And I believe that when you talk about souls, they suddenly fill the room, and you can feel them all around you. Even people who don't believe in souls know what I mean when I say this. Rub the bottle and out comes the genie. It's there.

My name is Hayley. I'm one of those surplus Chinese girl babies everyone began adopting back in the 1990s. Two decades later and still people in my town stare at me, and I know what's going through their minds . . . I was unwanted . . . Some people maybe pity me . . . definitely some racist stuff going on . . . and sex fantasy stuff too . . . I'm not dumb. They're probably waiting for me to magically produce a violin and play like I'm in the Boston Pops.

A lot of people assume I speak Chinese, even though the closest to China I've ever been geographically is the outlet malls in Vermont. But whatever the people in my town are thinking, it can't be anything like what it feels like to be inside my own head.

Here's my thing: I'm a complete alien. Not an immigration alien, but an *alien* alien. The UFO that brought me here from my home planet is lost beneath the waters of nearby Molasses Pond. When it crashed, it marooned me on this planet populated by minivans, divorce lawyers, Rubbermaid storage bins and trail mix. Which is to say, I guess, that this planet is neither paradise nor hell, just a place called Maine, which seems like that's all it's ever going to be. And here I am: the outsider, with people always being too nice to me because in the end they don't think I deserve to be here with them. I somehow cheated by being both surplus and a girl baby—*can't kill a baby!* People look at me and think I'm smarter than I really am. And none of those people, none of them, know that I come from a place they'll never know—from wherever my UFO got made. I know what you're thinking: *How cute, she thinks she's an alien. How* banal. *What next—black lipstick?* Well, so what. Screw you.

Last summer, just after I graduated from my junior year, our neighbour's basset hound, Henry, went missing. I liked Henry a lot—we all did. He was an old soul, his eyes ringed with hamburger-red lids, even though he was only a year and a half old. When he slobbered on me, it felt like he was forgiving me for anything bad I'd done that day. And he never barked; I liked that because there used to be a dog three houses down from us that barked all day and all night and it drove me crazy.

Henry lived outside mostly. Our town's small enough that using a leash would be an embarrassment or an admission of some kind of dog-ownership failure. Dogs are like honorary people here.

I remember hearing the doorbell. I was eating a red Popsicle around sunset, and it was Leeta, Henry's owner, wondering if we'd seen him anywhere. Me and my two (non-Chinese/non-alien) sisters, Emily and Rochelle, went out into the street and started calling for him. It's amazing how quickly our tone turned from "Henry! Here, Henry!" to "Oh God, he's probably dead." Rochelle is much younger than me and was wearing her bejewelled ice-skating onesie. She began suggesting worst-case scenarios and started crying.

My mother told Rochelle to shush and say a prayer. My mother's pretty churchy. People think only liberals adopted Chinese girl babies, but we're distributed across the board politically and religiously. I never minded church because, as I said, I believe in the soul. Churches are just bureaucracies to handle the paperwork, so they don't interest me much. And I like it that aliens can have a soul just as much as humans. Why not?

Emily, who's two years older than me, arrived late for dinner. She'd been a few streets over looking for Henry. No luck, so after dinner my dad and I went out in his car, trawling the streets and calling out Henry's name, but we didn't find him. Nobody did.

My senior year passed quickly, and in the fall I went to a college in Portland, at the University of Southern Maine. I was lucky to get accepted, as my grades have never been very good. I liked being away from home, and I liked not having to always drive by the lake where my UFO sank. I liked that people at USM didn't assume I was a surplus Chinese girl baby, and I started to find it easier to pretend I was a human being, that unwantedness was no longer so central to the core of my being.

I made some friends and earned okay grades, but only okay. I got a part-time job at a doughnut place that I didn't take too seriously, so it ended up being fun. Other kids from USM worked there too. It was like a TV sitcom where everyone's witty and looks good and has good lines right on cue. I never discussed souls there. It would have felt out of place.

A few days ago I went down to Nashua, New Hampshire, with my friend Sara. We wanted to go to the Bloomingdale's at the Merrimack Outlets, and we also wanted to blow off class, so it was a double win. For some reason there were way too many people at the mall; Sara and I got peopled out and we decided to bail after doing just three stores. We were headed back to the car and there was a woman with a basset hound on a leash. It looked just like Henry, so I called out, "Here, Henry! Here, Henry, Henry, Henry!" The basset hound froze. He turned around, looked at me and yelped, yanking his leash out of the woman's hand. He came bounding over and started squeaking and circling me, like those dogs when they see their owners returning from duty in Afghanistan.

It was Henry, no mistaking it—the strange patch of brown he had on his left ear—and I was confused. Henry started slobbering all over my face, and then I twigged on to what was happening and said, "Sara. Get out your iPhone now. She's trying to get away." The woman who'd had Henry on the leash was desperately trying to get out of her parking spot, but she'd put her car in the wrong gear. She was stupid to try to drive away. She should have just ran away while we stood there in shock. In any event, she slammed her car into the car parked in front of it, then squealed her tires as it went into reverse and she peeled out. Sara got it all.

So I sat there with Henry on the parking lot's asphalt, in shock, while Sara posted the clip online to some sort of shaming website. Henry scrunched himself up to me and wouldn't move, and when I stood up, he thought I was leaving and freaked out. So I had to pick him up and carry him to Sara's car, and he sat in my lap as we drove to the police station.

As you can imagine, Sara's clip went viral. It turned out the dog thief was Leeta's sister-in-law—I can just imagine Christmas dinners at their houses for the next fifty years. I became a mini-hero and got to be on the WSCH TV-6 local news, and Henry was home again and a blanket of peace fell over the neighbourhood.

Then a few days ago I was visiting my parents, and my mom said, "What do you know—some technicians were doing a sonar test and they located a large metal object in Molasses Pond. They think it's a car. I'll bet you it's that Anderson boy who went missing in 1972."

Needless to say, I was at Molasses Pond within minutes, and I saw they had big winches and a diver was attaching them to whatever it was down there. The Channel Six news reporter was there and said, "Well, hello there, it's you again. Wherever you go, there's action."

"I just can't help it."

It was sort of fun and insider, knowing the reporter. A neighbour, Jeanie, stopped and came over to join us. "It's that Anderson boy. That's what everyone's guessing." Then Jeanie looked at me. "Hayley, how does it feel to have rescued Henry like that? That's got to feel good."

"I didn't rescue the dog. I was just in the right place at the right time. You would have done it too."

The car was emerging from the water, and everyone was correct—it was Tony Anderson's 1971 Mustang, all covered in brown mud, like it was having a spa day. At the wheel were the bones that remained of Tony. I was the only person not shooting this on a cellphone.

To be honest, I was sad to be wrong about the UFO, but I was right in thinking there was something potent down there. Of course everyone on the lakeshore gawked and kept on shooting iPhone movies. It was genuinely awesome to see a ghost car complete with skeleton, and we'd waited enough time for the privilege of gawking—we'd *earned* it. But then the muddy car went onto a flatbed and everyone else left, and it was just me standing there looking at the now flat void of Molasses Pond. I thought about how quickly water, which is clear, turns into darkness. Shouldn't lakes be colourless? I threw a few white stones into the water and they vanished almost immediately.

I remembered driving back from Nashua with Henry sitting on my lap while Sara drove. Henry was whimpering a little bit because he knew he was going home. It was around sunset and we were on this patch of freeway where there are eight lanes, and cars and their white headlights kept coming toward us relentlessly. I began to think about how many people die on Earth in any given minute, and I figured out that each bright set of headlights was a soul that had just died and was vanishing off into the Great Beyond.

I sometimes get to thinking about what I say when people ask how it felt to find Henry at the outlet mall. What I don't tell people is that, more than anything—anything, anything in the entire universe—I wish that someone would find me the way I found Henry. They'd look at me and call me by my real name, whatever that may be, and I'd recognize it. Because I don't believe the one I have.

Mrs. McCarthy
and Mrs. Brown

Mrs. Brown

I'm Collette Brown. At the age of thirty-seven I was living in Grosse Isle, Michigan, a sleepy suburb of Detroit. On an early afternoon in March 1963, I had my friend Peg McCarthy over to my place for weekday lunch and a bit of venting. Each of us had a brood of five children who tried us constantly, but it was really just venting, as we both knew our blessings.

That afternoon it was cool and cloudy out, and we each had our two youngest downstairs playing together. It was nice and quiet, certainly a respite from our nightly chaos of dinners for seven. Before lunch Peg knit a baby bootie for a neighbour friend, and then around twelve-thirty I made sandwiches with a tin of tuna from the local A&P, some Hellmann's mayonnaise, Land O'Lakes butter and slices of bread from a warm, fresh loaf from a nearby bakery. I called to the kids down in the rumpus room and asked if they wanted tuna fish or peanut butter and jelly, and they unanimously chose peanut butter and jelly, and because of that, they lived and I didn't.

After Peg left, I got ready for the predictable after-school onslaught and then started getting dinner ready. I was so busy I didn't really pay much attention to the fact that my vision was blurring and I felt a bit weak, but just chalked it up to a long day.

Before turning out the lights at bedtime, I made a decision to go to the eye doctor the next day, assuming that the weakness wasn't the start of flu, which I truly didn't want.

I died in my sleep.

Mrs. McCarthy

I'm Margaret McCarthy—Peg—and in March of 1963 I was thirty-nine. Like my friend Collette, I had my own brood of five. After knitting and lunching at Collette's house, I drove to the market for some ingredients for spaghetti. I ended up using a bottled sauce because I was feeling oddly tired, and come sundown I was too lazy to even dice up some onions and sauté them in butter. My mother always added onions to everything because she said it would prevent scurvy, which is a disease pirates used to get, and I thought it was funny, but we get these superstitions from our parents and they stick.

Come bedtime I was in bad shape. I was vomiting almost non-stop, my eyesight kept coming and going like I had blinds on my eyes, and my throat hurt something fierce. In the powder room mirror, I saw that my eyelids weren't closing correctly. I couldn't speak and could barely hold up my head, so my husband called an ambulance and around three a.m. I arrived at Outer Drive Hospital in Lincoln Park. The doctors there looked at me and poked and prodded, and I could see (in between vomiting and losing my eyesight) that they were in a state of confusion, which didn't help my confidence much. I was worried I'd somehow caught polio. I didn't want to end up in a creepy iron lung like I once saw at a freak show in Fort Wayne when I was twelve. I was so scared I didn't sleep for a week after seeing that thing. Why didn't they just kill people?

The doctors pumped me full of drugs, and I'd come to and go out of consciousness, but mostly I'd go. I was just so relieved when, amid all the hubbub, I heard them say I didn't have polio. But . . . botulism? Botulism was a kitchen bogeyman I remembered from home ec class in high school. I didn't think people ever actually *got* it.

About twenty-four hours after I got to the hospital, I couldn't move my facial muscles. The doctors thought I was asleep, but I wasn't, and I could hear what they were saying, which was that Collette was dead and they'd done swabs to see what botulism strain we'd contracted. Apparently our strain was type E, found only in Arctic fish, and it was so rare that there was no antitoxin available in the United States. They had to bring in some from Toronto, Canada, of all places. But because it was a marine botulism, they quickly figured out that the tuna was the culprit. They found and swabbed the can in Collette's kitchen trash can, the can of A&P Chunk Light Tuna from lunchtime, batch number WY3Y2-118X, one of 5,760 tins shipped to Detroit from a San Francisco firm called the Washington Packing Corp.

Botulism is actually everywhere, but it becomes pernicious only when it encounters a warm, protein-rich, anaerobic environment in which to grow: the can of tuna. My type E botulism inhibited the release of acetylcholine in my nervous system, a chemical that produces synaptic bridges by which nerve cell axons and dendrites connect. My botulism symptoms started with my facial muscles and then spread toward my limbs, leading to paralysis of the breathing muscles and respiratory failure. After five days of fighting it, I died. It made *Newsweek* magazine. I certainly never would have thought that a bad tuna sandwich could become national news. Maybe it was a slow news week.

In the end, the fish-packing company was able to show that the tuna had been packed under scrupulously stringent conditions,

UPI

Seized shipment: Did a leak kill . . .

. . . Mrs. McCarthy and Mrs. Brown?

Image spread taken from "Two Tuna Sandwiches," published in *Newsweek*, April 1, 1963, author unknown. Courtesy United Press International.

cooked at 242 degrees Fahrenheit for seventy-seven minutes, and samplings of other tins from the same batch showed no signs of botulism. They ultimately chalked up the botulism to a mechanical failure—maybe someone dropped a can and put it back in the wrong part of the tuna-fish canning machine. We'll never know. The botulism that killed Collette and me came from nowhere, killed us anonymously and then vanished. I don't think there's any moral to be learned from our deaths.

Andy

I'm Andy Warhol. I died in New York City at 6:32 a.m. on February 22, 1987. I was in hospital for a gallbladder operation. I don't really know what happened, but I woke up and it was still dark out, and it felt like there was chlorinated swimming-pool water going up my nose—like when I was thrown into the Catholic swimming pool in Pittsburgh, growing up, before they realized I was a sissy and that throwing me into the deep end was almost like murder. Apparently I had cardiac arrhythmia, but I didn't know. I could feel the gurgling in my lungs, as if I was drowning. I know that's not what a heart attack is supposed to feel like.

And then . . . I don't remember anything hurting, so I guess that's what dying feels like—not so bad. And when I realized I was dead, I began wondering who'd show up at my funeral and whether it would be open coffin or not, because if it was open coffin, afterwards people would only talk about whether the hair and makeup were any good. I always used to say that a funeral was usually the most glamorous moment in most people's lives, just because of that—afterwards people only talk about the hair and makeup— but I didn't want that. Honestly, if it was going to be open casket, then just a dash of Christian Dior No. 425 concealer, then apply a tiny bit of rouge on the cheeks, and then add a fake zit just so people know it's the real me and not a fake me. I found out later that they put me in a solid bronze casket with gold-plated rails and white upholstery. They dressed me in a black cashmere suit, a paisley tie, a platinum wig and sunglasses, which is kind of a cheat, but sunglasses got Jackie O through the last three decades of her life. They're always well advised, and let's face it: eyes are really hard for morticians to get right.

I don't know if death is such a big deal. Wherever it is I am now, it's not that exciting; it feels like I'm waiting to get a driver's licence renewed. They have buffet tables set up, but the people in the lineup are so unglamorous: Some guy who got run over by a bus in Lagos, Nigeria. Some woman from Uzbekistan whose husband murdered her by pinching closed her nostrils and clamping shut her mouth while she slept. And there are so many old people here too. I hate it. I want to hold a sign saying, "I normally hang out with younger and much better-looking people."

I'll be out of here soon enough, I guess, but in the meantime they won't let me have any film for my camera. So for all of those people who know and recognize me, I have to pretend to be taking their picture to get them to stop bugging me—but fortunately not all of the world is into fame, so it could have been a lot worse. Being recognizable cuts both ways.

My mother's here, but she's almost at the front of the line for getting a driver's licence or whatever it is, so we don't have much time—whatever time is. It's nice to be with her again. We cut snowflakes out of tissue paper a little while back, and she teased me because I always used to say that dying was like going to Bloomingdale's except you never came back. She thinks it's funny because there's no shopping for me here, so it's really boring. There aren't even garage sales or flea markets. It's like Abu Dhabi in the 1970s—just nothing to buy. Someone could make a killing if they could just figure out a way to make money out of Purgatory.

Halston's here, but he's a bit too grand and mostly hangs out with Mrs. Vreeland, who still looks terrific, even though she's what—a million years old? I'm wondering if Halston and I were ever really friends or if it was just a sort of arranged marriage set up for us by magazines. He's trying to butch it up a bit because of dying of AIDS and all—he doesn't want to be treated like a fruitcake. I called him on it and he said, "Darling, you weren't there at the end. I looked like those Nazis at the end of *Raiders of the Lost Ark*, with their faces melting off. I want people to think of me as a hunky Iowa boy who made good in the big city." Well, it's his image, not mine. And all these old people here couldn't care less. Mostly they sit around wondering what's for dinner next. It's like a cruise ship.

So I was with my mother, thumbing through really worn-out copies of *Paris Match* from the mid-1970s when Steve Rubell popped by and said, "Andy, you'll *die*. You just have to meet these two gals I just bumped into. They're fan*tas*tic!"

My mother made a face at me. I knew what she meant: Steve was really wired. Wait . . . how did Steve manage to find coke in Purgatory? Oh my God, someone was dealing coke! I was so jealous. I just wanted to get in on it because at least it would be something to buy and sell.

"Andy, here they are now. May I present to you these two lovely ladies . . ."

I was hoping for Babe Paley and Suzy Parker, but instead he introduced these two frumpy mom-looking women with drugstore glasses and Sears cardigans from the early 1960s. They looked like they bought Tide and Brillo pads and gave their kids vitamin supplements and hula hoops.

"Andy, this is Mrs. McCarthy and Mrs. Brown."

I looked at these women. "Uhhh . . ." It was embarrassing. I never did figure out a way of glossing over the fact that you don't

Jasper Johns' 'Three Flags'

Solomon R. Guggenheim Museum

Solomon R. Guggenheim Museum
Roy Lichtenstein's 'Ice Cream Soda' and Andy Warhol's 'Dick Tracy': 'Is it art? Yes and no'

Image spread taken from "Pop Goes the Easel," published in *Newsweek*, April 1, 1963, author unknown. Courtesy Solomon R. Guggenheim Museum.

recognize a person in front of you who you're supposed to know. So I said, "Uhhh . . ."

"Andy, come on now. This is Mrs. McCarthy and Mrs. Brown. Think *Tunafish Disaster*."

Oh my God, it was *them*—Mrs. McCarthy and Mrs. Brown, those housewives who died of botulism back in 1963. I did a bunch of paintings about them. This was really cool. "Wow. Uh, hi. It's so cool to, um, meet you."

"Well, it had to happen sometime. I'm Margaret . . . Peg."

"And I'm Collette."

Steve sat there beaming like he'd just set me up on a date with a really great-looking Swiss Guard, but I mean it's not like I'm going to give him a discount on a portrait for it. In any event, he could see that my encounter with these two women wouldn't be very interesting for him, so he vanished.

Mrs. McCarthy removed a copy of *Newsweek* from her purse. It was dated April 1, 1963, so I kind of knew what was coming next. "You'll remember this issue, surely, Mr. Warhol."

"Andy."

"Andy." She flipped through the pages to near the end, page seventy-six, the magazine's medical section. There, right in the centre of the page, were two postage-stamp-size photos of the two women underneath a can of tuna seized by the FDA. Mrs. McCarthy said, "Quite flattering, don't you think, Andy?"

"Uh, yeah. You look great."

Mrs. Brown added, "I liked that photo. It was spontaneous and I was using my real smile, not my fake camera smile."

"Smiling for a camera is so abstract," I said.

The magazine article was titled "Two Tuna Sandwiches" and detailed the process by which the two women had died of botulism. For my paintings of them, I blew up the images of the tuna fish can plus the two women, with the caption "Seized shipment: Did a leak kill . . . Mrs. McCarthy and Mrs. Brown?" I screened them with black paint on a silver background.

"You know," said Peg, "I heard that in 2009 the painting you made of us, *Mrs. McCarthy and Mrs. Brown (Tunafish Disaster)*, sold for $6.1 million."

I felt sick to my stomach. That sale wasn't in inflated future dollars; that was a real $6.1 million, and I was angry that I'd never broken six figures in my own lifetime . . . but then I wasn't quite sure what time meant in Purgatory. I didn't know how far in the future we really were. People would show up and we'd say, "Wow, Michael Jackson and Farrah Fawcett in one day!" But I don't know, it gets too abstract. Farrah looked really great when she arrived. She was a real star.

"But . . ."

Of course I knew what was coming next . . .

"But, Mr. Warhol—Andy—we couldn't help but notice what was on page eighty of the same copy of *Newsweek*."

"Ummm . . . yeah, I remember." On page eighty was the magazine's review of a pop art show I was in at the Guggenheim Museum.

"Andy," said Margaret, "I don't think it's just a coincidence that the review of your work was just a few pages away from the article about our deaths. Am I correct?"

"Gosh. Ummm . . . yeah, I guess there's a connection."

The two women stared at me, and it was obvious that there was no escaping without my confessing everything.

"Okay, one morning my studio assistant came in after being out all night and he was still really wired on amphetamines—his body was kind of vibrating. I don't know how he and his friends could do that all the time. That stuff is harsh. Before you know it, your skin looks like dried corn husks."

"I did an amphetamine diet once," said Peg. "After my third child, and it nearly caused a divorce. I went through my days feeling like Xavier Cugat's maracas."

"How much weight did you lose?"

"About ten pounds."

"So you looked good?"

"Yes, I did, actually."

"So, what does it matter if you were rattling around?"

Collette interrupted. "You were talking about this assistant."

"Oh yeah, right. Ummm . . . So he came in and he had a copy of the *Newsweek* you have there and he started waving it at me and told me I'd got a great big review in it, except he wouldn't let me see it. He'd go to page eighty, where the review was, and read half a sentence out loud and then he'd gasp and go silent. It was very funny, but I wanted to see the review. Pop art was still really new back then. When you get an art review in *Newsweek*, suddenly all those people in the middle of the country start to know about you, and it can really raise your prices."

"What then?"

"Then my mother phoned and whoever answered let her know I was right there, so I couldn't escape and I had to speak with her."

"You don't like your mother?"

"I do, but I knew that if she was calling me at work it meant I had to go home to help her with something, and I was right. She had some income tax forms and had really gotten herself into a state. She'd never seen tax forms before—my father handled that kind of thing—and she thought the government was going to confiscate everything, so I had to cab home and calm her down."

"You're such a good son."

"Uh, thanks, but I don't know about that, because all I could think about was getting a copy of *Newsweek* as quickly as possible so I could read my review. But my mother insisted on making me lunch. I was getting ants in my pants just itching to get out of there, and I finally did. I bought five *Newsweek*s—"

"Five?"

"It's more fun than buying just one. Try it some time. Buy five copies of a magazine and the magazine guy says, 'Hey, you in that magazine or something?' When you say yes, it makes their day, and when they go home at night, they have something to say at the dinner table."

"That's a lovely suggestion."

"Thanks."

"So you bought your magazines and . . ."

"I was angry because the Guggenheim's director flipped and flopped about pop art, saying, 'Is it art? Yes and no.' I mean, you think with your own museum you could be a bit more support-ive. Hilton Kramer trashed the show completely, which was no surprise, and it was kind of nice to triumph over him in the end. I bumped into him up here not too long ago and he just hissed and stormed away. But you have to remember that the Sixties hadn't happened yet, and to most people, art was just squiggles. So when you showed people something that wasn't squiggles, their brains froze because they'd spent the past fifteen years being told that only squiggles were art. It was hard on them. At the same time I wasn't the least bit surprised when I found out the CIA was underwriting almost all that abstract expressionism—all those expensive shows abroad, the lavish catalogues, the pretend sales to big collections."

"You mean the CIA funded modern art?"

"The American government didn't want Europe to be the intel-lectual king anymore. They wanted Americans to be the avant-garde. But, I mean, they spent fifteen years supporting squiggles and then there I was, painting really great American things like Coca-Cola and movie stars, and you didn't see me getting any CIA funding."

"What a shame."

"Thanks."

"So what happened then?"

"After reading the article I was kind of fidgety. I didn't know whether to say thank you or fuck you to *Newsweek* magazine. It was such a big publicity moment, but it was also so ambiguous. How hard is it to make up your mind? Finally, someone had made something to replace squiggles and they just sat there dithering. That was so un-American."

Collette looked at me. "So, let me guess. You started flipping the pages and . . ."

"Well, obviously I saw the article about you two."

"You painted car crashes and atomic bombs, yet two women getting botulism in Michigan counted as a disaster?"

"You guys look kind of like my mother. I thought of my mother and how scared she was about leaving Pennsylvania and moving here to Manhattan—at her age—and that I was a bad son for wanting to ditch her to go read *Newsweek*."

"That's so sweet."

"So it was kind of a painting about my mother. And death. And it was about me really being up there, now that I was in the weekly news magazines. So you can sit there and be a magazine bigwig who's indecisive about my art, but while you're doing that, I'm turning you and your magazine into whatever I want it to be. Because I get to decide what is and isn't art. I'm the one who gets to turn the world upside down. I took your deaths and I made them art. So you didn't die for nothing."

Then the two women got all mushy and started crying and hugging me, and it was all so abstract, so I pretended to take their picture and it made them happy again, and then I got mad at Polaroid for making such stupid business decisions and going broke. John-John Kennedy told me that. He's up here somewhere. He's so handsome. He should have been a movie star.

An App Called Yoo

yoo

Broadly,

yoo is a fantastically personal experience viewed only by you.

yoo allows you to see what's buried inside you.

yoo is yours. It's not meant to be shared.

yoo creates an intensely private onscreen experience by tapping into your many streams of personal data and metadata.

yoo allows you to experience your daily life played back to you, remixed with images, sound, video and visualized data.

yoo doesn't judge, and it allows you to increase or decrease the amount of sexuality and all other forms of NSFW content.

yoo brings previously unobserved life patterns to the surface.

yoo allows you to reinterpret any day of your life in an infinite number of ways.

yoo's onscreen experiences can be saved or they can be transient.

yoo finds connections in your life that you didn't know were happening and makes them for you, before your eyes.

yoo, poetically, allows you to reincarnate while still living.

Again, yoo is only for *you*. It's not really meant to be shared unless you want to.

Every new technology allows us new opportunities to explore our humanity.

That's what yoo is all about.

So . . .

You get home from work. The kids are asleep. The place is silent.
It's your cherished quiet time before bed. You think about the day
you've just had. What did you do? What did you avoid? Did it make
you happy? Have you forgotten something but you don't know
what? Are you getting older? Are you looking for a bit more mean-
ing from all this?

So you visit yoo. You press return and suddenly your screen
lights up with the view from a car driving down the street where
you grew up. It stops in front of your old place and then there's
a quick montage of photos that people over time have taken of
that same street, and then your screen sifts through photos and
comes to a regional newspaper site with a wedding announce-
ment: your high school crush is engaged to a dentist you've never
heard of. Suddenly Bryan Ferry's "More Than This" starts play-
ing overtop a YouTube clip of your ex-crush's proposal, filmed
by the dentist's son from a previous marriage. Overtop this, a
woman's voice with a slight British accent reads aloud a drunken
email you once wrote to your old crush but never sent, leaving it
in your Drafts folder.

Then text comes up telling you how many steps you took that
day, also telling you the farthest point you were away from home,
and then something NSFW appears onscreen—and then suddenly
you're inside a mesh model of the Guggenheim Museum Bilbao,
which lands you in the middle of a scene from *The Garden of the
Finzi-Continis*, a scene on a tennis court. A crawl at the bottom
of the screen reminds you that Wimbledon starts in a week. The
screen fades to white and a montage of products appears, but it's
not advertising . . . it's all the logos you walked past today while
wearing Google glasses. The music cuts to the soundtrack of *Days
of Heaven* while the screen cuts up into nine squares, each dis-
playing a kitten video. A male voice reads passages from *Lolita*

(you haven't thought of that book in ages!) while the screen now shows footage from a 1974 *Partridge Family* episode. Then we see scenes from your office life, except they're in slow motion, and then they're melting into . . .

And so forth.

This process of algorithmic association will continue for as long as you like. You can save the whole thing if you want. You can put sticky notes in places you'd like to return to. You're basically having your subconscious played out directly before your eyes.

 . . . in a bit more detail:

yoo takes images, sounds and text from the course of your day (or week or year) and weaves them together so that they morph, jump-cut and dissolve.

yoo seeks and blends into your experience the faces, spaces, audio feeds and experiences of all the people in your life, imported from various streams.

yoo options are multiplied with Google Glass, which pick up images and sounds throughout the day—details that you didn't notice but still registered in your subconscious.

yoo adds and weaves in fragments of movies, songs or other media you experienced that week—but does so by displaying similar or related content: cover versions of favourite songs; movies by the same director; movies with similar plots.

yoo connects you geographically and experientially to YouTube clips taken by people who've visited the same places as you.

yoo's voices read passages from emails you've sent and received that somehow connect to, say, a phone call you had today.

yoo makes you add two plus two in ways you would never have done otherwise.

yoo provides unexpected data visualizations: dietary statistics; medical advice; driving advice; flight data and so forth.

yoo users who wish to amplify their experience can fill out simple Q & A forms: Are both parents alive? Did you get along with them? Do you have a chronic health issue? Are you in difficult financial circumstances? Which politicians do you like/loathe? And so forth.

yoo can incorporate a matchmaker function as it locates blogs and diaries of people whose thinking you'd like, or maybe whom you'd like to meet in person.

yoo could ultimately be Channel yoo, a site that tells you data about yourself presented in a *whatever* sort of manner. Channel yoo would be a more complex and statistics-driven app than yoo. It would answer questions like: "Who is the person most like you in the world?" "Who is your opposite?" "Where and how do you fit into the human race?"

yoo is one great mixing board with many advanced controls and filters . . .

Choose your yoo experience length:
. . . snack-sized yoos
. . . one-hour yoos
. . . twenty-four-hour yoo, running all the time

Choose your yoo's scope:

    . . . today only

    . . . the past hour

    . . . the past year

    . . . from the moment you started

Locate your yoo:

    . . . your old high school

    . . . Rome

    . . . Mars

    . . . "Grand Theft Auto"

Pump up your yoo palette:

    . . . add kittens

    . . . add fail videos

    . . . nighttime only

    . . . generate light shows similar to iTunes

    . . . add whatever it is you want more of

Is there something you don't want in your yoo?

    . . . relatives

    . . . guns

    . . . anything from outside your own country

    . . . anything religious

Point of view can be altered to some degree:

    . . . different age

    . . . other sex or sexuality

    . . . different ethnicity

Speed: Some people will want to unplug their brain and sit back and watch a light show. Others are going to want a "textier" experience that allows them to stop and browse when something interesting comes up. yoo allows you to freeze or go backward to investigate something interesting you saw en passant.

Sounds and Music:
>   . . . Weave together voice, music and ambient sounds in all forms.

Voices:
>   . . . Johnny Hallyday?
>   . . . Boutros Boutros-Ghali?
>   . . . Dolly Parton?
>   . . . Tintin?
>   . . . sexy Russian spy?
>   . . . your own?

Adjective-driven yoos (mix and match adjectives):
>   . . . purple . . . relaxing
>   . . . goth . . . Bavarian
>   . . . family-based . . . cartoon
>   . . . psychedelic . . . slow dance
>   . . . Mormon . . . wildlife
>   . . . sci-fi . . . lame

Designer yoo experiences:
>   . . . Neil Patrick Harris designs an array of yoo data you can borrow or buy
>   . . . a Beatles yoo experience
>   . . . National Geographic yoo
>   . . . yoo goes WWII
>   . . . FIFA

yoo mood filters:
    ... one that allows only happy imagery
    ... one that takes a political stance
    ... one that injects campy horror
    ... one that feeds depressive tendencies

Visual texture filters:
    ... 1960s TV
    ... old *Life* magazines
    ... eight-bit
    ... fractals
    ... NASA

    ... so many to choose from ...

Daily news add-ons:
    ... Time-code yoo experiences with of-the-moment news
        feeds and crawls.

Branded taste filters:
    ... For example, a Monocle filter that formats all imagery
        to a standardized template.

Here's a list of support I think yoo requires:

Gmail
    ... access to emails
    ... access to all shipped files in all formats
    ... access to links embedded within emails
    ... access to personal search histories

What's most important for all data streams is a methodology for locating material that's psychosensitive and then linking it to similar sensitive material elsewhere in the user's datascape. It would also be necessary to psychologically correlate forms of charged content (sex/death, money/shit and so forth). I'm unsure if/how Google does this. I imagine it's part linguistics and part mathematics with a dash of psychiatry.

Linked material needs to be visualized in a way that's dynamic but not too frenetic and that segues into other material without jarring. This applies to all the other data sources listed here. And again, if you're in a texty mood, you can turn into an interface that finds text that is interesting to you, in much the same way Amazon recommends books.

Google Images
Obviously.

YouTube
A limitless supply of moving imagery.

Google Maps and Street View
A powerful nostalgia tool, plus a way of generating moving backgrounds.
Is it possible to go from street address directly to Street View?

Google Translate
. . . to read aloud text files in any number of voices
. . . to translate files from all languages

Google Glass
  An amazing trove of link options.

Google Trends
  Data visualization is important, whether it's a neutral
  display or dynamic/subjective.

  . . . basically Google everything.

GPS
  Preferably using a device that tracked all daily move-
  ments plus flight and driving data. This would link
  to data visualizations about driving. Most people are
  obsessed with statistics.

SketchUp
  For entering models in orbit mode and creating spaces
  using other 3D systems.

Film and photo archives
  As many as possible.

GIF ranching
  Punctuate yoo experiences with collections of animated
  GIFs.

Porn sites
  There must be one or two out there.

Sports
  Replays. Stats. Interviews.

Instagram
> Is it possible to access if users give passwords?
>
> . . . Create instant stop-motion animations from identi-
>   cally hash-tagged postings.
>
> . . . Dissolve and quilt together static images.

Tumblr archives
> Obvious source of all kinds of images. Image blizzards
> can be created.

Flickr streams
> Possible to access?

Ditto . . .
> . . . Facebook
>
> . . . Pinterest
>
> . . . Vine
>
> . . . Twitter
>
> . . . all the usual suspects—predictable, no?

The iTunes universe
> Is it possible to tap into this?

Wikipedia
> For facts and images. Entries can be read aloud by
> synthetic voices.

Screensavers and wallpaper
> I suspect there are thousands of underappreciated
> dynamic full-screen graphics out there just waiting to
> find eyeballs.

yoo can be shared . . .
　. . . between two people or by millions or billions.

There are situations in which people might want to share
aspects of their yoo data:
　. . . People in love can share deep levels of data to feel
closer to each other when separated.
　. . . Highly sexual people can lend one another sexual
yoos.
　. . . Political and religious yoos can be shared broadly.
　. . . Self-curated and modified yoo segments can become
funny beautiful tools to move people.

This document was created in Microsoft Word, which in the year
2014 is pathetic.

Afterword

Filtered by Experience: An Algorithm Called "Me"

If we look at historical photographs of Aby Warburg's *Mnemosyne, A Picture Series Examining the Function of Preconditioned Antiquity-Related Expressive Values for the Presentation of Eventful Life in the Art of the European Renaissance* (1924–29)—an organized set of images that Warburg arranged in such a way that they illustrate one or several thematic areas—we can see that each picture series strongly resembled a Google image search result, both in its ambition and layout. What to make of this resemblance?

From the cabinet of curiosities and the encyclopedic projects of Diderot and d'Alembert, to the iconographical studies of Warburg and the Google image search engine: where there is man, there is stuff, and man wishes to organize this stuff in a way that mimics the way he thinks. It seems that by now, the Internet is simply mimicking the way human brains have always worked, rather than invoking radically new ways of thinking, as some e-optimists might have us believe. If we were infinitely smarter than the first computers, the time has arguably now come where artificial intelligence has outsmarted us. Has it, though?

It is a platitude to say life imitates art, but it is less so to say that the Internet imitates a specific sort of thinking, one I would like to identify as artistic thinking.

The other day someone showed me a website that generated clusters of images based on some finely tuned algorithm. It struck me as a terrifying vision of future ways of creating collections and exhibitions. Or was this the ultimate curatorial tool? Logarithmic technology always raises the question: Who is making the data dance to his or her beneficial rhythm?

The exhibition *Bit Rot*, which prompted this eponymous publication, was made up of disparate and heterogeneous images and objects both by Douglas Coupland himself as well as others. What is then the glue keeping it all together? An algorithm called "Me." Or, in this particular case, called Douglas Coupland, born in 1961 on a NATO air force base in West Germany, etc., etc. You can look up the details online.

When reading Coupland's text "An App Called Yoo," included in this collection, it struck me as the description of a mindscaping tool, where logarithmic technology allows us to create something that would closely resemble the exhibition this book was named after. Did Coupland invent an app that mimics the way his brain works? Or, differently put: Does the Internet speak our language? Or have we learned to speak its? Are the search entries we have come to master actual reflections of our own thoughts and desires? Or are they, rather, mere substitutes for them, developed to match the by now barely concealed commercial interests of the World Wide Web?

⊗

As Coupland writes in his essay "Stuffed," also included in this book, people cannot help but collect or even hoard, and he is rightly suspicious of people who do not possess any accumulations of any sort. We crave more of what we enjoy most, be it Japanese bottles of detergent or empty space. The things we surround ourselves with are telltale signs: "Show me your house and I'll tell you who you are."

The art world's equivalent of this cliché of interior-design-pop-psychology might be "the artist as collector." Indeed, collecting can and should be seen as a creative act in its own right. However, as is always the case with art, what matters is not so much *what* an artist collects, but *how* it is presented. Whether they will share a set of references and interests beyond their own work is a personal choice artists must make for themselves. One can think of it as a mental group exhibition, a spiritual library, or a Warburgian mood-board. Some prefer to carefully shield their collecting from the outside world; others make an entire oeuvre out of displaying this inner database.

If the dialectics between collecting and deaccessioning always entail a sense of loss, as implied by Coupland in "Stuffed," and if these respective acts always occur through an applied filter—be it computed or human—we are left with the question: What are these losses we try to compensate for?

Recurring in Coupland's writing are characters who have lost their story: their lives stopped feeling like a linear event-based narrative. Certainly some acts of collecting are attempts to solidify the fleeting storylines that make up our lives. Art has always been a rich source of simulacra that tell our story for us. When life seems to be escaping us, we reel it close again in the shape of things, fragments possibly shored against some ruins.

In the realm of organizing stuff in order to make sense out of it, an artist's position is perhaps to be located somewhere in between Warburg and Google: not quite systematic and scientific enough, yet definitely not ruthlessly efficient or devoid of actual embodied knowledge either. It makes me cringe writing this, for it sounds so very cheesy, yet it seems necessary to write it today: there is no finer filter than a human brain thinking artistically. Intuition seems to have been replaced by algorithms, making it an obsolete notion to some, and the most precious and unique human capacity to others.

If you think about it, almost every human undertaking—increasingly so, even—seems to involve some degree of information filtering. And if art seeks to reveal what is not immediately visible, there is an unveiling to be done; some things need to be shown, causing others to remain hidden. A conceptual or formal grid is laid over the world and the world appears anew, altered, filtered. This is how an exhibition can be made, but it is also the process of organizing one's wardrobe, or arranging books on shelves.

I remember that when I discovered the colour filter options in Google's image search function, I thought, *This is amazing*. But like with most computer technologies that reach us today, the awe wore off after about five minutes.

Filters are supposed to be flawless. Yet the human brain and its output are far from flawless. Brain rot will always occur, causing glitches both devastating and beautiful. When filtered by one's life experience, the outcome will always be less than perfect, yet never entirely wrong.

Flying to Vancouver for the first time in early 2015, I thought about how, even when we've never been there before, we often already have some sense of the place we're going to. In my case Vancouver brought up mental images of Jeff Wall's landscapes and a quote I might be erroneously attributing to the photographer, which says that you can make Vancouver look like anywhere, hence the movie industry's interest in this Canadian city.

Vancouver also triggered a set of references related to Coupland, who in many of his books describes the city and its natural surroundings. Perhaps it was Coupland who said that the city he grew up in could be made to look like anywhere else. It sounds like something he would say. Of course I could look up who actually said it, and where and when. But this blurring of memory entries, this set of subjective data, is precisely what makes up our inner landscape, our mind and, as such, who we are and what we do.

Samuel Saelemakers

Bit Rot is the title of this book. Bit Rot is also the title of an exhibition of the author's visual work at Rotterdam's Witte de With Center for Contemporary Art in 2014-15, which then traveled in 2016-17 to Munich's Villa Stuck Museum. A small catalog, also titled *Bit Rot,* which contained material from this book was produced for the Witte de With exhibition.

"Vietnam"; "George Washington's Extreme Makeover (pilot script)"; "361"; and "Mrs. McCarthy and Mrs. Brown" are appearing in print for the first time.

"The Short, Brutal Life of the Channel Three News Team"; "Nine Point Zero"; "Fear of Windows"; "The Anti-ghosts"; "Beef Rock"; "Yield: A Story about Cornfields"; "The End of the Golden Age of Payphones"; "666!"; "George Washington's Extreme Makeover"; "Superman and the Kryptonite Martinis"; "Zoë Hears the Truth"; "The Preacher and His Mistress"; "The Man Who Lost His Story"; and "Bartholomew Is Right There at the Dawn of Language" were first published in Douglas Coupland's novel *Generation A*, published in 2009.

"Creep" was first published by *DIS* magazine online.

"Black Goo"; "Pot"; and "Grexit" were first published in *Vice* online

"Stuffed" and "Shiny" were first published by e-flux.

"Temp" was first published by Metro International.

"Nine Readers"; "Smells"; "Coffee & Cigarettes"; "Public Speaking"; "Notes on Relationships in the Twenty-First Century"; "Stamped"; "Future Blips"; "Futurosity"; "Worcestershistershire"; "Bulk Memory"; "The Mell"; "Little Black Ghost"; "New Moods"; "Globalization Is Fun!"; "Unclassy"; "Wonkr"; "The 2½th Dimension"; "Living Big"; "The Ones That Got Away"; "Duelling Duals"; "Got a Life"; "Peace"; "iF-iW eerF"; "McWage"; "Lotto"; "Frugal"; "IQ"; "My TV"; "5,149 Days Ago: Air Travel Post-9/11"; "Glide"; "Klass Warfare"; "3.14159265358"; "The Great Money Flush of 2016"; "Ick"; "World War $"; "The Valley"; "3½ Fingers"; "Bit Rot"; "Retail"; "Trivial"; and "Über That Red Dot" were first published in *FT Weekend* magazine and edited for this book.

"An App Called Yoo" was first published in *Monopol* magazine in Germany.